# IN SEARCH
*of the*
# MIRACULOUS

D1462445

# IN SEARCH *of the* MIRACULOUS

## Healing into Consciousness

Eliza Mada Dalian

EXPANDING UNIVERSE PUBLISHING
Vancouver, Canada

Photo credits: Cover photo by Marcos Armstrong; author photo by Mark Brennan: photos on page 120: Tornado Vortex, Galactic Vortex, and Black Hole Vortex are used in accordance with the public domain contract NASA's and STScl.

The excerpt from the poem "The Dream That Must Be Interpreted" on page 229 is from *The Essential Rumi*, by Coleman Barks published by Castle Books. Used by permission of Coleman Barks, Maypop Books, Athens, Georgia.

**Library and Archives Canada Cataloguing in Publication**

Dalian, Eliza Mada, 1952-

In search of the miraculous : healing into consciousness / Eliza Mada Dalian. -- Rev. ed.

ISBN 978-0-9738773-3-5

1. Mental healing. 2. Mind and body therapies. 3. Spiritual healing.

4. Consciousness. 5. Subconsciousness. I. Title.

RZ999.D34 2010          615.8'51          C2009-905406-X

Also available in electronic format.

*(Please purchase only authorised electronic editions, and do not participate in or encourage electronic piracy of copyright materials. Your support of the author's rights is appreciated)*

Published by
EXPANDING UNIVERSE PUBLISHING
P.O. Box 19168
Vancouver, BC, Canada V6K 4R8
www.ExpandingUniversePublishing.com
info@ExpandingUniversePublishing.com

Printed in Canada by Friesens Corporation on
post-consumer ancient-forest-free recycled acid and chlorine free paper.

*This book is dedicated*
*with love and gratitude*
*to all my past and present teachers, friends, and kindred spirits*
*who have been a loving light on my long journey to awakening.*

*Working on this book for seven years was my way of saying thank you to this beautiful planet, which so lovingly has nurtured and sustained me for so many lifetimes, providing the ground on which I can learn, make mistakes, experience pain and pleasure, create and destroy, be wise and foolish, and evolve into the consciousness that I am today.*

*Without the sustenance that mother Earth so generously provides to all her creatures, our spirits may drift aimlessly in the vastness of this unknowable universe without a home and an opportunity to be aware of ourselves.*

*I hope that reading this book may spark a light in your consciousness and inspire you to search for the miraculous hidden within your own being.*

*Eliza Mada Dalian*

# CONTENTS

## PART I

# PART II

# ACKNOWLEDGEMENTS

This book would not have been possible without the loving support, devotion, insights, and extraordinary editing and organizational skills of my editor and friend Jesse Carliner. He not only dedicated two years of focused effort to helping restructure and edit the entire manuscript, but also practiced with all the suggestions offered in this book. His on-going practice and questioning helped me to further crystallize the concepts discussed in this book, enriching my attempts to explain the indescribable multidimensional reality of our evolution into consciousness. I am also very grateful to all the other gifted and creative people, who at one time or another, have worked on the manuscript: Carolyn Bateman and Richard Therrien – for their revisions and suggestions; Leah Commons, Cody Curley, and Anna Comfort – for their artistic contributions in the design of the book; Marcos Armstrong – for the photos; My special thanks to Albert Sturm – for his devoted and unwavering support personally and professionally, and to my daughter Helen – for always standing by my side. My heartfelt gratitude to all my clients, students, and friends – for directly or indirectly inspiring and influencing me over the years and for helping me to recognize the importance of sharing my inner wisdom through words. Lastly, my deepest gratitude to my paternal grandmother and all my spiritual teachers from this and past incarnations, with special thank you to Gautama the Buddha of compassion, Georges Gurdjieff, and Osho – for being the beacons of light on my long journey of healing into consciousness.

# EDITOR'S INTRODUCTION

*"My words are only a husk to your knowing, an earth atmosphere to your enormous spaces. What I say is meant only to point to that, to you, so that whoever hears these words will not grieve that they never had a chance to look."*—Rumi

One of Mada Dalian's main teachings is: "To be a knower of Truth you must experience it for yourself." Mada asked me to write the introduction to this book in a way that illustrated this teaching. I've answered that request with my personal story of searching for healing and finding my own truth while working with her personally and professionally.

When I was eight years old, my mother's kidneys failed, and she became very ill. She spent the next seven years in and out of the hospital until she finally died at the age of forty-two. As she lay dying, she told me, "Don't live your life in a shell. I lived the first twenty years of my life in a shell, and the second twenty trying to break out of it, but my body became too weak to do it."

Her illness and eventual death led me to question the meaning of life and my life's purpose. Unable to relate to the concerns of the adults and other children around me I felt all alone. The more isolated I felt, the more lost, depressed, and anxious I grew. I was sent to counselors and psychologists, but they didn't know how to help me. I was told that I was thinking too much and not to worry about these questions. The religion on which I was raised discouraged this kind of questioning, or it offered me simple answers that didn't feel true or resolve my anxiety and restlessness.

Around the time I was fifteen, I was put on antidepressants. Over the course of my adolescence and university years, I was prescribed more antidepressants, anti-anxiety medication, stimulants, sleeping pills, and medication to counteract the side effects of the other medications. I felt better for a while, and on the outside I seemed to be doing well. But on the inside I eventually began feeling numb and disconnected from my emotions and my own life. I felt as if I was dying in my own prison. As the feeling of being disconnected and alienated from myself intensified, I decided that spending the rest of my life on medication wasn't the answer. Deep down I knew there had to be more to life than the way I was living it.

After graduating from university, I stopped taking my medication and began to search for another way of living. My search took me to the desert of Utah where I lived and worked for two years and then to Asia and around the world. As I traveled, I began to realize that my depression and anxiety were, at their root, a spiritual problem that would need a spiritual solution. I figured what better place to resolve my questions than in India. While in India, I began my search for a cure to my angst and depression in earnest.

I started my search the only way I knew how – by reading books. I read and read: books on meditation, spirituality, religion, psychology, and even science. From my reading, I understood that the Eastern mystics and the Western physicists were describing the same truth (one from the inside, the other from the outside): we and everything in the universe are all one and everything that appears solid and separate is only a temporary illusion. I realized that all of my stress and suffering was due to my ignorance of and resistance to this truth. I knew that beneath all my wounds and fears I was okay, and thought that *meditation* might be the cure to my depression. I wasn't sure how it would work exactly, but I felt as if I was at the end of the line. I desperately wanted to be free.

I signed up for a ten-day silent Vipassana meditation retreat. Vipassana is the key meditation method taught by the Buddha. It is the observation of the body, breath, thoughts, and emotions with the understanding that everything one experiences is impermanent. It was a revelation. Instead of staying in the chain of emotional reaction, I understood how to break the chain by simply watching and letting the thought or emotion or sensation be there. By doing this, I literally felt the layers begin to evaporate from my body. I started sleeping better and felt less anxiety. I felt a peace that I had never known before. I knew this retreat was just the beginning, a taste, but I was certain that I had found the way to free myself from unhappiness and depression. After the retreat, I continued to meditate faithfully every day.

Upon returning to the West my "high" gradually wore off, and deeper layers of unconscious thoughts and emotions began to surface. It became increasingly difficult for me to meditate without getting caught in my mind and emotions. Somehow, sitting and just watching wasn't bringing me the same peace it had in India. I felt I needed guidance, but I wasn't sure what to do or where to go. I thought about studying transpersonal psychology that incorporates mindfulness and meditation and at the same time prepare myself for a career as a counselor, but after visiting the school I was interested in I realized: How could I hope to help others when I was still becoming aware of my own unconscious? I decided that I had to continue to help myself before I would be ready to help anyone else.

A friend referred me to a transpersonal psychologist working in Vancouver, British Columbia. I traveled to Vancouver and worked with him for almost nine months. When I realized I had arrived at a point where he couldn't lead me any further I stopped seeing him. I was grateful that he could take me as far as he himself had come on his own journey, but I knew I needed to move further.

I understood that in order to awaken, I had to peel away the layers of unconscious thoughts and emotions I was carrying around with me, but somewhere along the way I had become lost in all the baggage I was "working" on. I had already tried many different therapies, including talk therapy, massage, reflexology, chiropractic, acupuncture, flower essences, Rolfing, tai chi, qigong, yoga, chanting, physical cleanses, as well as continuing to faithfully meditate. If anything, I had stirred up so many layers that I was now feeling even more lost in a cloud of my thoughts and emotions.

I hoped and longed for a guide who could take me to the other shore, but I wondered if any guide would come. I knew I wasn't looking for a traditional guru to follow, but I also knew that the modern self-help-style psychologist/teacher wasn't for me either. I didn't want to hear more ideas about positive thinking, love, enlightenment or awakening. I wanted and needed practical help so I could discover the truth for myself. I wanted help simply peeling away the layers – nothing more.

Then I had a dream. I dreamed I was in the Arctic, on the edge of the ice. Everything was bright and shining with light. The water was intensely blue like the water in the tropics. It was so bright it hurt my eyes. Polar bears were swimming in the water, and I was swimming off the edge of the ice with them. At first I was afraid and intimidated by the bears. But then I saw a woman standing on the shore and I relaxed. She guided me firmly yet encouragingly. I finally managed to make it to shore. Once I was out of the water she said, "It's time to take a break," and she suggested that we go have something to eat. I was struck by her power and fearlessness, but mostly I was impressed by her gentleness, warmth, and compassion. She was like a mysterious temple priestess and a down-to-earth mother at the same time.

Two months later, a yoga teacher I had met referred me to healer and spiritual teacher Mada Dalian. When I met her, I recognized her as the woman that I had seen in my dream. Words cannot describe the tremendous relief I felt. I immediately knew that she was different from anyone else I had ever met. I was overwhelmed by the stillness and silence that she radiated. I knew right away that she was a "knower," though I didn't want to admit it out loud, even to myself. It terrified me to contemplate it. She had experienced first hand what I was searching for.

I was nervous at first when I sat in front of her. When she asked me to tell her what had brought me to her, I spoke quickly without pause. I told her about the "work" I had been doing. After I finished, she asked me to close my eyes and focus on breathing into my belly. She too closed her eyes and began to "look" into my energy. After some silence, she said: "You have been doing all this work on yourself with all these different techniques and you have stirred up a lot of stuff, and a lot is happening, but it's all like a cloud covering your awareness. You are missing your center. You are just moving in a circle. You have been doing this for lifetimes, trying to find yourself through the mind, and you stay trapped in it. We need to break through your cloud. The only way out is through witnessing the cloud of the mind. Just jump into the center and watch whatever is happening. You are only the witness."

She said this in a light, almost humorous way, yet I could feel her compassion. I also felt her strength and wisdom and knew that she was not merely guessing or feeling things but, in fact, was truly "seeing" me and my life. I knew she was right. I didn't feel defensive or concerned that I had been wasting my time up until now. Rather, I felt relieved that she could see and explain to me why I felt so lost. I felt myself relax deeper as she continued to speak: "People who don't have the awareness of their own center have been misguiding you. What does it mean to be enlightened or awakened? Coming out of the illusion means coming out of your ego-mind and its desires. Part of your illusion is that you think you are the one doing things to heal yourself. You think you are the one doing all this "work."

I felt the truth of what she was saying. I had become so identified with working hard to heal myself, it had become part of what was keeping me in the suffering. I was actually fueling my ego through my attachment to healing myself. I was attached to my identity as someone who needed healing. I thought I wanted to heal, but in reality, I was afraid to let go of being wounded. As I was digesting this, she went on: "You have been staying in the illusion of your ego-mind because you are afraid of your own power. Living in your power means taking responsibility for your own life and living your life and your truth, regardless of what is going on in the world. You are afraid to live in your power because if you do, you will have to stand alone. Only by standing on your own two feet can you make a difference in the world. To make a difference in the world and your life, you have to destroy the false within yourself and around you. Right now, you are controlling yourself to fit in. You had to do that in the beginning because you had to survive, but now it's no longer an issue. The only way of the spiritual warrior is to face the truth. It's the only way to be free."

These final words frightened me, but I knew she was right. I had spent my life hiding, trying to fit in and live up to the world's standards. I had been afraid to speak up and live my life according to my own truth. Even though I was trying to find the truth, I was at the same time afraid of finding it because it would mean that I would be responsible to live it and would no longer be able to hide. My mother's words came back to me: "Never live your life in a shell." I had to risk letting go of my shell, if I was ever going to be completely free.

After Mada finished "reading" my energy, she moved on to the practical part of the healing session, explaining how she was going to help me experience my center for myself using a technique she had developed called the Dalian Healing Method®. I lay down on her massage table and she worked with my body and the suppressed thoughts and emotions that were in my energy. She told me that healing and experiencing my truth doesn't have to be a struggle.

During the session, I had a glimpse of my center for the first time and was able for a moment to step out of the cloud of thoughts and emotions I had been lost in. After the session, I felt such a profound sense of gratitude to her, to the universe, and such a sense of relief and joy, I wept and laughed at the same time. I thought that I had been doing a lot to improve myself by working with many different therapies and techniques, but I had been missing the most important aspect – the witness in the center. I could relax now and surrender to her guidance. No matter what obstacles I might run into along the path, I could trust she would lead me through it.

Like any good teacher, she assigned homework. She told me, "Over the next little while you may again feel a sense of struggle, but don't get discouraged. The struggle is simply the shift between the old pattern of thinking and your new emerging consciousness. It takes time for the new consciousness to integrate. Contemplate the question, 'If I was absolutely free, what would I do?' Come back and see me as a friend, but not to talk, just to feel the silence. So start focusing on your inner silence. Don't talk about yourself, just feel and be present. Talking takes you out of the present."

As I was leaving after my first session, I asked her, "Where are you from?" She laughed as if it was a strange question. She replied, "Here." I persisted and asked, "No, I mean, where were you born?" And, this time, humoring me, she replied, "Armenia." But she had told me the truth when she answered me the first time. She is from here. Or the Here-and-Now.

Mada belongs and has always belonged to the universe, like the serene, detached, temple priestess I saw her as in my dream. But she is also a blunt, firm, practical, and compassionate mother and woman. Although this was my first meeting with Mada, my real work with her did not begin until I attended my first twenty-one-day meditation and enlightenment intensive with her.

While attending her meditation intensives, where she used a combination of active meditations, group work, individual guidance using her gift as a healer and medical intuitive, Mada would point out the areas in my body where consciousness was not present and would instruct me on how to work with my unconscious. Her instructions were very spontaneous, practical, and direct. She talked matter-of-factly about even the most taboo things. Some called it blunt or even insensitive, but I found it to be the most helpful approach I had ever experienced. Sometimes what she would say would hit a nerve and expose a wound that was hidden in my unconscious, and although painful for me to see, it enabled me to have a breakthrough in my self-awareness and moved me one step closer to healing and freedom from suffering.

Several years after first meeting Mada, I came across a story called "Fire Poker Zen" from *Zen Flesh, Zen Bones*, compiled by Paul Reps and Nyogen Senzaki. It neatly encapsulates this aspect of Mada's teaching style.

*Hakuin used to tell his pupils about an old woman who had a tea shop, praising her understanding of Zen. The pupils refused to believe what he told them and would go to the tea shop to find out for themselves.*

*Whenever the woman saw them coming she could tell at once whether they had come for tea or to look into her grasp of Zen. In the former case, she would serve them graciously. In the latter, she would beckon to the pupils to come behind her screen. The instant they obeyed, she would strike them with a fire-poker. Nine out of ten of them could not escape her beating.*

Mada will frustrate every notion you might have about what enlightenment is, or what an awakened person is like. She doesn't fit into any stereotypes. Her contradictions are a gift to her students and clients, but it is also what makes her so challenging to them and others. Though she can be called a healer and a spiritual teacher, she is most of all a mystic – one who has had direct experience of the divine. She is truly a Bodhisattva who after her awakening has committed herself to helping others wake up.

Mada's style of teaching may not be for everyone, but I find it to be incredibly and wonderfully refreshing. She is like the master Lao Tzu writes about in the *Tao Te Ching* who "…leads by emptying people's minds and filling their cores, by weakening their ambition and toughening their resolve. He helps people lose everything they know, everything they desire, and creates confusion in those who think that they know."

She is no-nonsense and completely and utterly practical. She doesn't spend a lot of time talking about love, enlightenment, or abstract concepts and philosophies. Instead, she spends her time and energy practically directing us so that we can have the experience and know the Truth for ourselves.

I admire Mada for declaring the age of guru over. She does not encourage her students to be dependent on her. She never sets herself up as some figure on a pedestal. She insists that she is a human being like the rest of us with her own lessons and life to live, and she pushes her students to take responsibility for their own lives and choices. One of her main messages is: you have to do the work for yourself – no one else can do it for you. No one else is responsible for your happiness or your pain. To be a student of Mada's, you cannot just listen to or parrot her ideas – you must practice it and embody it for yourself. You must be courageous and absolutely sincere in your efforts. There is no getting around it.

I focused most of my energies over the next three years on my meditation practice and my work with Mada. After three years of studying with her, she asked me to help with the editing of her book, which she had been working on for several years. I then spent the next two years working with her on the manuscript. If anything, working with her day after day on the book was more transformative than anything I had done with her previously.

While working on the book with Mada I felt as if I was unlearning everything I had known, and becoming like a child again. Being in her presence, my consciousness naturally evolved. This meant I had to be always present and stay in my heart and my innocence, watching my mind and its judgments, fears, and reactions.

It wasn't easy. Mada was like a waterfall, gradually and continually wearing down the shell of my ego. There were many days when I went home and needed to scream or cry in my room because something Mada had said or written had hit my ego and exposed its wounds and fears. Being with her helped me truly understand what Rumi meant when he said, we need to tear down the house of the ego and dig under its foundations in our unconscious to find the treasure of our true Self.

As the Buddha said, "Regard the person who sees your faults as a revealer of treasures. Associate with the skilled person as one who is wise, who speaks reprovingly. Keeping company with such a person, things get better, not worse."

Every moment of working with Mada was an opportunity to shed more and return the next day to work on the book a little bit lighter. As time went by, I gradually learned to observe my mind and its thoughts and emotions without reaction. I felt lighter and lighter, to the point where my life itself became a meditation and it felt paradoxically both more ordinary and extraordinary. I now know that the whole universe is my home and I can never be lost.

If Mada's teachings can be said to have a purpose or goal, it is to help every sincere seeker make the leap into the boundless unknown of no-mind – the silent stillness that exists within our center. What sets Mada apart from other masters is that she is also a practicing hands-on healer. What sets her apart from other healers is that she is not primarily concerned with fixing symptoms but rather with helping people heal from unconsciousness into consciousness.

Mada calls this book *In Search of the Miraculous: Healing into Consciousness* as an homage to two important twentieth-century mystics, Georges Gurdjieff and Osho. It follows in the footsteps of P.D. Ouspensky's book on Georges Gurdjieff's teachings, *In Search of the Miraculous: Fragments of an Unknowable Teaching* (the book that sparked Mada's own journey), and Osho's book *In Search of the Miraculous*, which further spurred her quest for enlightenment. To me, these three books about the search for the miraculous are attempts at speaking of the unspeakable.

In this book, Mada shares her own unique perspective on enlightenment and healing and their relationship to spirituality and growth in consciousness. Through her own personal story in Chapter 8, she illustrates everything covered in the book and shows how she herself has lived and experienced what she now teaches to others.

Mada calls both the journey to awakening and the awakening itself "healing into consciousness," and describes the journey we all take as we evolve into consciousness. She illuminates the purpose of our ego and takes us through the stages of its development, and of the need for its final surrender. She also offers practical guidance and an array of exercises for breaking through the illusion of the ego-mind.

By its very nature, a book like this can never be complete because the journey is full of paradoxes that cannot be adequately described using the linear mind and language. However, Mada describes the paradox of the spiritual journey: on the one hand the idea that we even need healing is an illusion; on the other, to get to this understanding we need to do the work of healing and becoming more conscious. Or, as she is fond of saying, "It takes effort to get to effortless effort." In other words, only by "trying" and "pursuing" healing and awakening with 100 percent of our mind and energy can we exhaust the mind of all effort and realize the natural and whole state of our being.

Above all, Mada emphasizes the need to strengthen our inner witness and teaches that each one of us can find ultimate health and wholeness only by witnessing and disidentifying from our ego-mind and surrendering to what is. She offers clear, simple guidance and instruction so that we may know this truth for ourselves.

In essence, this book is a how-to manual on transforming our unconscious into consciousness. It is packed with exercises, meditations, and visualization practices you can turn to over and over again on your healing journey.

Although you can read and practice with each chapter alone, each chapter also prepares you to understand the deeper truths and wisdom in the following chapters. You will get the most out of this book if you practice with the suggested exercises and meditations; however, if you only work with one exercise, look within and practice watching your breath. This practice alone is the key to awakening. Reading and reflecting on the book while maintaining a regular meditation practice is the ideal way to walk your healing journey.

If you feel overwhelmed while reading this book, don't be discouraged. It isn't meant to be read quickly. Read it slowly, and let yourself digest it. Our intellect alone is not enough to understand life or find healing. The concepts discussed in the book could be at times overwhelming

– they certainly were for me. What we can grasp with the mind is limited compared to what we can grasp through experience. Don't worry about trying to understand everything; instead simply practice with the exercises and understanding will happen on its own.

This book is like a mirror that reflects whatever is within us. Something ugly or beautiful might be revealed. Every line is a potential arrow that might expose something hidden within your unconsciousness and help you come a step closer to your true Self. To get the most benefit from this book, look inside and sincerely reflect on each line you read. Maybe you have heard it before. Maybe you already feel as if you know it, but are you living it? Does your life reflect what you think you know?

It is my sincere wish that reading this book is every bit as powerful for you as editing it was for me. I hope that it becomes a helpful guide and inspiration for you on your healing journey into consciousness. I am forever grateful that I was blessed with the opportunity to be part of its creation.

*Jesse Carliner, MA, Eastern Classics*

# 1 HEALING INTO CONSCIOUSNESS

While sitting in meditation one day, a deep sadness and despair at the state of the world enveloped me. I felt a thick dark cloud of pain surrounding the planet like a heavy blanket. The pain and weight of it in my soul and in every cell of my body was excruciating. I knew that it was we humans who were creating this cloud of pain. Tears welled up from the depth of my being and I wept for myself, for humanity, for the trees, for the animals, and for the planet. I felt like I was in a dark cave without one ray of sunlight that could light up my soul. I sobbed and sobbed. Then, like the calm after a storm, the sobbing stopped and everything became quiet and still. A ray of light suddenly penetrated the dark cave, bringing the warmth of the Sun with it.

I realized then that the Earth is suffering because we are suffering. Regardless of how much we feel separate from one another and the world around us, we all live on the same Earth and breathe the same air. What happens to the animals, trees, and humans anywhere on the planet affects us all. The differences between us are superficial. They only exist in our appearances and minds. Our diverse personalities, perceptions, body constitutions, and the different paths we take on our journey determine how we live in the external world. Internally, however, we are inseparably the same.

1

Our attachment to our identity and the material world creates our pain and suffering. To create a better world, we must first let go of our attachment to our differences. Every one of us needs healing from pain and suffering created by our ideologies, fears, hatred, jealousy, arrogance, blame, judgments, and lust for power.

Our conditionings and beliefs, and identification with our thoughts, emotions, and desires keep us in unconsciousness. We think if we get more money, the dream job, house, car, and perfect relationship we will be happy. Yet, when we do get what we want, we still feel unfulfilled and want more. We continue to follow our mind's desires, even if they harm us, others, or our planet and its creatures. We continue to suffer when we fail to recognize that satisfaction and inner fulfillment can never be found outside of our being.

To find happiness, we need to surrender our ego-mind and grow in consciousness. Joy and peace are a direct result of a surrendered ego. To surrender the ego and grow in consciousness, we must look inside and understand that our ego-mind has nothing to do with our being. Our being is as mysterious and unknowable as the universe, untouched by the suffering created by the mind.

Love, joy, and peace always exist in the present moment independent of the past or the future. Joy is our true nature, an innate part of who we are. Our being has nothing to do with our thoughts, emotions, beliefs, or self-identity. Our being does not need healing – it is already healthy by nature. It is like the hollow core of the bamboo flute, empty and silent yet full of divinity and joy of creation when played. The music arises out of the hollow emptiness of the flute the way joy and love arise out of the emptiness of our being.

When you experience your inner truth, you unlock the door to the miraculous nature of existence, and, for the first time, recognize that you have everything you need within yourself. Your feelings of aloneness, insecurity, abandonment, alienation, and not feeling loved evaporate the moment you experience the purity of your silent being. Within this silence, there is balance, peace, freedom, love, health, and all the happiness you long for. The closer you get to your innocence, the healthier, more conscious, and whole you become. When you understand and experience first-hand that joy, peace, love, and abundance are the qualities of your own inner being, you begin to manifest the limitless creativity hidden within yourself.

Our being is our most precious treasure – the miracle that we all seek consciously or unconsciously. This miracle exists at the core of each one of us regardless of our gender, the color of our skin, our beliefs, or religion. To find this miracle, we must tear down our ego's false identity and let go of our attachment to our beliefs, desires, and conditionings.

Experiencing and knowing the being has been called enlightenment, self-realization, awakening, liberation, and union with God. I call it *healing into consciousness*. Healing into consciousness includes both the search and the sudden moment of awakening to the truth that "I am what I have been searching for." Like the phoenix that is reborn out of its own ashes, we are healed into consciousness through the fire of our destroyed ego-mind.

## LOOKING IN: THE CONSCIOUS SEARCH

Everything within the universe, including humans, already exists in its true nature. Unfortunately, we try to discover the truth of existence outside of our own nature. Instead of looking within to find the source and mystery of existence, we focus our eyes on the horizon outside of ourselves. Whether we are aware of it or not, our genuine search for truth begins when we ask the most fundamental questions: *Who am I? Where did I come from? Why am I here? Why do I do what I do? What will happen to me when I die?*

To find the answers to these questions we must let go of our attachment to who we think we are. If we keep looking in and continue questioning, we will eventually realize that it is impossible to find the answers with the mind alone. It is not enough to hear or think about the truth, we must experience it for ourselves if we are to truly know it.

In Zen, they call the search for Truth the search for the "original face." The original face is our pure essence before our personalities, beliefs, and conditionings covered it like layers of the onion covering its inner emptiness. Each one of us is responsible for searching and finding the original face for ourselves. To uncover it, we must embrace the present moment and the unknown it contains.

What stops us from finding the original face is our mind's fear of losing our ego-identity and disappearing into the unknown. We are afraid of the unknown because in the unknown our ego-mind cannot function. Out of fear, we cling to what we know and are familiar with: our past, our beliefs, and our relationships. Instead of embracing the unknown moment to moment, we avoid it by distracting ourselves with different activities like working, eating, having sex, watching TV, smoking, fantasizing about the future, etc. When we search for happiness in the future, we miss living the abundant joy that is already present inside us every moment.

To live in joy and fully manifest our true potential, we must let go of our desires and attachment to the past and the future and be excited about living in the unknown. If we can live in the unknown, no matter how afraid we are of losing what is familiar and known, all our problems will quickly vanish. The miraculous is the unknown, which is always revealed moment to moment in the stillness of the present.

# HEALING:
## THE JOURNEY INTO CONSCIOUSNESS

Health is a state of consciousness. It has nothing to do with age, illness, or even the health of the body or mind. Whether you are aware of it or not, every step you take towards healing is a step towards consciousness. Everything you do in life is part of your healing journey towards the ultimate health of your true nature.

Only consciousness can heal our pain and suffering. Each moment contains an opportunity to awaken from the suffering of the ego-mind into the health of consciousness. Our bodies are full of suppressed thoughts, emotions, fears, desires, insecurities, and judgments. These create and sustain our ego-mind. In our unconsciousness, we keep our identification and attachment to our body, emotions, desires, and the world. Many unconscious thoughts and emotions are stored layer upon layer as patterns hardwired into our body's cells. These patterns create energetic blocks in the body and cause physical and psychological pain and suffering. We heal into consciousness by peeling away these layers.

Only in our thoughts is there happiness and unhappiness, right and wrong, birth and death. When we stay identified with this ever-changing play of opposites that only exists in our mind, we fail to see what is permanent – the eternal presence of our being. As we get closer and closer to our being, we gradually move away from the duality of the mind and transform our ego into consciousness.

All our physical and psychological ailments point us to where we need to focus our attention so we can transform our unconscious energy into consciousness. Usually, we believe that our pain is a misfortune that needs to be fixed, but in fact, all pain (physical, mental, and emotional) is a necessary step towards becoming conscious. When we try to avoid pain, loneliness, and death, we also avoid finding our eternal being.

In a very real way, all pains are growing pains. When we are ready to heal from an unconscious belief or behavior pattern, we experience symptoms such as pain, anxiety, depression, and ill health. If we try to fix something on the outside instead of trying to find out the cause of our ailments from within, we continue to suffer. When we let go of our identification with who we think we are our body and DNA literally change.

Healing into consciousness is the most arduous task that can ever be undertaken. There are many fears, obstacles, and ups and downs along the way. You need courage and trust to face the darkness of your unconscious. If you persevere and stay committed to your awakening, the journey will become easier and you will even begin to enjoy it and be excited by it. No matter how intense your pain and suffering, if you stay devoted to your healing journey, you will undoubtedly come face to face with the miraculous universe that abides within your own being.

# WHERE AM I?
# THE SEVEN STAGES OF THE HEALING JOURNEY

For those of you who are beginning your healing journey consciously, and for those of you who are already on your way, it might be helpful to think of your healing journey as a kind of "school of life," a process similar to our educational system. The school of life can be divided into seven stages that correspond to *Pre-school, Elementary, High School, Undergraduate University, Graduate University, PhD Student,* and finally *Professor.* Unlike the school system, however, this process is not linear, and the stages are not distinct, but rather subtly blend into one another. The stage at which you start your healing journey depends on the level of self-awareness you bring from your previous lives and your understanding of the journey itself. As you progress through the school of life, your awareness of yourself and the world increases and your consciousness expands. Depending on your choices and level of consciousness, you may move through some stages faster than others.

*Stage 1:* **Pre-school**
Your attention and awareness are primarily focused on healing your physical body. You have no understanding that you are here on Earth to know yourself and evolve into consciousness. When you experience physical pain or illness, your attention moves into your body. You go to a physician and try to fix your problem with medication or surgery. Allopathic medicine temporarily treats or suppresses the symptoms of your ailments, but because it does not heal the psychological root cause hidden in your energy, your physical "problems" resurface.

*Stage 2:* **Elementary School**

At this stage, you know through experience that medication alone will not fix your problems, and due to its side effects, may even be making you sicker than before. You explore alternative healing methods such as physiotherapy, chiropractic, traditional Chinese medicine, acupuncture, naturopathy, and others. You understand that to improve your physical health you need to take care of your body by exercising, changing your diet, and using supplements. You take relaxing baths, spa treatments, have massages, and listen to soft music. You engage in yoga, qigong, or tai chi practices purely to take advantage of their physical benefits. In this stage, your focus primarily remains on your physical well-being. Your physical condition improves, but you soon realize that you are still unfulfilled and that something more meaningful is missing in your life. You re-evaluate your life's priorities and begin to explore other options to find happiness and contentment.

*Stage 3:* **High School**

After realizing that physical health alone does not make you happy, you begin to focus on your mental and emotional well-being. You try to understand your psychological problems and heal your mental and emotional wounds through counseling, psychotherapy, and personal development groups.

You realize that your mental and emotional health affect your physical health and you try to change your negative thoughts and behavior patterns. You read psychology and self-help books, and practice positive thinking and affirmations. Your life begins to change, and you temporarily feel better, but a point comes where you feel that you are still unfulfilled and are missing something. You finally understand that you cannot find happiness and your life's purpose with your mind alone, and you begin to explore the dimensions of spirituality and religion.

*Stage 4:* **Undergraduate University**

In this stage, you recognize that to find true healing you need to find a spiritual connection to the divine. You explore different spiritual paths, such as Christianity, Buddhism, Taoism, Sufism, Kabbalah, and others. You read spiritual books, attend lectures and workshops given by spiritual teachers, join spiritual groups, meditate, pray, and devote yourself to a spiritual path. You investigate the paranormal, past lives, the tarot, psychics and psychic healers, near-death experiences, channeling, astrology, and other occult practices. You experiment with visualization, chanting of mantras, and tribal ceremonies. You try to be a better and more loving person, and to bring more peace into your life and the world.

Most people get stuck at this stage, believing that they now "know" the truth. When life continues to challenge you with more difficulties, and you are not able to maintain your inner peace and contentment, you realize that you haven't yet explored your own inner truth and haven't found your own authentic being. You start to question who you are and what you are doing on this planet. You begin to understand that the only way to find the answers is to do the hard work of going in and looking into the darkness of your unconscious.

### Stage 5: Graduate University

After all the seeking outside of yourself for healing and salvation, you finally understand that the only person who can save you is you, and you can only do it by taking the responsibility of facing and surrendering your ego-mind. You work hard to understand and disidentify from your mind and emotions. You begin to meditate not simply to feel better, but to find who you truly are. Through meditation and learning to witness your body, thoughts and emotions, you begin to see how your ego-mind creates all your problems and keeps you in suffering.

As you move deeper into yourself, a time comes when you are forced to decide if you are willing to continue facing and exploring the agony and pain of your own mind. Many people stop their introspection here because the pain and fear of facing the unconscious darkness intensifies. It now becomes more difficult and painful to confront the ugly faces of the ego and disidentify from them. It also becomes more difficult to remain a detached witness to the deeply ingrained behavior patterns related to past lives. Cultivation of the inner witness becomes crucial in order to continue moving into the unconscious darkness.

To pass through this challenging stage of your development, you need to take full responsibility for your own pain and suffering. Observe both your beautiful and ugly faces, and understand that you are neither. Through detached observation, your sense of self-identity begins to break down, and what you thought you knew about yourself no longer seems as clear and true as before. You may feel more confused and recognize that the more you know, the less you know. Life begins to feel like a meaningless dream. You realize that you need a guide, someone who has passed through the darkness of their own unconsciousness, to help you move through your own darkness and take you beyond it. Consciously or subconsciously, you begin to search for a teacher or master who can point you in the right direction and guide you to liberation.

A teacher is someone who may or may not have experienced the truth of his own being but tries to help others through speaking about the truth and taking them as far as he or she has gone. A master is someone who has fully awakened from the illusion of the ego-mind and knows how to help others also wake up.

As you search for a guide, you first must face the challenge of discriminating between a false and a true teacher or master. A false teacher or master may promise to liberate you from your ego-mind and in doing so creates a relationship of dependency. A true teacher or master will never allow you to become dependent on him because he knows that he can only point to your own unconsciousness. Ultimately, it is your own courage, effort, and surrender to the will of existence that will liberate you.

To know the difference between a false and a true teacher or master, listen to your own inner knowing and intuition and be absolutely honest with yourself about your motives. If you can't discriminate between the false and the true within yourself, you will not be able to discriminate between the false and the true in others.

Once you find a teacher, or, if you are fortunate enough, a master who will take you on, you face another challenge: trusting him or her and surrendering to his or her guidance. It is not easy to follow a true master because he or she will use any situation to help you become aware of your own ego-mind. You need to stay alert and be aware of any judgment, blame, or neediness you might project on to this person. If you can stay in your innocence and heart, you will be able to see and surrender your ego-mind and eventually experience true liberation and awakening.

## Stage 6: PhD Student

In this stage, you deepen your personal meditation practice and start to feel more at peace with yourself. As you pass through your personal unconscious in the previous stage, you purify yourself of your past unconscious actions. You understand that all your "problems" (physical, mental, and emotional) were there to teach you something about yourself. You cultivate trust, and your fears no longer have a hold on you. You master your ego and are no longer a victim of your mind and emotions. You transcend fear of the unknown and live more and more in a state of acceptance and surrender.

You now move into the collective and cosmic unconscious, which includes the collective human beliefs and behavior patterns as well as your animal survival instinct – all of which fuel the illusion of separation of your being from existence. Every step you take in facing and becoming aware of the collective and cosmic unconscious allows you the freedom to move higher in consciousness. You now have enough clarity, awareness, and inner strength to support your guide in his or her work of raising individual and collective consciousness. You are ready to unconditionally share your gifts and the light of your consciousness with others.

*Stage 7:* **Professor**

You are liberated from your ego-mind and have transcended your fear of death and the unknown. You have broken through the veil of illusion created by the mind. You now know through your own experience that you are one with everything that exists within the universe. You have experienced the universal Joy your guide was pointing to. You welcome and celebrate the emptiness of your being and your oneness with the boundless universe. You feel grateful to the Earth for sustaining and nourishing you and for everyone you have met along your journey, whether they have helped or hindered you. Most of all, you feel grateful to your master and to all the awakened beings who have guided you through your many lifetimes of trials and tribulations. You now understand that the journey is endless and is the goal in itself. You surrender your ego-mind to the universe and become a vehicle through which it can express itself, guiding those who are still searching for their way out of suffering.

# WITNESSING:
# THE KEY TO HEALING INTO CONSCIOUSNESS

We can only heal into consciousness through witnessing. Witnessing is an alert watchfulness of whatever is happening moment to moment without mental or emotional engagement. In other words, it is the detached, unidentified, and non-judgmental observation of what is. When you experience that you are not your mind, body, and emotions, you are in consciousness. The only way to understand this is to observe your body, mind, and emotions.

Through self-observation, you can see that all of your sensations, thoughts, and emotions are impermanent – they always change and move like passing clouds. Seeing their impermanence helps you understand that your pain and suffering is created by your ego-mind.

All your problems exist because you are unable to witness and disidentify from your thoughts and emotions. When you don't witness your mind and emotions, you remain caught in the story created by the ego-mind and continue to suffer. When you witness the mind and its story, you realize you are not the story but the observer of the story. When you simply observe your body and its sensations, thoughts, emotions, and everything that happens around you, you are out of the story.

You heal into consciousness with each moment of witnessing and disidentification, no matter how brief. Once you know you are nothing but consciousness, you are healed out of suffering.

Your ability to witness is innate. The witness is part of your being. It is with you eternally, even after your body dies. Even though the witness is always present watching everything coming and going, your awareness goes in and out of it. Witnessing is like a muscle that you need to strengthen through experience and practice. Meditation is the practice.

## MEDITATION: THE TOOL FOR STRENGTHENING THE INNER WITNESS

Although there are many meditation techniques, meditation is not a technique. Meditation is the practice of witnessing. Meditation gives you an opportunity to disidentify from your body, mind, and emotions and experience your inner consciousness. It allows you to step out of the chattering mind and transform your beliefs and conditionings into pure consciousness.

The essence of meditation is a pure witnessing of whatever is perceived inside and outside the body, mind, and emotions without reaction or judgment. Through detached observation, you stop fueling your ego-mind and find the stillness and silence of your being. A dedicated practice of meditation leads to inner silence, relaxation, and improved health as well as increased self-acceptance, confidence, and understanding of oneself and others.

Traditionally, meditation has been practiced through passive sitting and watching the breath, body, and mind. This meditation technique is known as Vipassana and was devised by the Buddha 2,500 years ago. In Buddha's time, people lived closer to nature and were more relaxed and heart-centered. Passive sitting and observation was much easier to practice in Buddha's time than it is today. Presently, our bodies and minds function at such a high speed that passive sitting feels like an almost impossible task.

To aid the modern-day seeker to experience their inner silence and stillness a lot faster than what can be achieved through a long practice of passive sitting, the contemporary Indian mystic Osho created several active meditation techniques that are practiced by thousands of people around the globe. Active meditations use activity and movement such as shaking, dance, catharsis, laughter, crying, jumping, chaotic breathing, or gibberish to first release stress and purify the body of its many layers of repressed thoughts and emotions. Once the repressed thoughts and emotions are released, it is much easier to sit silently and experience the inner stillness of your being.

At their core, there is no difference between active and passive meditations. Their intent is the same – to empty the mind and help us connect with and strengthen our inner witness. I like to use active meditations in all my workshops because they help participants experience relaxation and inner peace even after meditating for the first time. *(For more details about active meditations and how to practice them visit, www.madadalian.com).*

# NOW IS THE TIME AND YOU ARE THE PLACE

Our body is a gift from the universe. Without it, we cannot heal into consciousness. Like a rechargeable battery, the body has a limited life span. In the same way that we recharge a battery with electricity, we recharge the body with food, sleep, and rest. After a while, like an old battery, it can no longer be recharged and inevitably dies. When the body is young and healthy, we often neglect it and take it for granted. We usually wait until it is sick or old to start our healing journey.

Don't wait! Life is short! Start healing into consciousness when you are young and have plenty of energy, vigor, and enthusiasm. The later you start your inner search, the harder it becomes because you will have less energy and be burdened with more responsibilities. When you invest a lot of time and energy on things that are impermanent and can never fulfill you, you miss many opportunities to discover the ultimate joy of your eternal being. The sooner you transform your unconsciousness into consciousness, the sooner you can start enjoying life, and the more fulfilling and joyful it will become.

## QUESTIONS AND ANSWERS ABOUT THE HEALING JOURNEY

*I find it hard to avoid the distractions of the world and stay focused on my healing journey. How can I stay committed to my inner work while working and raising a family?*

You may think you do not have any time for yourself when you are working and raising a family. However, if you examine how you spend your time, you will discover that you can always find twenty minutes to an hour a day to do spiritual work, such as reading, introspection, meditation, and sometimes even participating in personal growth groups.

For example, if you usually watch TV for an hour or two a day to unwind, try meditating instead. Even if it's only for ten minutes, just sit

14

silently and watch your breath. If you find that silent sitting is difficult because you are stressed and you have many thoughts racing in your mind, you can try the active meditations described in *"Healing into Consciousness with Active Meditation & Visualization Practices"* e-book available at www.madadalian.com.

If it is difficult for you to allocate time for meditation, then turn your work and chores into meditation. For example, when you are washing the dishes, watch your breath, watch your body movements, feel the water on your hands, watch the thoughts and emotions you are experiencing. Be fully present and aware of everything you are doing and whatever is happening in the moment, both inside and outside of yourself. You can do the same with any task or activity, whether it is cleaning the house, gardening, grocery shopping, cooking, sitting in front of your computer, running, playing sports, or walking your dog. Whatever you do, do it with full awareness.

If you keep practicing breath awareness during your daily activities and during meditation, eventually you will see that everything you truly need to do arises naturally, spontaneously, and effortlessly out of your inner silence and emptiness. If you can live this way, your home and work life will become more balanced and relaxed.

You don't have to renounce the world to be true to yourself and your journey. What you need to renounce is your attachment to the world and your identification with it. The world needs only to be renounced in your mind. Everything in your life, including your work and family, is here to help support the goal of you finding your being. If you are presently working and raising a family, then this is what your soul and existence needs you to do.

Although the world can distract you from your introspective work, it can also help you by forcing you inward. When life is going well, we remain identified with worldly success and often forget to look inside. But when life isn't going so well and we feel sad or depressed, we begin to look inside. If rightly used, every life situation can help us become more aware of our inner reality. Don't miss any opportunity to look inside in whatever situation you are in, no matter how worldly or mundane it may seem.

*Are visualization exercises the same as meditation?*

No, they are very different. Visualization engages the mind and meditation observes the mind. Visualization uses imagination and keeps you in the mind and its illusion of good and bad. With visualization, you may judge one thing as good and another as bad and try to change the existing reality and create a new one. With visualization, you try to imagine something positive replacing something negative. Visualization is helpful for healing, or changing negative thoughts and emotions into positive ones. This may give you temporary comfort and a feeling of "okay-ness," but it also may keep you identified with one part of your ego-mind and cause you to deny other parts that you would rather not face and take responsibility for.

Meditation does not use imagination. Meditation is the witnessing of what is. In other words, it is the detached observation of reality with full acceptance of both positive and negative, good and bad. Meditation helps you to center in your being and observe whatever is happening in your mind and emotions. With meditation, you simply witness the duality of the mind and its judgments of good and bad and move beyond both. Meditation is the only path out of inner turmoil and suffering. Just as regular exercise is essential for your physical health, meditation is essential for your mental, emotional, and spiritual health.

*How can following a teacher or a master help me become free of my ego?*

It doesn't. Following someone can never liberate you from your ego and make you conscious. You need to do your own work of searching and looking in. Many people gravitate towards a teacher or a master hoping he or she can do the work for them, but they don't understand that it is impossible for anyone to live another person's life.

You can sit in the presence of a spiritual master and receive guidance, but if you don't meditate and do your personal work you will never find your being and experience the truth the master is pointing to. No matter how great the spiritual teacher or master is, he or she can point the way but cannot liberate you. You must understand that you live your life based on your own conscious and unconscious choices. No one can interfere with these choices no matter how good their intentions may be. Your choices are your freedom and your responsibility.

You must become the captain of your own ship because no one else can navigate it to your soul's destination. This is what Jesus meant when he said: "The path is long and narrow and only one person can walk on it." What I am doing here is only sharing a little of my own experience and understanding. Perhaps hearing my words will be an inspiration for you to chart your own path.

*Does becoming enlightened mean that you no longer have an ego, need to meditate, or have anything else to learn?*

You are asking a very important question. It arises out of a misconception that many people have about enlightenment. Enlightenment, or self-realization, does not mean that you no longer have a mind. As long as you have a body, you will have a mind because the mind is part of the body's survival mechanism. Enlightenment simply means that you have come to experience your being and have realized that your mind was creating the illusion of separation. The experience of enlightenment liberates you from the psychological pain and suffering created by the ego-mind and brings a clear understanding that you are not your ego, body, thoughts, and emotions, and that your being is untouched by anything external. With enlightenment, your attachments to things and people, as well as the existential angst that kept you searching, drops. Enlightenment frees you of insecurity and fear of the unknown.

The growth and expansion of consciousness does not end with enlightenment. Evolution of consciousness continues eternally through new experiences and learning. Each day brings many opportunities to learn something new. There is no end to how much we can learn. An enlightened person continues to learn and evolve just like everyone else, but his or her learning arises out of joy, creativity, and compassion, not out of resistance, fear, and suffering. An enlightened person longs to share out of pure joy and abundance, not out of a need to receive something in return.

You also asked, does an enlightened person still need to meditate? Have you ever seen a house that doesn't accumulate dust? Whether you are enlightened or not, as long as you live in a physical body, you need to clean your house. Meditation is a way to remove the dust that the mind accumulates. The dust of the mind clears just by sitting and watching your breath.

Because the mind is goal oriented, from its perspective enlightenment is the end. The mind cannot comprehend that by being a detached witness you can know what action you need to take the next moment. Your question shows that you are still identified with your mind and are still searching for enlightenment outside of yourself.

*Can you say something more about consciousness and unconsciousness?*

The energy that makes up the universe is either conscious or unconscious. Unconscious energy has no self-awareness, while conscious energy is aware of itself. Our bodies contain both conscious and unconscious energy. The level of conscious energy is determined by how aware we are of our being in the present moment, and how aware we are of our body, thoughts, emotions, and whatever is happening around us. Consciousness exists within the unmoving center of everything that moves. In humans, consciousness is awake and in animals, trees, and rocks, it is asleep. Humans are aware of their existence, while animals, trees, and rocks are not aware of their existence. In other words, animals live in their being, but they are unaware of it; humans too live in their being, but unlike animals, they have the ability to become aware of it.

Consciousness arises out of detached observation of what is, whether it is an experience, a thought, an emotion, or a physical sensation.

*How does my unawareness affect my spiritual growth?*

It is impossible to evolve without awareness. When you live in unawareness, your life is filled with fear, mistrust, and judgment, and your actions create unnecessary pain and suffering for yourself and others. When you are unaware, you live mechanically, moving in a circle, but not really going anywhere. Your unawareness keeps you trapped in a little box made up of your fears and beliefs.

Spiritually speaking, awareness and growth are synonymous. Awareness leads to growth, and growth leads to awareness. With awareness, you can disidentify from your mind-generated fears and live every opportunity that life presents fully and fearlessly. With awareness, you can squeeze the juice out of life, instead of life squeezing the juice out of you. Awareness keeps you present and able to create, grow, and expand as the universe grows and expands. Only with awareness can you bring peace and joy to yourself, others, and the world.

*Do we carry our unexpressed thoughts and emotions from one life to the next the same way we carry over our behavior patterns?*

Anything unresolved from a previous life remains in the unconscious part of the mind and is carried over from one life to the next. We carry all our unconscious patterns from life to life until we become conscious of the lessons they contain. And because patterns are created by unconscious beliefs, completion happens when we become conscious of the causes of our beliefs and disidentify from them.

Thoughts, emotions, and behavior patterns carried over from other lives become harder and harder to recognize and break. They become even harder to see and break through as we get older. Don't postpone facing, feeling, and exploring the causes of your thoughts, emotions,

19

and behavior patterns. Don't procrastinate; deal with things as they arise and complete them. Embrace every situation and treat it as an opportunity to learn and grow. Learn to trust and surrender to whatever life brings you, so you don't miss the many opportunities it offers you to heal into consciousness.

*I think I have changed and moved past my old behavior patterns, but whenever I am with my family, I suddenly find myself acting in the old way. Why does this keep happening?*

It is normal to slip back into your old patterns, especially when you are with your family, because this is where you first started learning them. When you are with your family, you slip back into mechanically repeating the old patterns because your awareness of your center is not strong enough. Until your awareness is strongly rooted in your center, you will go back and forth many times. Don't worry about slipping back. Each time you see yourself behaving in the old way, remind yourself to remain a witness. Watch what kind of thoughts or fears arise when you are with your family and, without reacting to anything, bring your awareness into your center. Your consciousness is like a seed – it will take time for it to grow and strengthen.

It may help you to look at your parents as fellow travelers who are learning just as you are. Don't be afraid to show your family you have changed, even if you think they will not be able to understand you. If you stay true to yourself, without blame or reaction, you may indirectly influence your family with your awareness instead of being influenced by their patterns.

*You've said that permanence is the goal of the mind, and that the goal of the spirit is the journey. How does this concept work in relationships when the mind seeks permanence and the journey is ongoing?*

We are all here together for the time being, but eventually our paths will part, if not in life, then in death. In that sense, every relationship is temporary. Every relationship helps us heal a part of ourselves that we may not be able to heal alone. Each partner contributes to the other's growth in his or her own way. If one person is not able or willing to continue learning and healing into consciousness, then that relationship will end, and you will move on to the next.

Make the best of your relationship while you are together, and instead of struggling, try to be more loving and accepting of each other. Don't hold back from surrendering to love, and keep reminding each other that your relationship is there to help mirror something about yourself so you can heal into wholeness. Nurture your individuality and help your partner do the same. Reminding each other that you are only walking together on this journey temporarily will help you accept each other and give each other more freedom. With both of you keeping your freedom intact, your relationship will grow into deeper intimacy and friendship. When you know that every relationship is temporary and your journey is ongoing, your mind will be at rest and you can be more relaxed, accepting, and open to enjoy the time you have together.

*Is it possible to have a sick body and be truly healthy?*

Absolutely. We think of health as something physical, but the body's destiny is ultimately to get old, stop functioning, and return to the earth. Your being and consciousness are always healthy and can never die. When you find the truth of your being, you find true health. You may think: *How can anyone who is enlightened have cancer?* Ramakrishna, an Indian mystic, died of cancer. Georges Gurdjieff, a well-known Western mystic, also died of cancer. Many people die of cancer or some other fatal illness, but they can die absolutely conscious and healthy.

We reincarnate into a physical body as many times as we need to, until we fully transform our unconsciousness into consciousness. It is through illness and physical and emotional suffering that we learn and complete our spiritual lessons. Regardless of whether the body is sick or healthy, when it is time for it to go, it will go just as mysteriously as it had appeared. We don't and can't take our bodies with us when we die, but we do take our being and our consciousness. A physically sick and dying person can be even healthier than any physically healthy person if he is conscious of himself and life's temporary nature.

# 2 THE DEVELOPMENT OF THE EGO

*"Before you can lose your ego, you must attain it.*
*Only a ripe fruit falls to the ground."*
– Osho, My Way: The Way of the White Clouds

In this chapter we will discuss the ego, what it is, its purpose, the seven stages of its development, and its final surrender and dissolution into pure consciousness.

## WHAT IS EGO?

The ego is a cloud-like illusion created by our thoughts, emotions, fears and beliefs. It is the source of all our personal and collective problems, pain, and suffering. Our desires and judgments about ourselves and others and identification with the past and future sustain the illusion created by the ego. This illusion separates us from the truth of our inner being, from one another, and from everything that exists in the universe. We stay in the illusion of the ego when we believe we are our body, thoughts, emotions, and beliefs. In short, the ego is who we think we are, and who we truly are is pure consciousness.

Most people think that having an ego means being selfish, but in the sense that I am using the word, the ego or the ego-mind is any aspect of our energy that is unconscious. (I will be using "ego-mind" alternately with "ego" throughout the book as a reminder that it is the mind that creates the ego.) When we struggle with the ego, what we are really struggling with is our mind. We judge and condemn the mind and struggle to be free from it without understanding that we are in fact using one part of the mind against the other, and therefore, keep moving in an endless circle. We maintain our pain and suffering by protecting our pride, beliefs, and conditionings, instead of understanding and transforming them into consciousness.

The mind is as much an inseparable and necessary part of our mysterious existence as is consciousness. By battling with our mind and emotions and projecting them out onto others and the world, we create more suffering for ourselves and others. The only way to be "free" of the ego-mind is to see that it is an illusion.

Look inside right now and see if you can pinpoint where your ego-mind is located in your body. You will discover that it is impossible to find any specific place because the unconscious that makes up the mind is everywhere in the body.

We become conscious of the mind through awareness. Normally, our identification with our mind is greater than our awareness of what it is and how it works because our focus is mainly in the past or the future. What makes our ego-mind challenging to see is our inability to be present in the Now. In the Now, the ego-mind simply vanishes. The Now is like an open blue sky without any clouds where there is only pure space within which we can effortlessly see what passes by moment to moment. In the Now, we stay watching the passing clouds without identifying with them and judging that they should be different.

If you close your eyes and look inside right now, you will see darkness, feel an emotion, or see a thought. If you identify with the darkness, the emotion, and the thought, then you are in your ego-mind. If you remain a witness to them without judging anything as good or bad, you are in the Now and in consciousness. In other words, you are in the ego-mind if your focus·is on the object (tangible or intangible) instead of the witness that itself sees the object. If your witnessing awareness is not strong and centered in the body, it is difficult not to identify with the illusion of the mind that always comes and goes within the infinite Now. To be conscious and live in the Now, we need to continually witness our thoughts, emotions, and experiences.

Those who keep looking in and focusing on their inner witness eventually come to discover that their ego-mind disappears with the observation of what comes and goes. Through continuous observation, the only thing that remains is a detached witnessing awareness in the center of your being. This awareness always sees whatever is happening around you without identifying with anything.

We often experience moments of no-mind and presence in the Now throughout our lives but fail to recognize them. When we look at a colorful sunset by the ocean, or see thousands of sun rays explode through the trees in the forest, our mind stops and we are held in the wonder of the present moment. These are moments of transcendence. We don't realize we have experienced a moment of no-mind and quickly return to the mind, labeling the already past experience as beautiful or breathtaking. This way we completely miss the next moment that has arrived with its own unique presence. We don't recognize how we go back and forth between the mind and no-mind because our witnessing awareness is not fully centered in our body. With growing awareness of our being and inner center, we begin to have more experiences of no-mind and begin to recognize how it would be to be in the Now all the time.

## THE PURPOSE OF THE EGO

On the path of healing into consciousness, our ego is both the obstacle and the teacher. Anyone desiring healing into consciousness must understand four things about their ego: *what it is, its purpose in their spiritual journey, the stages of its development,* and *how to heal and transcend it.* I have described what ego is in the previous paragraph. In the rest of this chapter, I will outline the ego's purpose and the seven stages of its development. Later on, in Chapter 6, I will give practical suggestions on how to heal and transform the ego-mind into consciousness.

While reading, take time to contemplate over where you are on your own journey of evolution, and how you can hasten the development and transformation of your ego into consciousness.

Like everything in existence, our ego has a purpose. It is like a womb that cradles, nurtures, and protects the body while the energy within it evolves from unconsciousness into consciousness. Our ego is the soil upon which the seed of consciousness germinates, develops, and flowers.

Although all life forms have an instinctual intelligence that maintains their body's survival, only humans need an ego to protect themselves from unwanted outside influences. Unlike most animals that need a relatively short time to become self-sufficient, it takes a human baby many years to be mature enough to take care of itself.

The ego-mind helps to protect the body from the dangers in the world until consciousness within the being can care for its physical, mental, and spiritual needs. Once there is enough awareness in the body to take responsibility for its own existence, the search for the being begins. With awareness of the being and its oneness with existence, our ego's purpose is fulfilled and our self-realized consciousness is freed back into the universe to continue its journey through eternity.

We struggle with our ego because we don't understand its purpose. Just as we need darkness to see light, noise to recognize silence, fullness to understand emptiness, ugliness to appreciate beauty, we need the ego-mind to become conscious of our being. Like the blackboard that illuminates the white letters, our ego provides the background upon which the light of consciousness becomes visible.

Without seeing what is impermanent (the ego-mind), we cannot recognize what is permanent (consciousness). Without the misery and suffering created by the ego-mind, it is impossible to surrender the mind and recognize the bliss of no-mind. The more conscious we become of the fleeting, illusory nature of our ego-mind, the more conscious we become of the everlasting presence of our being.

Understanding the ego's purpose makes it easier to embrace it instead of suppressing and struggling with it. Condemnation of the ego only delays the development of consciousness and keeps us trapped in the wheel of life and death. Those who accept, embrace, and understand their ego-mind hasten their liberation into consciousness.

## THE SEVEN STAGES OF THE EGO'S DEVELOPMENT

The ego-mind and consciousness grow and evolve hand in hand. In other words, consciousness develops in proportion with development of the ego. To experience what has been called self-realization or enlightenment, and what I call healing into consciousness, the ego and consciousness have to develop to their fullest and highest peak. The more aware and disidentified you are of your ego (emotions, beliefs, conditionings), the more conscious you are that the ego is not your true Self.

The irony of spiritual growth is that the more conscious you become of your ego-mind, the bigger it may appear to others. The most conscious people sometimes appear as the most egotistical because they have no fear or insecurity about themselves. This is so because they have grown to see that they are much more than their ego-mind and they no longer have any need for other people's approval or validation of them. People with developed ego-mind and consciousness no longer live according to others' expectations and beliefs of what's right or wrong and feel no need to follow others' ideas and standards. They prefer to follow their own inner knowing because they know that no one can know them better than they know themselves. They don't judge or impose their beliefs onto others, and don't allow others to judge and impose their beliefs on them. They feel centered within themselves and know they are enough unto themselves.

A developed ego-mind is not selfish, as we might normally perceive it. Selfishness is a characteristic of an undeveloped ego. A developed ego-mind is conscious of itself, whereas an undeveloped ego-mind is unconscious of itself. A developed ego-mind is fearless, self-sufficient, and is closer to enlightenment, while a selfish ego-mind is immature and always looks outside of itself for approval, protection, power, and recognition. An undeveloped ego-mind is needy, insecure, judgmental, and clings to others and life. This kind of ego-mind is farthest from self-realization. The developed ego-mind can give to others fearlessly and unconditionally, and can easily surrender itself to the universe and the unknown. The undeveloped ego-mind on the other hand is fearful, incapable of giving to others unconditionally, and always feels the need to take from others or protect itself from life and the universe.

As the Chinese mystic Lao Tzu put it, "If you want to get rid of something, you must first allow it to flourish." It is impossible to transcend the ego-mind without strengthening it and allowing it to flourish first. To understand this paradox, imagine the ego as a balloon (the rubber shell), and consciousness as the air inside the balloon. The size of the balloon (the ego) and the amount of air inside the balloon (consciousness) represent the level of self-awareness within the being. In the beginning, there is no air in the balloon and no consciousness or self-awareness. As the air inside the balloon increases, the balloon stretches and expands. The more air that comes into the balloon, the more it expands. This is how our ego and consciousness develop. At a certain moment, when the balloon grows to its limit and becomes fully transparent, we begin to see through it. If we continue blowing the balloon up, it eventually explodes and all the air returns into the atmosphere, where it originally came from.

The same thing happens to the developing and expanding ego-mind and consciousness. When consciousness (the air) expands the balloon, the ego (the balloon's shell) turns to a thin veil that separates the air inside the balloon from the outside air. The ego-mind can now see the consciousness inside the balloon and the vast consciousness of the universe all around.

With a little puncture in the balloon, the air (consciousness) inside the balloon begins to merge with the air all around it and the ego-mind begins to think, "I am the universe." Though this is true, the thought "I am," still carries a notion of separation from the whole. This thought is the last bit of ego-mind that separates the individual consciousness from the universal consciousness. When this last thought and the ego's fear of completely dissolving into the vast unknown space is surrendered, the ego-mind bursts like a balloon and its purpose is fulfilled. The now self-realized individual consciousness merges with the universal consciousness all around.

Before this can happen, though, the ego-mind must pass through seven stages of development: *Formation, Strengthening, Suffering, Contemplation, Introspection, Healing,* and *Transcendence.*

It takes many lifetimes for the ego-mind to develop through these stages. Everyone experiences each of the seven stages at different times according to the age and history of their soul. These stages are interconnected and happen simultaneously. The growth the ego-mind undergoes in one stage affects its growth in other stages. One stage may be more predominant than others, depending on the soul's maturity, level of awareness, and the lessons the soul is learning. We cannot heal into consciousness without passing through all these stages.

Although the stages appear to coincide with certain age groups, such as child, teenager, adult, and old age, physical age has nothing to do with the stages of the ego's development. Many adults have childish egos, while there are children with developed, mature egos.

We can avoid unnecessary suffering, and move through the stages of our ego's development faster, if we embrace every opportunity to know our true Self and focus on learning the lessons hidden within the many layers of our unconscious.

*Stage I:* **Formation**

At its most infantile stage, our ego-mind begins to form the moment we discover that we exist. In this stage we become aware that we have a body, voice, likes, and dislikes. Absorbing ideas, emotions, language and beliefs from our environment, we develop attitudes and behavior patterns in order to survive. Entirely focused on our own needs, our formative ego-mind perceives itself as separate from everyone and everything that surrounds it. It feels that the world revolves around meeting its every need and desire, and when its needs and wants are not met it feels rejected and experiences its first pain of separation. In this stage we either form a belief that the world is at our disposal and we can do as we please, or that it is harsh and unsympathetic. So, we develop a behavior pattern of either engaging with the world or retreating into ourselves. Our ego-mind in this stage of formation thus sees itself either as a powerful conqueror or a helpless victim.

When our developing ego-mind is nourished and supported by our parents and the environment, it forms a belief that the world is a safe and supportive place. As a result, we either openly share ourselves with the world, or at the other extreme expect the world to always take care of our needs.

Gradually, the first glimpses of competitiveness begin to emerge and our newly forming ego-mind struggles to learn to share and cooperate with others' needs. The initial attitudes and behavior patterns in the ego's formation stage determine how it will develop in the other stages.

*Stage II:* **Strengthening**

After feeling dependent on others for its survival in the formation stage, the ego-mind moves into its adolescence and strives for independence. At this stage, you either rebel against your early conditionings and try to break through the inhibitions that you felt during your ego's formation stage, or you retreat in fear by conforming to and defending what you were programmed to believe. Through rebellion and standing up to others and the world you begin to strengthen your will power and develop courage. Most of the time, you do a mixture of both in order to experience both the positive and negative polarities of the mind. In this way you come into true strength, which arises out of self-awareness and the realization of your innate freedom and independence.

As your ego-mind begins to strengthen, like a growing teenager, you strive to be more self-sufficient and independent of others and the world, believing you are now capable of doing whatever you want. Thinking that what you know is the truth, your ego-mind is ready to defend its ideas with words or actions. To prove your self-worth you begin to compete with others, experiencing both victory and failure. When you experience victory you feel strong and superior, and when you experience defeat you feel weak and inferior and begin to struggle with your initial self-centered attitude that the world should revolve around your needs and give you what you want.

In this stage, your ego-mind believes that it can receive recognition by achieving power, status, and material success. When you don't achieve the sought after power and recognition, or receive it prior to ego's maturity, you become aware that something inside you is unfulfilled. Here, your ego-mind moves into the suffering stage to continue its development.

## Stage III: **Suffering**

In the same way that coal transforms into a diamond under great pressure, pain and suffering are absolutely necessary for the development of our ego-mind and consciousness. The pressure of suffering helps to transform our unconscious into consciousness. Suffering helps us learn the needed lessons to grow in intelligence and consciousness because unless we suffer we don't see the need to come out of suffering.

Suffering allows us to change how we perceive reality and to recognize how our ego struggles to keep its will and self-identity alive. Realizing that you don't know everything, that you cannot force your will onto others, and cannot always do as you please creates suffering for the ego. Seeing that others are stronger, more powerful, more beautiful or intelligent, your ego-mind begins to struggle with itself. This inevitably causes you to suffer emotionally and physically.

You suffer the pain of your own self-imposed ideas and feel powerless against the realities of life. You suffer through many ups and downs of life, feeling strong and powerful one moment and powerless the next. Your suffering intensifies when you struggle to hold on to your beliefs, expectations, the people you know, and the things you own. With rejection, failure and defeat, in order to hold on to your identity you manipulate, lie, and compromise – and suffer even more. You protect your feelings of hurt by judging and blaming others, seeking revenge, or by blaming yourself and feeling guilty and ashamed for your choices and actions.

After recognizing that what you were really looking for all along was love and acceptance, you feel the pain of separation and of having missed out on many opportunities to experience love and intimacy. As a result, your ego-mind now begins to pursue love in the same way it pursued worldly success. When you continue to experience rejection, you begin to suffer even more, until you finally understand that you cannot buy or conquer anyone's love.

Through rejection your ego re-experiences the wound of separation and the pain of feeling alone increases. At this point, if you continue to search externally for fulfillment, your suffering intensifies. More suffering ensures the ego-mind to eventually accept others' needs, and understand that it is not better or worse than anyone else. As a result of experiencing pain and suffering your selfishness begins to diminish. This shift towards humility moves your developing ego-mind into the contemplation stage.

### *Stage IV:* **Contemplation**
In this stage, the most fundamental questions like, *Who am I?* and *Why am I here?* begin to arise and you try to understand the causes of your suffering. Through dawning new awareness you begin to contemplate

the purpose of life and the reason for living. You examine the consequences of your past actions and try to understand how your beliefs and desires have led to suffering. You recognize that your ego-mind has been the cause of your own suffering and your actions have been selfish and self-centered and therefore have not led to happiness and inner fulfillment. You begin to understand that you need to take responsibility for your own life and actions.

Through increased consciousness, you become aware of how your inhibitions and conditionings have limited you and kept you from enjoying life. You realize that whatever you have thought of as right no longer seems right and understand that you have nothing to lose by facing your fears and acting in spite of them. You now see how your negative thoughts and emotions sabotage your physical health and happiness and try to improve yourself by changing your negative thinking and behavior patterns into positive ones. You try to discipline your body and strengthen your will power. You begin to assert your individuality and try to find and live your life's purpose. Through contemplation and growing awareness, a true conscience begins to arise, and consciousness supersedes unconsciousness.

Your ego-mind matures into adulthood when you realize that you are responsible for your own welfare and happiness and move from selfish taking to compassionate and unconditional giving. When you feel exhausted by giving, you recognize that no matter how much you give, you cannot satisfy others; you still feel alone and unfulfilled. You now understand that you cannot find peace and happiness outside of yourself and begin to look inside. At this point, your ego-mind moves into its introspective stage to begin its conscious search for Truth.

## Stage V: Introspection

The humility and suffering of the contemplative stage gives rise to the introspective stage, where instead of focusing outwardly to find answers you move your attention inward. You now realize that to be free of suffering you need to examine the causes of your feelings, thoughts, and hidden unconscious motives, and take a leap from focusing on fulfilling your desires to focusing on awareness.

Through introspection, the identity that your ego-mind had built in its contemplative stage begins to crumble. You realize that your giving was conditional and you feel like a fraud. You begin to understand that no matter how hard you have tried to improve yourself and help others, you still have judgments, fears, and desires. You experience the agony of seeing your falseness and attempt to become more aware of your thoughts and actions. You now attempt to reconnect with your being more seriously through introspection and meditation.

This is the stage where consciousness begins to gain mastery over unconsciousness. Through increased consciousness you begin to see and understand how your ego-mind creates your own pain and suffering and you begin to take responsibility for your own creation.

As the ego-mind evolves through the introspective stage, the positive and negative thoughts and emotions become clearly visible and you begin to understand that positive and negative, good and bad are only parts of the mind and have nothing to do with the truth and reality of your being. All social and religious beliefs and conditionings begin to break down and lose relevancy. You now realize that there is a greater wisdom unfathomable to the mind alone; something greater to your existence than the mundane reality. Consciousness now comes to the forefront.

The introspective stage lays the foundation for you to learn to listen to and trust the language of intuition, and to direct your actions according to intuition instead of the conditionings of the mind. Listening to and trusting intuition, further increases and strengthens your consciousness, and the ego starts to take a back seat. Now, only the knowledge that comes from intuitive knowing becomes important, and you learn to surrender to your intuition.

For example, some time before meeting me, one of my students was backpacking through Asia. While waiting at an airport in Thailand to catch a flight to Nepal, he noticed a young woman sitting against the wall. The moment he saw her, he had a strong intuitive feeling that he should talk to her. Even though his ego-mind questioned it, he followed his intuition and started a conversation with her. Within twenty minutes, they had decided to trek in Nepal together and ended up becoming good friends. Later on, he moved to her hometown of Vancouver, Canada. After a year in Vancouver, he met me and started meditating and studying with me. Three years later, he became the editor of the book you are now reading. If he hadn't followed his intuition at that airport in Thailand, his life, my life, and the lives of the people he has met and affected here in Vancouver would have been different. By listening to and surrendering to his intuition, he transcended his ego-mind and as a result enriched his and other people's lives.

*Stage VI:* **Healing**
Many people think that healing means curing physical, mental, and emotional problems, or changing something that is "negative" or "unhealthy" into something that is "positive" or "healthy." Although this kind of healing is a necessary step in the ego's development, it is still part of its suffering and contemplative stage. Only after experiencing the consequences of our beliefs, choices, and actions do we truly begin our healing journey consciously.

As I mentioned earlier, we usually think that a fully developed ego is selfish, but selfishness is an attribute of an undeveloped ego and is only the beginning of its formation stage. To heal the ego-mind into consciousness, you first need to heal your wounded negative ego into a healthy positive one. Unless your ego-mind is completely positive, it's difficult to transcend it.

The wounded ego keeps you fearful and small and stops your consciousness from growing. (You'll recall that as part of the ego's formation stage, not getting what it wants naturally leads it to feeling wounded.) Unfortunately, most people live their lives in a wounded ego-mind. The wounded ego-mind has a poor self-esteem and image and is full of negative and self-defeating thoughts and emotions. The wounded ego-mind sees itself as a victim and life as a big struggle. When it does not receive unconditional love and acceptance, it thinks others are against it and begins to shrink.

Your wounds inhibit your ego's development and cause your energy to leak out. Healing is the process of closing the holes created by the wounded ego. Understanding that only a healthy ego can support the growth of consciousness can ultimately lead us to let go of the pain and suffering created by our wounded ego-mind. Healing the wounded ego-mind is part of our spiritual work. Although painful, healing the wounded ego is a necessary part of growth in consciousness.

The beliefs and attitudes that you acquired during your ego's formation stage determine what you need to heal in the healing stage. Healing happens when you take the responsibility to nurture your wounded ego and give to yourself what you didn't receive during your ego's formation stage. Only a healthy ego-mind is able to take full responsibility for itself and understand the importance of trust and surrender, which are absolutely necessary for taking the leap from mind to no-mind.

The healthy ego-mind has a positive self-identity and embraces life unconditionally. A healthy ego-mind does not judge and blame others but views everything that life brings, including rejection and hardships, as opportunities to learn and grow. It is sincere, generous, trusting, and always able to see life as an opportunity to grow. Although we commonly think of having a healthy, confident ego as boastful, in reality, a healthy ego is the doorway to liberation.

To heal your wounded ego you need to travel back through the unconscious history of your soul to the time of birth and into your past lives. This means peeling away the layers of personal and collective conditionings and beliefs, the karma of your past unconscious actions, and the layers of pain and suffering accumulated over many lifetimes. You must consciously work back through all the stages of your ego's development and transform your unconscious into consciousness. In a way, healing is like a thread that links all the stages of the ego's development and its final transformation into consciousness.

36

To heal the wounded ego-mind, you must be willing to embrace your wounds, take full responsibility for them, and learn the lessons they contain. This means accepting all your pain and problems as signs pointing to the lessons that you need to learn. To learn your lessons, you must be willing to explore the unconscious thoughts and emotions suppressed in your body, and let go of all your beliefs, conditionings, judgments, negative emotions (jealousy, envy, etc.), and allow your old ego-identity to die. In other words, to heal your wounded ego you must pass through the dark night of the soul and disidentify from all your thoughts, emotions, and beliefs. You must also break through your social and religious taboos and conditionings. This is a painful and arduous process. Absolute honesty, courage, and committed effort to do whatever it takes to heal the wounded ego is needed because only a healthy ego can welcome its own death and liberate your being into consciousness.

At first, you attempt to heal your wounded ego-mind with the mind itself, using counseling, psychotherapy, affirmations, and reading self-help books. Trying to heal your wounds using the positive mind accomplishes some results. However, unless you are willing to go into your body's cellular memory to feel, understand, and release the initial imprints and conditionings suppressed there, you will not be able to fully recognize and disidentify from the illusion created by the wounded ego that believes itself to be wounded.

Like fuel that keeps a car running, your identification with your negative thoughts and emotions fuels your wounds and keeps them alive. Once you stop feeding your wounded ego with attention and simply remain a witness to it, you eventually transform the ego into a healthy, positive one.

Healing the wounded ego may seem like a struggle in the beginning, but with perseverance, the journey becomes lighter and more exciting. When your thoughts change from: "I am not good enough; I hate myself; I cannot do this; I am a failure; others are smarter and better than me; I am a victim; why is this happening to me?" to: "I love myself; there is no one like me in the whole world; I have my own unique gifts to offer to the world; I can create the life I want; I am responsible for myself; there is nothing that I can't do; I'm willing to face all my fears and do whatever I need to be free of misery and suffering," the wounded ego is healed into a healthy and fully developed ego. Through the healthy ego you become conscious of the need to transcend the mind and find your being. But, before this can happen, all identification with the healthy ego-mind must be dropped as well.

The ultimate healing and transformation of the ego-mind into consciousness happens when you witness and disidentify from both the wounded (negative) and healthy (positive) parts of the mind. Through witnessing both, you become conscious that you are not your thoughts or emotions, whether positive or negative.

To heal into consciousness, don't judge or suppress your ego. Welcome it, accept it, and observe it as a detached witness. Suppressing your pain and judging your thoughts and emotions will only delay your healing into consciousness.

### Stage VII: **Transcendence**

Transcendence of the ego-mind (both wounded and healthy) concludes our healing into consciousness. With transcendence, a full consciousness of the being and its oneness with the universe arises. The experience of transcendence is known as liberation from the mind and the wheel of life and death. With complete disidentification from the body, thoughts, emotions, and personal will, the witnessing awareness transforms the ego-mind and only a pure consciousness remains. With consciousness, the anxiety that was created by the mind ceases to exist. Within consciousness lies a knowing that fear and death are illusions and that nothing in the universe ever dies. Consciousness now bursts open the balloon of the ego, and the purpose of the protective shell of the ego is fulfilled. With transcendence of the mind, recognition of the being and its eternal presence within the universe come to the forefront and the door to the universal Mind and the unknown mystery of existence opens.

As the ego-mind ripens for transcendence, its survival fears gradually begin to dissolve. Certain physical signs may appear when the mind begins to dissolve, i.e. energy movement, which may cause a feeling of falling into a whirlpool of spiraling energy or a feeling of nausea and fear of death. There may be disorientation, as if you are waking from a dream and are between two realities. Fear may give rise to thoughts that what is happening is "weird" and should be stopped. If you experience these things, you should not worry. Understand it is just the ego's fear of crumbling and dying. The key is to stay alert, surrender to whatever is happening, and simply watch the experience as a detached observer. Remind yourself that what you are experiencing is what you have been preparing for. This will help you to let go of the mind and the ego's fear of disappearing and will allow your experience to continue, leading to full consciousness and liberation from the mind. Keeping your witnessing awareness anchored in your silent center about two inches below your navel – and reminding yourself that *you* can never die – will enable you to move through the experience and celebrate your transformation.

## QUESTIONS AND ANSWERS ABOUT THE EGO'S DEVELOPMENT

*Will the fear of exposing my ego-mind stop its development?*

Most definitely! Any fear or suppression of the ego-mind will delay its development and the evolution of consciousness. You are afraid to expose what you think and feel because you are conditioned to believe that you are not okay as you are. As a result, you go on hiding your thoughts and emotions. Experience has taught you that if you expose your true thoughts and feelings, you will be criticized and rejected. And because you are afraid of rejection, you learn to suppress and compromise your truth.

If you want to heal your ego-mind into consciousness, you need to cultivate courage and trust. This would require you to honestly look at your fears and expose them to yourself and others. Looking at your fears with courage will help you see their illusory nature. Remind yourself that your fears have nothing to do with your being and are only a part of your ego. With right remembrance, and the practice of trust and courage, you will soon realize that your fears, thoughts, and emotions are only illusions created by the mind. This will help you develop a healthier outlook on life and eventually transform your ego-mind into consciousness.

*You've talked about our thoughts and emotions creating our ego. I've noticed that my mind goes crazy and I feel fearful whenever I am around you. Why am I so afraid in your presence?*

You are afraid because somewhere you know that my presence can expose your inner turmoil. If you stay present and don't identify with your mind, you will have no fear. Your fear indicates that you judge yourself and think that if you are spiritual you should have no anger, likes or dislikes, and should live a certain way.

Don't fight with your thoughts and feelings. Instead, embrace them as friends and try to understand why they are there. Be patient with yourself and keep in mind that whatever you are feeling and thinking simply exposes part of yourself to you. My presence only triggers what you need to see in yourself. As you continue to feel and observe your thoughts and fears, you will begin to understand their cause and disidentify from them while small windows into your inner silence slowly begin to open. Whenever you are relaxed and in your inner silence, you will feel trust and joy in my presence instead of fear because I am simply inviting you to take a leap into your being and enjoy the moment.

*Can I know myself without letting go of my desires?*

You normally hear that if you become desireless, you'll come to know yourself. As I see it, the opposite is more accurate: if you come to know yourself, you'll become desireless. This is difficult for most people to grasp. You want to know yourself, so you try hard to let go of your desires and attachments. You think to yourself: "I am working hard. I meditate. I tell myself I have to let go and be free of this and that desire," and simultaneously something in you does not allow the letting go to happen. And when your mind hears that desires and attachments cause suffering, you struggle with them even more. Yes, attachments and desires cause suffering, but this is only half the truth. On one hand, you think you want to be free of desires so you can know yourself, but on the other hand, you are not aware that you are not yet willing or ready to let them go. This creates an inner turmoil.

All spiritual teachings say that you need to be free of your desires and attachments. When you hear this, you try to suppress your desires. After hearing me say that your ego needs to develop to its peak before it can drop, your mind is confused. The idea of developing the ego-mind goes against your beliefs about spirituality.

Don't try to be "spiritual" by suppressing parts of yourself that need to be lived. Don't condemn yourself for having desires, and don't condemn your ego-mind. You heal into consciousness when you find the courage to fully embrace and face your ego and its desires. Expose your ego-mind and let it come out into the light from its hiding place in the darkness of your unconscious. Once you give it permission to be exposed, you will be surprised how quickly it can be transformed into the light of consciousness. With consciousness, you will be able to effortlessly discriminate between your mind's desires, which can be easily surrendered, and your existential needs that demand to be lived. By living and experiencing your existential needs, and facing the consequences of your actions, you will start to know yourself and will be able to detach your consciousness from the desires that arise out of your ego-mind.

41

*I keep encountering people who seem to attack me and are aggressive towards me. How can I protect myself?*

The way you posed your question shows that you are looking out instead of in. To understand why people are aggressive towards you, first look inside yourself and ask, "What gets triggered inside me when I feel attacked? What feelings and thoughts come up? What do I need to discover about myself as a result of what's happening outside?" Perhaps people are aggressive towards you because that's how you treat others and yourself. Or perhaps you have a need to be accepted and treated in a certain way, and when you are rejected, you feel disturbed and angry. People and situations always show us what we need to see and learn about ourselves, and when we take responsibility for our own feelings, how others treat us also changes. Everything in life is there to teach us something about ourselves. Don't blame others, or try to separate yourself from them. Be grateful that they are helping you to become conscious of yourself and your own ego-mind and consciousness.

Whenever you feel "attacked," move your awareness into your center and from there watch what's happening inside and outside of yourself. This way you will know exactly why something is happening the way it is. Perhaps someone is "attacking" you because they feel envious of you and they want to pull you down. Or perhaps they are pushing you away because they feel your judgments and aggression towards them, and this may seem to you as if they are attacking you. Whatever the situation, observe what gets triggered inside you, take full responsibility for your own thoughts and feelings, and understand the lessons that the experiences bring. Until you understand your lessons, similar situations of feeling attacked by others will continue.

And there is no need to be fearful. Trying to protect yourself keeps you in the illusion of your ego-mind, instead of helping you understand and become more conscious of what is truly happening inside you. This, of course, doesn't mean that you should allow someone to harm you. If you are not reacting but are simply taking care of yourself, your inner peace will not be disturbed and your response to protect yourself will not come from fear but out of your inner strength. When other people's opinions about you don't disturb you, you have found the way into your inner power and center of being. Being in your center will free you of the recurring pattern of attracting situations where you feel attacked, and people's behavior towards you will automatically change.

*How does pain and suffering lead to compassion?*

Compassion flowers out of suffering like the lotus grows out of muddy water. Suffering is a necessary part of growth. Unless we experience pain and suffer in our own skin, we will not understand the pain and suffering of others. Our pain and suffering force us to understand ourselves and others and helps us learn forgiveness. When we take responsibility for our suffering, instead of blaming and criticizing others or ourselves, our heart opens and we are able to truly understand and experience compassion for ourselves and others. Compassion is the healing power of unconditional love that arises out of an understanding and forgiving heart.

*Sometimes, when I just watch my anger, I feel separate from it and experience a sort of peace in my body similar to when I release it by expressing it out loud. Is one way more effective than the other?*

If you can witness your anger, that is the best way, but sometimes you need to express the anger out loud. As long as you don't throw it at someone else and blame them for the way you feel, expressions of anger can be healthy. Healthy anger exposes the deeper part of you, which is not willing to live with the situation at hand or the old limiting beliefs. Perhaps you are angry that you are forced to compromise your inner truth and what feels right for you. If you take responsibility for your anger and express it with awareness, watchfulness, and without blame, it will release your blocked energy and help you break through many other layers of your unconscious beliefs and behavior patterns. If, however, you are afraid to express your anger because it is not socially acceptable, or you are afraid of rejection, then you continue to feel trapped and frustrated. Without feeling, watching, and understanding the cause of your anger, no internal or external change is possible.

It is usually easier to experience peace after an outward release of anger because it does not require any witnessing. But it is impossible to understand yourself or the cause of your anger without witnessing. Ultimately, you need to watch the anger before, during, and after it is expressed and understand its cause; otherwise you will go on releasing the tension that comes with anger, but no transformation can happen. When you watch the anger as an observer, you jump out of the movie created by your thoughts and emotions and separate your consciousness from it.

You cannot transform anger, or any other negative emotion, into love, peace, and joy through control. To transform any negative emotion into a positive one, you need to accept your feelings and watch the sensations that arise in your body as a result. If you continue observing your feelings of anger, the energy of anger will eventually transform into inner joy and peace, simply by your watching.

*Does birth trauma have a bigger effect on our spiritual development than other traumatic experiences?*

The birth trauma may have the biggest effect on our spiritual development because it is our first experience of separation. When the child is pushed out of the mother's womb where it felt fully taken care of, as if in paradise, the child for the first time feels rejected and alone. So in that sense the birth trauma is the first trauma, and has the biggest effect on our spiritual development. The birth trauma is the root cause of all our fears of rejection, separation, aloneness, and death.

All traumatic experiences generate thoughts and emotions that create blocks in our body and energy. Our physical bodies are full of suppressed pain related to many "traumatic" experiences that create our ego-minds. Any identification with an experience maintains the ego-mind and hinders our spiritual transformation.

Ultimately, all traumatic experiences cause feelings of woundedness, but we need to remember that our wounds are only temporary stepping stones on our journey. All our mental and emotional wounds help us grow in consciousness and find our true Self. To heal from a traumatic experience, it will be helpful to remember that on some level, your soul chooses what you need to experience in order to learn the particular lessons you need on your journey.

*How do I know if my healing from a trauma is complete?*

What keeps the imprint of a traumatic experience alive is your identification with the pain it has caused. The pain could be physical, psychological, or both. Your healing from a trauma is complete when you have disidentified from your pain, and the memory of the experience no longer triggers an emotional reaction. When you disidentify from the pain, you also disidentify from your ego-mind and become conscious that your soul and your consciousness are separate from the experience and the pain. Although the memory of the experience will always remain in your consciousness, it will no longer disturb your mental and emotional well-being. Whenever you remember the experience, you simply view it as a past event without emotional reaction.

You can disidentify from a traumatic experience and heal your wounded ego-mind when you take responsibility for your feelings of pain, learn its hidden lessons, and forgive those who have "hurt" you. With forgiveness and understanding of the needed lessons, the pain, sorrow, regret, fear, anger, and blame that you experienced as a consequence of a trauma are transformed into compassion, forgiveness and gratitude, and your energy is restored to wholeness. When you feel whole, your life becomes more creative and joyful, and you become more relaxed, present, and content.

45

If the memory of a traumatic experience triggers an emotional reaction and affects your psychological and physical well-being, it means you are still identified with the experience and have not healed from it yet. Your reaction indicates that there is pain, anger, sadness, or blame associated with the experience that you are still suppressing in your body. You need to go deeper into your body and your feelings and release what is suppressed. You will postpone your healing from the trauma if you continue to hold on to your pain, thoughts, and emotions associated with the experience. Your emotional pain could eventually manifest as physical pain or illness. Once you let go of your attachment to the pain, you hasten your healing from a trauma and the quality of your life improves.

*I feel my being wants to expand and do something new and different, but at the same time I am afraid. It is exciting and terrifying at the same time to know that I am more than what I think. What can I do to break through the fear that keeps me small and allow my being and consciousness to expand?*

Your being wants to expand but the fear of the unknown holds you back. Your instinct is to run away. Even a small experience of expansion beyond the familiar shakes up the conditioned ego-mind and destroys your perception of reality. The ego-mind is afraid to disappear, so it tries to do anything it can to take your awareness out of the experience of expansion. When your energy expands everything that was familiar begins to crumble. Expansion is scary for the ego-mind but it is exciting for the being because it can finally live itself fully and freely.

To allow your energy to expand, stay in your center and observe the fear and the mind that try to stop the experience. Let the experience of the expansion happen on its own while you continue to observe what is happening. The more you observe, the less fear and anxiety you will experience, and the more your energy can begin to expand.

Your work is to remain an observer so your mind, fear, and excitement don't stop the experience of expansion. Continue strengthening your inner witnessing awareness and preparing your body through meditation and purification to allow the experience of joy that comes with expansion to settle in your body.

Also, watch your breath. Watching your breath while you experience fear or expansion will enable you to continue experiencing whatever is happening until the experience of expansion stops on its own. Tell yourself: "I can watch and continue experiencing whatever is happening in spite of my fear." By doing this, you gradually learn to contain the joy that comes from an experience of expansion inside your body. When you understand that your fear, thoughts, and excitement are only passing illusions, you will suddenly realize that you are not your mind or your fears and your energy and consciousness will be free to expand far and wide into the universe.

*I want to let go of my pattern of needing attention from people. I have moments when I think I have let it go, but then I find myself repeating the same pattern again. How can I permanently break this pattern?*

If you want to break a pattern, you cannot do it just by wishful thinking. As I said earlier, if you are truly serious about letting go of a behavior pattern, then you need to look inside to understand why it is there, and then take responsibility for it. Unless you take full responsibility for your behavior pattern and understand its cause, it will be impossible to break it and let it go. If you are unconscious of the cause, you will keep repeating the behavior. Only by becoming conscious of the cause can you break the pattern. If the cause is suppressed in your unconscious, no matter how much you try to change it, you will not succeed because the power of your unconscious is bigger than your wishful thinking.

Our unconscious can be compared to the bottom of an iceberg, and our consciousness to the part that is above the water. No matter what the top of the iceberg decides to do, it is the bottom part that ultimately decides where the iceberg will be moving. That's why every time you decide to let go of a pattern without going into your unconscious, it feels like a struggle and nothing seems to change.

First, ask yourself why you want to break this pattern. Is it because others say that you should, or is it because you feel fed up with how your neediness keeps you small and fearful? Feel the answer inside and be honest with yourself so you can understand why the pattern is there. If you feel it is your mind that wants to let it go but something inside resists, then it will be impossible to break it. If, on the other hand, the need comes from understanding that this pattern does not serve you any longer, then you are close to learning the needed lessons and breaking the pattern. So, go on looking inside and exploring the causes of your neediness until you see why you are holding on to this pattern.

*I feel a need to experience a deep intimate partnership, but each time I am in a relationship it doesn't work out. I am left unfulfilled and frustrated. I recognize my pattern of neediness, but I don't know how to come out of it. Is the best way to deal with it to say to myself, "I'm not going to be needy anymore," or is just watching my neediness enough?*

Any relationship based on need exposes the wounded ego and is sooner or later bound to fail. To experience intimacy with another being, you first need to experience it with yourself. Intimacy requires openness, honesty, and full acceptance and love of yourself. If you can't be open and honest with yourself and can't accept and love yourself as you are, it will be impossible to truly accept and love someone else. You can only relate to others as deeply as you can relate to yourself. It's important to understand why you get sad, angry, or frustrated when your needs are not fulfilled. Intimacy requires understanding, and if you cannot understand yourself, how can you understand someone else?

It is impossible to change your pattern of neediness by rejecting it. Just to say that you are not going to be needy any longer is not enough. Changing any pattern requires more awareness of yourself. You stay needy because you don't know yourself. As a result, you stay insecure and always look to others for validation. To stop being needy, you must see your wounded ego and understand your selfishness. To see your selfishness is painful. To admit that you are insecure is painful. Unless you understand that your partner is not responsible for fulfilling your needs and making you feel secure, you won't be able to mature and take responsibility for your own life. Your partner has his own needs to take care of.

If you want to break your pattern of neediness, first accept it, then understand its cause and take full responsibility for it. Without understanding the cause of your neediness and taking responsibility for it, you cannot find your inner truth and power. Without finding and living your own truth and inner power, it is impossible to break any pattern. To come out of neediness you need to learn to give to yourself what you hope to receive from others. Without this, you will remain a beggar and your needs can never be fulfilled.

Instead of trying to find ways to satisfy your needs from outside, find ways to satisfy them from inside through your own creativity. Watch your needs and remind yourself that you are not the needs but simply a witness that sees and feels them. Watching your needs from inside will help you see them from a distance, understand their cause, and disidentify from them.

Normally, instead of understanding and taking responsibility for our needs, we struggle to change something about ourselves so others will love and accept us and give us what we want. When our needs are not met we feel rejected, insecure or angry and try to justify our feelings by blaming others or ourselves. When you blame others or think of yourself as a victim, you either feel self-righteous and push yourself onto others, or retreat and withdraw from them. Either way you manipulate to get your needs met, and your heart remains closed. It is impossible to have an intimate and meaningful relationship this way. Staying in neediness and insecurity only creates more unhappiness for yourself and others. There is a basic universal law that applies to everyone: when we try to take because we perceive that something is lacking, we cannot truly receive; on the other hand, when we are full and content within ourselves, we are in a true state of reception.

So to just say, "I'm not going to do that anymore" without awareness is useless because this will not stop your feelings of neediness. To transform your neediness into love and intimacy, you must look inside and take responsibility for how you feel. When you take responsibility for your own feelings, you simultaneously become conscious of your creative potential and realize that you already have everything you need.

What you are looking to receive from outside is already inside you. Your being is always full and content. Existence has already given to you everything you need; it has given your being, your life! What more do you want? It is your responsibility to find and live what is already yours. Who else can find your hidden potential and live it? Everyone is responsible for finding and living their own creativity and true purpose.

How can anyone else heal your wounded ego or live your inner joy? If someone else lives it for you, you will be robbed of your own experience. You must recognize how your neediness keeps you in unconsciousness and learn to give to yourself what you are hoping to receive from others. You also need to see and take responsibility for how you blame or manipulate others to get your needs met. Most people prevent their spiritual growth by keeping their neediness hidden. Have the courage to expose it. This is how you are going to see your selfishness and heal it into consciousness.

Intimacy and unconditional giving and receiving can happen naturally and joyously if each partner is self-sufficient and content within himself or herself. To be self-sufficient means to understand that there are times when you or your partner need to be alone. The world ceaselessly demands our participating energy and tries to take our attention out of our inner Self in order to operate. Once in a while, we need to withdraw from the world and rejuvenate our energies if we want to continue giving. The same is also true for any balanced relationship. Every once in a while, we need to have time alone. When we are full, giving and receiving become effortless and bring more joy to ourselves and others.

It's a good sign that you don't want to stay in your pattern of neediness any longer. I know that you have a lot to offer, but you don't seem to realize that wanting to give something to someone is another need. You are imposing on others what you like to give. Trying to give something when the other does not want to receive what you are offering is another form of insecurity and neediness. People somehow sense that your giving is not unconditional and you want to give because you want to receive something in return. When your giving is conditional, then it is not true giving. If it is unconditional, you will not feel frustrated, depressed, or insecure when the other rejects what you are offering. If your giving is unconditional, you just give out of your inner joy and abundance and because giving enriches you and allows your energy to expand. If someone does not want your offering, then you simply move inside and enjoy your own presence.

*I am beginning to see that I enjoy seeing other people suffer because it gives me a sense of power. I manipulate and control them by not giving them what they want, yet leading them to believe I might give it to them. I use people to meet my needs but don't give in return. Behind this is a vile hostility and hatred towards others, and a feeling of righteousness and enjoyment in withholding. I feel power in this anger and giving it up feels like "giving in" and "losing." When people don't play into this dynamic, I feel insecure and undeserving of their friendship and I abandon the relationship.*

*I feel I'm not good enough so I'm always trying to be better, which includes being better than others; I use people to help me feel more full inside. It seems like this behavior is coming from a place of pain and a feeling of inadequacy. It happens when I don't feel good enough and I want somebody else to make me feel good. So, it is like taking what they have, which was exactly what happened to me when I was sexually abused as a child. I see this pattern and how it keeps me in suffering, but I am having a hard time letting it go so I can fully heal. I feel the incredible value and power that my actions could have if I used this awareness to act differently in my relationships. What can I do to heal myself?*

51

First, understand that nothing in life happens by accident. No one knows your soul's history the way you do. Perhaps you needed to experience the abuse so you could recognize that part of you that enjoys abusing others. The desire to have what someone else has, such as possessions, love, beauty, power, success, intelligence, wisdom, happiness, health, innocence, etc., creates jealousy and is at the root of all types of power struggles and abuse – physical, mental, and emotional.

You can see the cause of the abuse only if you look inside yourself and take responsibility for your thoughts and emotions. Otherwise, you will stay believing yourself to be a victim and powerless to come out of the pain caused by the abuse. It is good that you have seen how you enjoy seeing others suffer and how you manipulate to get your needs met. With this understanding, look at why you compare yourself with others and feel a need to hurt them if they appear better or happier than you are. If you take responsibility for your feelings, instead of being revengeful, your energy will have a chance to transform into love and compassion for yourself and others.

Once you accept that you are capable of hurting others and forgive yourself for hurting them, you will be able to also forgive those who have hurt you. This will allow you to heal and move further in your spiritual development. True healing arises out of understanding and compassion for yourself and others. Once you begin to love and accept yourself as you are, your heart will open and transform your hurt and anger into understanding and compassion.

Both the abuser and the abused need healing into consciousness. Sometimes the roles change, and the abuser becomes the abused. But regardless of which perspective you are healing from, it is about healing from unconsciousness into consciousness. We hurt others and are hurt by them when we are unconscious. We are healed and start loving ourselves and others when we become conscious.

When you withhold your love you maintain your false sense of power and control over others and continue to suffer. If you enjoy making others suffer then you too will suffer because your heart will stay closed. So the more you love yourself and enjoy your life, the more you can let others enjoy theirs. With this understanding, you'll stop being nasty towards others and will stop manipulating or putting them down so you can feel better.

Even a murderer will become a Buddha one day. A murderer is only exposing the state of his unconsciousness. A person who is conscious cannot commit murder, and yet he or she does not condemn the being of the murderer. The only thing that can be condemned is the unconsciousness of the person who acts violently. The murderer's being cannot be condemned because it is not separate from everyone else's being. This is why, when Jesus was on the cross, he said: "Father, forgive them, for they know not what they are doing."

*One moment I feel very centered, free, and peaceful, but then the next moment I feel like I have fallen back into my old unconscious habits. What am I not getting?*

What you are not getting is that you are still trying to choose one over the other instead of just remaining a witness to both. There is nothing wrong in falling back as long as you get back up and continue your search with more awareness. Through the process of going back and forth, your witnessing awareness gradually strengthens and you become more centered and grounded.

To become conscious of yourself, you need to welcome your unconscious darkness as much as you welcome the light. Knowing both is how you can distinguish unconsciousness from consciousness. If you suppress your darkness, you also suppress your light. Both darkness and light are needed to serve as guides and to point you toward the silent stillness of your being. With increased awareness of your center, you can move there any time at will and maintain your inner peace regardless of what happens on the outside.

Everyone, consciously or unconsciously, is looking for inner peace. People who talk and work towards world peace don't realize that they are talking and working towards their own need for peace. They are actually searching for their inner peace from the madness of the world. The world may never be at peace: that is not its purpose. Only individuals can be free and at peace. The outer world is only a reflection of our inner madness. When we focus on trying to change the outside world, we go astray from our own path. Individuals make up the world, and only individuals can make the world a better place to be by finding and living their own inner peace.

Find your inner peace by becoming more aware. Understand and be conscious of who you are. Manifest your calling, but don't do it for the world. Don't allow your ego to mislead you into believing that you are doing something for the world. Do it just for the sake of doing it. Do it because you enjoy what you do. Do it because you feel a call from within your being. You simply contribute the purity of your essence because that's the only way existence can express itself and enrich the world. The world is here only to help you come to your own flowering. You can benefit the world only by realizing and living your authentic truth. If you live your truth, you will help others to see and live theirs. How consciously or unconsciously you live your life will either contribute to the expansion or contraction of the universe. As your energy opens and expands, the universe opens and expands. As your energy contracts, the universe also contracts. Allow your being to expand. The more consciously you live your life, the more you become a blessing to yourself, others, and the world.

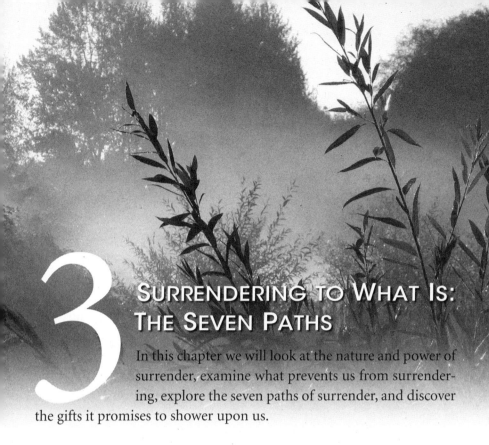

# 3 SURRENDERING TO WHAT IS: THE SEVEN PATHS

In this chapter we will look at the nature and power of surrender, examine what prevents us from surrendering, explore the seven paths of surrender, and discover the gifts it promises to shower upon us.

We heal from ego into consciousness by surrendering. In surrender we let go of our ego-mind and personal will and accept whatever life and existence bring us. When we stop struggling with what is, we bring peace to ourselves and the world, and free our energy of the pain and suffering the mind creates. Surrender requires acceptance of whatever existence brings us without grudge, blame, or complaint. It requires acceptance of everything that life presents us with – without fear, resentment, resistance, or repression. If existence doesn't support our desires but brings us pain and sorrow, surrendering to what is means not fighting with the circumstances or suppressing our emotions, but accepting them as messengers and teachers. If it brings us success, love and happiness, surrendering to what is means not holding back from enjoying and sharing these uplifting and joyful feelings.

Surrender requires a positive outlook on life and a pure and grateful heart that blesses others instead of judging and competing with them. Surrender happens instantaneously the moment you move from your mind to your heart. Surrender makes your life more meaningful.

Let go of any desire that life should be different from how it is this very moment, and you are in surrender. Accept success and failure without being attached to either, and you are in surrender. Trust whatever the universe brings you from moment to moment, and you are in surrender. Understand that existence gives you and everyone else exactly what is needed to heal into consciousness, and you are in surrender.

Surrender is not a withdrawal from or renunciation of life. Neither is it a sign of weakness or avoidance of responsibility. Only through strength, wisdom, and fearlessness can you surrender to what is. In surrender, you become the master of your own life instead of the servant of your existence. In surrender, you learn to rise and fall with the tides of life, while remaining untouched within the purity of your being.

## WHAT PREVENTS YOU FROM SURRENDERING?

All struggles and unhappiness arise out of your rejection of what life brings. Instead of enjoying the life you already have, you seek what your beliefs and conditionings dictate. If you were prepared to accept what life gives you and able to watch your ego-mind from moment to moment, there would not even be a question of needing to surrender. In the absence of the ego-mind, you would already *be* in surrender.

What prevents us from surrendering is our need to always be right and in control. When we are afraid to let go of our beliefs and attachments to people and things we prevent ourselves from receiving what life abundantly showers upon us with all of its creation. It's impossible to accept and surrender to life when you negate it through fear and insecurity. Your fear of the unknown and your worries of survival turn your life into a struggle that inevitably jeopardizes your own health and happiness.

You bring peace to yourself, others, and the world when you let go of your struggling ego-mind and gracefully accept what life offers you. By surrendering to what is you free your energy of the pain and suffering that your desires, beliefs, and conditionings create and discover many new and exciting things about yourself, others, and the universe.

## LEARNING TO SURRENDER

We cannot think ourselves into surrender. We are either surrendered or in the mind thinking about it. To surrender to what is, we must move our attention from the mind into the heart where the seed of true wholeness and transcendence resides.

To learn to live in surrender, you must develop courage and trust that existence takes care of you and always gives you exactly what you need. The divine wisdom of existence, or if you choose, God, can only be understood through learning to accept and surrender to whatever lessons the universe brings you. Whether it is through success or failure, poverty or riches, pain or happiness, the universe always gives you exactly what you need to heal into consciousness.

There is a beautiful story in the Old Testament of the Bible about a man named Job. Job was a wealthy, powerful, and influential man who did his best to live an honorable life. He faithfully fulfilled his family and social obligations and was regarded by others as a religious and trustworthy man. He was grateful to God for his good fortune and felt rightly rewarded for his efforts and commitment. One day, at the peak of his success, a disaster struck him. Job lost all his wealth, and all his animal stock and servants were consumed by fire. He also lost all his children when a hurricane struck his elder son's house while they were gathered there to eat and drink.

Job was devastated and in shock that God would forsake him after he had been so faithful to Him, but he held on to his beliefs. Outwardly, he tried to accept and surrender to the will of God, but inside he struggled with anger and disappointment at what he thought was God's betrayal. His inner anguish brought about an excruciatingly painful skin disease that covered his body in oozing sores from head to toe. He suffered intensely. His wife further added to his misery by showing no sympathy and blaming him for all their misfortunes. He felt completely alone and isolated. He had gone from feeling like a somebody who had everything to a nobody left with nothing.

When his friends came to comfort him, Job broke down and cursed the day he had been born. He raged against himself and his existence, complaining that he had done nothing to deserve what was happening to him. He went back and forth between fearing God and accusing him of cruelty and injustice. He demanded that God give an explanation. What was the point, complained Job, of being God's faithful servant if he was only made to suffer? Why were things given to men then taken away? Why was there creation if it was going to be destroyed? Why was awareness given to man on one hand and the truth hidden from him on the other? Why was there life at all if everything was going to turn to dust? He questioned, but found no answers. He felt hopeless and confused and saw no end to his suffering. In despair, he contemplated suicide.

Job's friends were shocked by what had happened to him. They judged him for his anger and thought he must have done something wrong to deserve his misfortunes. They insisted that God was punishing him for some sin he must have committed. They told him to repent so that he could be forgiven.

Job argued that he had faithfully lived by the commandments he was taught. He insisted that he had not made wealth or power his goal, nor had he put himself above others. He had been a loyal husband and father. He had never taken pleasure in another's misfortune, had not hidden anything to protect his reputation, and had generously given to those in need.

Then the youngest of the men, who had been silent out of respect to his elders, spoke. He expressed his anger at Job for trying to use reasoning to justify himself in the face of God's mysterious ways. He also rebuked the other men for believing that God was simply punishing Job for his hidden sins, and condemned them for not being sincere and truthful. Then the young man asked Job if he believed the commandments through his own understanding and experience, or if he was just blindly following the scriptures. Did he know the laws of the universe? Had he seen the depth of darkness and the gates of death? Had he grasped the vastness of the Earth and its creatures, knew who provided the animals their prey and who made the rain to quench their thirst? Had he truly found where darkness and light dwelled?

Then the young man reminded all of them that God does not despise or judge anyone, because everyone and everything is his creation. He only creates situations so that everyone can know themselves and gain wisdom, compassion, and understanding. It is not the mind, he said, but the spirit within man and the breath within his heart that enables him to understand the wisdom of God. He reminded them of the need to surrender to God's will and trust that whatever God gives is for everyone's higher good. The young man then asked Job to stop cursing and judging what had happened and accept it gracefully, so he could find true wisdom.

Job remained silent. His confidence in himself and his righteousness were shaken. He realized his ignorance and saw what God was trying to teach him. He understood that both the successes and the catastrophes were a blessing bestowed by God so that he could become conscious of the laws and power of creation and his own inner truth. He understood that God is both light and darkness, and there cannot be good without evil. He understood that pain and suffering were nothing to be feared or avoided but welcomed as teachers of wisdom, humility, and compassion. In gratitude, he surrendered to the will of God. His wisdom grew with time, and God blessed him with a long life and restored everything that he had lost many times over.

59

## THE POWER OF SURRENDER

By surrendering to what is, you end your ego's struggle to survive and come into alignment with your being and the universe. In surrender, your vulnerability and judgments are transformed into strength and compassion. Surrender opens your heart and authentically connects you with others. Surrender helps you to align with your inner wisdom and allows you to let go of anger and pain and forgive those who you believe have hurt you. All wars between people, religions, and nations would end if everyone could learn to surrender their ego-mind and learn to live through the inner silence of their heart and being.

The ego-mind thinks that by surrendering you become a "loser," but in reality, the reward of true victory hides within surrender. Through struggle and denial you strengthen your ego-mind; through acceptance and surrender, you strengthen your heart. By not surrendering, your attention stays focused on superficial thoughts and desires; in surrender, it moves into the wisdom of your inner knowing. By not surrendering, you stay closed, frustrated, and depressed; while in surrender you open to the many miraculous gifts the universe waits to shower upon you.

When you stubbornly persist in pursuing your beliefs and desires, you create stress and anguish for yourself and others. Even if you get what you want, you ultimately don't feel fulfilled. Understanding that existence doesn't support your desires when they are not in your best interest, allows you to relax and accept what is, without resentment or struggle, trusting that existence has something else planned for you.

Your intelligence and inner wisdom know that when one door closes another always opens, so you can easily change direction. When you let go and accept life as it is, it suddenly starts to reward you in the most unexpected ways. This is how we experience and live the miraculous.

For example, instead of trying to hold on to a relationship that does not work, if you can surrender to what is and let go of your fears and expectations, a better one will be just around the corner. But if you stay afraid of change or are afraid to be alone, you will either stay in a relationship that does not work and keeps you in misery and unhappiness, or attract a relationship similar to your previous one.

True religiousness can only arise out of surrender. Job thought he was religious, but only after he fully surrendered and accepted everything that had happened to him did he become truly religious. By surrendering to God's will, he found true wisdom and everything that he had lost was given back to him many times over. Surrender allowed him to experience the fullness of his being, which is not dependent on anything external. Through surrender he left behind fear, anger, ignorance and grief, and found authentic humility and true faith in God.

## HEALING INTO CONSCIOUSNESS THROUGH THE SEVEN PATHS OF SURRENDER

If you reflect back on your life you will realize that you have already had many moments of surrender, some more profound than others. Although the circumstances in which we surrender are different each time, the inner experience of understanding, gratitude, and expansion that results from surrender is always the same. Each experience of surrender expands our consciousness and influences our life in a positive and profound way. Since the best way to learn about the healing power of surrender is through experience, I have chosen seven basic ways that you can practice surrendering to what is and have called them the seven paths of surrender. These paths are:

*Surrendering to Your Sexuality*
*Surrendering to Life*
*Surrendering to Your Inner Power*
*Surrendering to Love*
*Surrendering to Your Individuality*
*Surrendering to Your Inner Wisdom*
*Surrendering your will to the Will of Existence*

61

These paths are closely interconnected and relate to the seven chakras or energy centers of the body as well as the seven stages of the ego's development. I'll be talking about the chakras in more depth in chapters 5 and 6; this chapter offers a practical way to heal and transform the ego-mind into consciousness through surrender.

To help you choose a path of surrender that is right for you, take a moment to contemplate and answer the following questions:

*Do you find it difficult to surrender to your sexuality?*
*Do you worry about your survival?*
*Do you have difficulty standing up for yourself?*
*Do you find it difficult to surrender to love and intimacy?*
*Do you find it difficult to follow your intuition?*
*Do you find it difficult to surrender to your inner knowing?*
*Do you find it difficult to accept and surrender to whatever life brings you?*

If you answered "yes" or "sometimes" to any of the above questions, and have gained enough insight into the nature of your mind and the behavior patterns that prevent you from surrendering, ask yourself: *What do I usually do when I don't like what is happening in my life?* and *If I could surrender to just one thing, what would it be?* Depending on your answer, choose a path of surrender you most resonate with and practice it for at least three months. You can practice with more than one path at a time, but I recommend staying with one or two at the most, so your energy stays focused on the path that is most relevant to your current life circumstances. Decide how much time you will allocate to your practice daily, and find ways to help you discipline your practice with ease. It is important that you enjoy what you do without struggle. Once you have created a suitable schedule, be diligent with your commitment. You can move on to other paths when you feel ready.

The paths of surrender will continually change as your life changes, but the main thread between all the paths will remain the same – it is moving from acceptance to understanding, from understanding to surrender, and from surrender to transformation. Surrendering to what is will bring you more joy, silence, and inner peace and will eventually lead to total transformation of your ego-mind into consciousness.

*1st Path:* **Surrendering to Your Sexuality**

Surrendering to your sexuality means accepting that you are a sexual being. Existence gave you a body, and sexuality is part of it. To deny your body and its sexuality is to deny God who created it. Usually, we struggle with our sexual desire by either suppressing it or immediately needing to satisfy it.

If we repress our sexuality because of social and religious conditionings and think that sex is sinful, we fuel the struggle between our body and mind. If we compulsively strive to gratify our sexual desires, we keep ourselves stuck in the animal realm and stunt our spiritual evolution into greater consciousness. Either way, we cannot grow solid roots and will always find it difficult to surrender to love, life, and existence.

*To practice surrendering to your sexuality, practice acceptance and understanding of your body, desires, inhibitions, and conditionings about sex.* Before you can surrender to your sexuality, you need to first accept it with an understanding that it is an undeniable part of you. Begin exploring your sexuality objectively, like a scientist. Whenever sexual desire arises, look inside and observe your body, beliefs and judgments about sex. Observe your feelings, breath, and energy movements in your body. Be a detached observer of what is happening without judging or acting upon your desires. Watch your sexual desire and remind yourself that you are simply a witness to whatever is happening in your body and mind. Then, write down your observations and take time to contemplate them. Ask yourself, *Is my desire coming from my mind or my body? Did it start with something that I saw, heard, thought, or imagined, or did it arise spontaneously without me thinking about sex? Was I alone or physically near someone when I felt sexual desire?*

63

With the practice of observation, you will be able to learn to discriminate between the sexual needs of your body and the desires of your mind. If sexual arousal occurs without the imagination or thought, then it is the body's natural physical response to energy and sexuality. If it is triggered by a thought, by the imagination, or by visual stimulus (i.e., pornography), it is from the mind.

If you see that your sexual desire arises out of your mind, don't feed it with your attention. Release your attachment to it and let your focus and energy rise higher into your heart. If the desire is naturally arising from the body, surrender to it and give yourself permission to enjoy your sexuality when appropriate while you still remain a witness to it.

To discriminate between the two is not an easy task and requires much focus and awareness, but if you persevere you'll find the golden key to freedom from attachment to your body and its needs. Surrendering to your sexuality will allow your sexual energy to be channeled into love, intimacy, creativity, and higher consciousness. It will also prepare you to surrender to life, death, and existence.

*2nd Path:* **Surrendering to Life**

To surrender to life means understanding and accepting your responsibility in needing to take care of your physical, mental, emotional, and spiritual needs and well-being. Life always takes care of you and offers many opportunities for growth in consciousness, but you need to take responsibility to fulfill your part. Most people resist life by either worrying about their survival, withdrawing from life or contemplating suicide when life is difficult, or by struggling with how it unfolds.

They impose their will on life by either wishing things were different or by fighting against and manipulating it. When you surrender to life and ride with its ups and downs you not only grow and evolve individually but also contribute to the evolution of others. By taking responsibility for your own well-being, you also affect the well-being of others.

To surrender to life is to surrender to both the simple and complex tasks that life requires, such as cooking, cleaning, eating, working for a living, and caring for your children. It's not what you do but how you do it that matters. When you do these things mechanically, or with resistance, you miss their value for your spiritual development. Surrendering to daily tasks helps to put your energy into motion and takes you away from the chatter of the mind.

Surrendering to life doesn't mean to remain passive. It means to take responsibility for how your life is and has been, and for how you would like to see yourself in the future. To improve your quality of life and to live a more meaningful and fulfilling life, you need to educate yourself and find the sources of creativity within.

Life is always wiser and greater than our small ego-mind. When we surrender to what life brings, we can see and understand the hidden lessons and the new direction that life is pointing us in. By resisting and rejecting the guidance that life offers, we miss learning our lessons and stay in ignorance and suffering. When you accept and surrender to your own life, you also accept and surrender to other people's lives instead of resenting, judging, and competing with them.

*To practice surrendering to life, accept everything that life brings you without a grudge or complaint.* To do this you need to learn how to read the signs that existence gives you each moment. If you stop spending the energy that you normally waste on complaining, judging, and resenting what life offers and instead follow its wisdom, you can use your energy creatively and purposefully. Surrendering to life without complaint will bring you greater understanding and peace of mind.

One way to practice surrendering to life is to use your breath. You can practice this at any time and anywhere. Whenever you feel fear, resistance, or judgment towards anything that is happening, take a moment to look inside and bring your attention to your breath. Move your breath and attention into the center of your body, just below your navel. As you inhale, watch your breath reaching deep into your center in the second chakra *(see illustration on page 121)*, and as you exhale watch how it leaves your body through your nostrils. With the inhalation, say to yourself: "I accept whatever is happening in my life right now, and I take full responsibility for my part in what is happening." With the exhalation, say to yourself: "I let go of my struggle and surrender to the will of existence. I will focus on understanding the lessons that existence is showing me."

Practice with this exercise only if you sincerely feel these words are resonating with you. If you practice with them mechanically, they will not be of much help. You can also use your own words to suit what feels truer to you. You can practice with this exercise either with something current, or by working with a memory from the past with which you are still struggling.

While practicing surrendering to life, allow any thoughts or emotions to be there, feel them, let them come up, but keep your focus on your breath and the task at hand. You will notice that you may get identified and distracted by your thoughts and emotions, and your breath may become shallow, especially if you start to feel sadness, fear, shame, or resistance to what you are doing and saying. When you notice this, make a conscious effort to take deeper breaths and stay focused on your breath. As you exhale slowly and fully, feel the sensations of surrender in your body and observe how your sadness, shame, fear, or resistance dissipate and transform into love, peace, and joy.

Breath helps us to go inside and anchor our awareness in the center of our being. When your awareness is anchored in your center, you don't struggle with how things should be, you simply witness and accept how they are. Then you can easily let go of whatever you are struggling with and find the answers that will help improve your life. If you keep practicing surrendering to life, you will begin to act effortlessly from a place of acceptance and understanding instead of struggle and insecurity, and your life will become more exciting.

### 3rd Path: Surrendering to Your Inner Power

Surrendering to your inner power means living your life without compromising your own truth. From childhood we have been taught to suppress our inner truth and power. As a result we become insecure about our uniqueness and learn to suppress our true voice. We learn to doubt and criticize ourselves and others. We learn to lie, deceive, and manipulate to get our needs met.

To regain your integrity and authenticity you must develop the courage to surrender to your inner power. To do this, you must live according to your awareness and remain true to yourself even if others disagree with you. You must stay alert not to allow anyone, including your own mind, to manipulate or in any way control your inner truth. Only by surrendering to your inner power can you gather the courage to manifest your unique gifts and talents and be of help to others.

Surrendering to your inner power doesn't mean imposing your will on others. It simply means not allowing your fears to stop you from doing what you know you need to do. Normally we think of people who have social, religious, or political status as powerful, but in reality true power lies in letting go of our ego-mind and fears, and in not maintaining power struggles created by our own beliefs (economic, political, religious). When you consciously surrender to your inner power and stop compromising your true nature, the need to have others agree with you naturally drops. Then your ego-mind loses its need to prove itself or interfere in the lives of others.

*To practice surrendering to your inner power you must acknowledge and accept your instinctive knowing (gut instinct) instead of following your conditioned mind.* Trust your gut feeling and take risks by saying "no" to things that don't feel right for you. The best way to practice surrendering to your inner power is to cultivate courage. Dare to be different and do what feels right even if others disagree with you. Watch how when you suppress your feelings of anger, resentment, insecurity, neediness, weakness, jealousy, or competitiveness you are diverting from surrendering to your own truth and power. For example, if you usually agree with others out of fear of conflict, or because you don't want to offend them, observe your thoughts and feelings that get triggered as a result. Ask yourself: *Why am I compromising?* Understand that no one is responsible for your choice to suppress your power – in spite of your fears and the possible consequences, courageously and honestly express what you truly feel. If you can live this way, you will not only give yourself a chance to live a more authentic life but will also become a source of inspiration to others.

First, make a list of all your fears, insecurities, and anything that makes you compromise your own truth and power. Opposite each point write what you do (your usual behavior pattern) when you compromise. Then take some time to contemplate the following questions: "What do I gain by compromising my truth and having others agree with me? What will I lose if others disagree with me?"

Next, choose three behavior patterns that you are ready to break. Write them on a separate sheet of paper. Opposite each point, write the thoughts and emotions that you normally have when you act out this behavior.

Finally, surrender to your inner power and break your old behavior patterns by beginning to act from the place of courage and without hiding, suppressing, or manipulating. By being prepared to face all the consequences and staying true to your inner truth you regain your dignity and honor and start feeling good about yourself. If you still feel paralyzed in the course of this exercise, return to the 2nd path, *Surrendering to Life* exercise, and try practicing them simultaneously. Once you feel you have broken through one stumbling block you had been working on from your list, move on to the next.

If you continue to practice with surrendering to your inner power, you will be surprised at the many positive results that follow. With time, you will not only feel stronger within yourself but will become an inspiration to others who also want to free themselves of their fears and freely live their own truth. While practicing with this exercise, if some people react to your honesty and judge and criticize you, know well that it is not because of you but because of their own fear of surrendering to their authentic truth and power.

Like anything in life, it is impossible to have everyone agree with us or be our friend. Some people will leave and some will come even closer. I would rather have a few friends who love and accept me as I am, including my "faults" and "mistakes," than hundreds of friends who would quickly judge and criticize me if I don't fulfill their expectations. Most of all, remind yourself that everything eventually passes and keep your sense of humor. Practicing surrendering to your inner power will prepare you for moving into your heart and surrendering to love.

### 4th Path: **Surrendering to Love**

Surrendering to love means understanding that you are more than your body, mind, and emotions and our challenges in life are similar. The ego-mind thinks that your pain and suffering is unique to yourself and that you are separate and alone, but in reality, no one is ever alone. When you think you are alone your heart stays closed to experiencing the love that connects us all and is in essence the very nature of our existence. Surrendering to love is a personal experience and has nothing to do with other people. Love permeates the whole universe. Love arises from within our being as the fragrance arises from within the flower.

When we judge, blame, manipulate, and criticize one another, we stomp on the flowers that could have opened in the garden of our heart. Judgment and blame separate us and keep us feeling uprooted and alone. When we allow our greed and ambition for worldly success and power to overpower our heart, we stay closed and unfulfilled. By fighting and putting each other down, instead of opening our hearts and surrendering to love, we waste the precious energy that can help our creativity and consciousness to flower. When we surrender to love, we learn from one another and grow richer within.

Normally, our heart opens when we feel accepted and loved by others. But when we are rejected, we feel hurt and our heart immediately closes. By holding on to our hurt and expectations, we rob ourselves of experiencing the divinity and bliss of love that is within us. When we open our hearts and surrender to love, we begin to feel what others feel and realize that we are not different.

The things we often criticize in others or want them to change are the very same things we need to see and change within ourselves. When we keep our heart open, we understand that we all travel on the same journey and learn through the same mistakes. When we truly and unconditionally surrender to love, we begin to love and accept ourselves as well as others, and even if others continue to be against us, our feelings of love stay untouched.

*To practice surrendering to love, you must break through your fears and prejudices and accept everything about yourself and others.* You must allow yourself to be vulnerable and expose your pain and feelings of isolation and need for love. If you are feeling rejected and hurt, instead of blaming others or feeling sorry for yourself, look inside and observe the thoughts and emotions that are triggered as a result. Watch your reactions when others criticize, judge, and reject you, and instead of getting angry or feeling hurt, simply accept all your feelings and completely love yourself as you are.

Look closely at the people that surround you and try to understand what each one of them is showing you about yourself. If you are judging another person's neediness or selfishness, ask yourself: "Why am I triggered by how they behave?" Perhaps you don't like your own neediness and selfishness, or perhaps you feel love and compassion for them and want to see them move higher in consciousness. In any case, always take responsibility for your own thoughts and emotions.

If you keep looking in, you will eventually come to realize that you are not alone in your trials and tribulations. As you continue to observe your thoughts and emotions, you will realize that your behavior has not been so different from the way others also behave. When you see and recognize a behavior that is also true for you, humbly and gratefully accept the lessons that the other person helped you see. What you need to see and accept might be something beautiful or something ugly about yourself. Regardless of what it is, by accepting something in yourself, you can also accept it in others and your heart will stay open to the blessings of existence. Your acceptance will transform your judgments into understanding and will open your heart to yourself and others, so that true love and compassion can grow inside you. When you surrender to love, you experience oneness with yourself, others, and the universe. Surrender always expands your heart and consciousness.

### 5th Path: **Surrendering to Your Individuality**

Surrendering to your individuality means discovering and living your unique essence, gifts, and dreams. Although many people talk about wanting to find and live their unique individuality and life purpose, very few actually do. Those who have found and lived their individuality are the people who have surrendered to their inner truth and power. The way each person manifests his or her unique gifts and talents depends on their personality, mind, and level of consciousness. Regardless of what we do, it is always our unique individual essence and truth behind what we do that makes a difference in the world. We can only truly contribute to our and humanity's evolution when we surrender to and live our own individuality.

We miss living and sharing our unique gifts and individuality when we compare ourselves to others, or try to be like them. We don't understand that by imitating others we try to live their destiny and miss living our own. Out of fear of rejection and criticism, we even try to suppress and hide our own gifts or play them down. At times, we may even feel embarrassed by what we have, and as a result feel insecure, stressed, and depressed. We don't understand that by suppressing our essence and creativity, or pretending to be modest and humble, we keep our true potential dormant. Resentful and jealous of those who live their gifts, we often try to undermine, destroy, or rob them of their success.

To surrender to our individuality, we need to surrender to our inner power (the 3rd Path) and gather the courage to expose ourselves – our deepest longings, thoughts, and feelings without fear, censorship, and judgment. When we take risks and don't hold back from expressing and living our own truth, we honor and respect who we are and how beautifully different we are from others.

Our minds will give us an endless supply of reasons why we shouldn't or couldn't express ourselves freely. If we don't allow our minds to interfere, we can take risks to expose our true essence and let the seed of the individuality that resides there blossom. Surrendering to our individual essence in spite of our fears automatically opens the door to living from the inexhaustible well of creativity and joy that is within our being.

*To practice surrendering to your individuality, risk doing what you know you need to do to manifest your dreams into reality, and don't be attached to outcomes.* We often have ideas that we want to manifest into reality, but we let our fear of disapproval or failure stop us. Break your pattern of holding back by expressing your truth in spite of your fears.

When you surrender to your individuality, you may feel overwhelmed by the vast freedom and multitude of opportunities existence makes available to you. Take a deep breath, bring your awareness into your center (the second chakra below the navel), and remind yourself that existence created you the way you are because it wants and needs your unique gifts and talents. Only by living your unique gifts and talents can you and others benefit. The moment you understand this, you will joyfully embrace who you are and surrender to your individuality.

Only by living your individuality can you experience true freedom, the kind that does not depend on anything external. In such freedom, there is no fear of success or failure; of being right or wrong. In such freedom, you can fully express who you are – your creativity, your joy, and your uniqueness. Let go of your fear of disapproval and freely express yourself regardless of how others receive what you say or do. Allow yourself to enjoy your unique gifts and be playful.

### 6th Path: **Surrendering to Your Inner Wisdom**

Surrendering to your inner wisdom requires learning to listen to and trusting your intuition instead of the ego-mind and its beliefs. Your ego-mind struggles and tries to steer you away from trusting because trust kills the mind. By trusting your intuition and surrendering to your inner wisdom, you come closer to the truth of your being and the universe. You can only surrender to your inner wisdom when you know and trust that existence always takes care of you, even if on the surface it appears otherwise.

We learn surrendering to our inner wisdom through life experiences and understanding that no matter what we desire, existence always has the last word. Usually, our mind tries to stop us from surrendering to our intuition by tricking us into believing it knows what's best for us and others. It stubbornly insists on holding on to its desires and beliefs. It may even pretend to be surrendered in order to stay in control, but our inner wisdom knows it is not a true surrender.

To surrender to your inner wisdom and trust your intuition, you need to let go of what you think you know and allow existence to decide what is right for you by listening, understanding, and following the signs it gives. When you surrender to your intuition and inner wisdom, you will know and trust that the universe takes care of you. Existence created you and will always love and take care of you – it cannot do otherwise. The more you struggle with, hold on to, and resist what existence gives, the less you can receive. This isn't the case because existence doesn't want to give but because by not trusting and surrendering you keep your fists tightly closed and remain unable to receive what is offered. It's the same in all your relationships. The more controlling you are, the less others are inclined to give you what you want. The more receptive, trusting, and surrendered you are, the more others can give you what you need because you are open to gracefully receive what they want to offer.

*To practice surrendering to your inner wisdom, begin by saying "yes" to everything that life brings you, even if it may look like a setback or an obstacle.* Saying "yes" will help you stay open and receptive to the new direction existence is pointing at. Saying "yes" will also help you become more understanding and trusting of yourself and others.

When you desire self-fulfillment with your ego-mind and keep persisting in spite of outside obstacles, you wear yourself and your energy down and miss other opportunities existence is offering you. Outside obstacles are a sign that existence doesn't support your ego's wishes and has something else in store for you. This doesn't mean that you withdraw from life or stop doing what you intuitively believe in. It simply means changing direction and letting go of your attachment to, or investment in, the outcome your ego-mind wants to achieve. Take time to step back from the situation and ask yourself: *Why can't I let it go, and what would happen if I did?* Understand your ego's stubbornness in not wanting to surrender. The ego always wants to be right and have things its own way. This is how it stays alive. When you don't willingly surrender the ego's will to the will of existence, you suffocate your inner wisdom and continue to create more pain and suffering for yourself and others.

Learn to discriminate between what is false and what is true within yourself. When you look inside honestly, you will see that the judgments and desires of your mind have nothing to do with the truth and clarity of your inner wisdom. When you see this and still feel resistance to letting go, be intelligent and don't feed your ego but be true to your inner wisdom instead. By surrendering to your inner wisdom instead of protecting your ego, your false self begins to dissolve and you receive the blessings and support of existence and your authentic Self.

### 7th Path: **Surrender Your Will to the Will of Existence**

To surrender to the will of existence you need to surrender your mind's fear of death. Surrendering to the will of existence brings about the ultimate death of the ego, dissolves the notion of separation created by the mind, and reunites our being with existence. Each time we face and surrender our mind's fear of death we move a step closer to experiencing the pure emptiness of our being and becoming conscious of the vast unknown mystery of existence.

What makes surrendering to the will of existence difficult is your identification with your body, mind, emotions, and your fear of losing everything that you think is familiar. Your mind resists surrendering to the will of existence because it is afraid to disappear and be useless. It thinks death is real, and it stops you from experiencing the vastness of the unknown.

Fear of death keeps you small and operating out of a fear of fear. Because of the mind's fear of losing itself, you avoid looking at something that is inevitable – your body's mortality. You distract yourself with desires, material things, food, sex, and relationships, to avoid seeing that eventually everything will be taken away.

Surrendering to the will of existence is easier if you welcome the unknown. By welcoming the unknown, you welcome the death of your ego-mind and realize that you are eternal consciousness that can never die. When you forget that you are one with the Source of Creation you stay identified with the fear of death and continue to suffer. To disidentify from your fear of death and the unknown; face, feel, and watch the fear and remind yourself that you are not the fear.

*To practice surrendering to the will of existence, watch your fear of death and say to yourself: "Even if I die and disappear into the unknown, I will welcome and watch the experience."* Don't try to distract yourself by thinking about or trying to justify the fear. Understand that what keeps you identified with the fear is your body's survival instinct *(see Chapter 7)*. This fear has nothing to do with who you truly are.

When you willingly confront the fear of death, you will be surprised to find that what you have been really afraid of more than death is Joy, because Joy, just like death, also kills the ego-mind. In truth, beneath the fear of death hides our fear of Joy because in the death of the ego-mind is the Joy of finding our being. And Joy can only be experienced in total surrender of the ego's will to the will of existence.

To help you surrender to the will of existence, remind yourself that there is something higher and more powerful than the small will of your ego. This power knows you, loves you, and unconditionally takes care of you. It also takes care of everything and everyone in the universe.

Enlightenment happens when you face your fear of death and the unknown and surrender to it. With the first glimpse of self-realization, you'll know that even when you thought you were doing something yourself, it was always the will of existence that made things happen through you. You'll understand that even though your mind claimed things as its own creation, it was always the will of existence that was creating through you. This realization will bring a deep relaxation into your life and regardless of what happens in the outside world your inner peace will remain undisturbed. When you understand that everything, including your ego-mind belongs to existence, you gracefully and joyously surrender to its will.

## THE PARADOX

One of life's paradoxes is that the ego-mind cannot be surrendered without first making an effort to surrender it. Before we can surrender to existence, we must gradually learn to surrender to its parts. This is like surrendering to the individual waves of the ocean before surrendering to the ocean as a whole. We first strengthen our ego through the struggle to surrender. When we come to recognize the futility of struggle, we are finally ready to let go and surrender to the will of the universe. Like a plant, we must go through the whole life cycle by seeding, germinating, sprouting, growing, blooming, and finally releasing our fragrance into eternity.

# QUESTIONS AND ANSWERS
# ABOUT SURRENDERING TO WHAT IS

*I'm always afraid that existence won't support me and I'll die if I let go of control. In my fear, I close off to life and others. How can I break free from this fear?*

Your fear is a blessing. It is giving you an opportunity to disidentify from your mind and learn to trust the unknown. The mind can never trust or surrender. Trust always happens through intelligence and consciousness. The mind always asks for guarantees, but life never offers any. Life unfolds moment to moment, and each moment arises as a result of the moment that was surrendered before it. Life is a surprise that always arises out of the unknown. You can either embrace the unknown and live it fully and joyously, or resist it and live in pain, fear, and struggle.

To break free from the fear of the unknown embrace the fear and let go of your concern about the past or the future. Don't hold on to what has already happened or control what is to come. Then, try to understand the cause of your fear. Go into the fear and feel it fully. Don't run away from it by diverting your attention. Stay focused and watch. As you are feeling the fear, ask yourself what will happen if you surrender to it. Observe any thoughts and emotions that come up without judging or avoiding what you see and feel. Then, give yourself permission to express out loud to yourself what you think and feel, as many times as you need, until you feel that the fear changes into awareness and trust. Expression will help free your energy of the suppressed thoughts and emotions associated with the fear and will naturally transform your unconscious energy into consciousness. This is the fastest and easiest way to understand the cause of your fear and transform it into trust.

*I experience moments of surrender, and I feel love showering down on me from all directions. I feel at home, and I can see how struggling with "what is" is meaningless. I have no idea how I get to the experience, but just as quickly as it happens, it's gone again. Why can't I stay in a state of surrender all the time?*

This happens to everyone. It is impossible to make any of our experiences permanent. To surrender to what is means to accept everything, including the moments of non-surrendering. There is nothing wrong with changing experiences. Our experiences are like the weather. When it is cloudy and cold, we contract and withdraw. When it is warm and sunny, we feel open, energized, and uplifted.

You are not separate from anything in existence. Whatever is happening in the universe is also happening in you. Your ego cannot comprehend or accept this. It always wants to make things permanent so it can stay in control. It's impossible to make any experience stand still. If you could make one experience permanent, there would be no possibility of having other experiences. You would be trapped in a static photograph with no growth, creativity, transformation, or evolution. Life is impossible without continually changing experiences. To be fully alive means to be open to change with each moment regardless of what it brings. To be able to live life this way you must continually let go of every experience. Enjoy the experience while it is happening but once it passes, let it go.

If you can understand that the only thing that is permanent in life is change and accept that everything will pass, you will be able to surrender to ever-changing moments and transcend your mind. Watch each experience as it is happening and let it go. Accept that one moment you will feel happy and the next you will feel sad or angry. Observe your mind's tendency to push away what it doesn't like or thinks as wrong. With observation and meditation, you will slowly start to notice the in-between gaps where there is no movement, where everything is still and calm regardless of the changing experiences. As your awareness of the silent and still gaps between experiences strengthens, you stop identifying with the ups and downs of life, and your consciousness starts to take root in the gaps. When you experience a peak, you will know, even before the next moment arrives, that a valley will be coming. Then you can simply be there, welcoming and watching the mystery of both the peaks and the valleys.

*How do I surrender to someone when I know they are lying to me?*

First, look inside to see if you are being truthful with others before you ask others to be truthful with you. Are you opening your heart and exposing what's in your own mind? By not surrendering to your own truth and freely expressing your thoughts and feelings, you are being untrue to yourself as much as to others. You may think you are not exposing what you feel because you don't want to hurt that person's feelings. This is part of your social conditioning. In my opinion, a lie hurts us deeper than truth. Truth may be painful at first, but it always liberates in the end because it allows us to grow in consciousness. By expressing what you feel truthfully you expose your vulnerability, but at the same time you expose your courage and ability to surrender to your inner wisdom and power. Don't be afraid to speak your truth and take responsibility for the consequences. Your surrendering has nothing to do with others, but it has something to do with your innocence, sincerity, and inner strength.

*My girlfriend and I go back and forth from having peace and love in our relationship to getting into huge hurricane-like arguments. We've always worked our way through the arguments and kept going with the relationship on the assumption that we're working towards ending the conflict for good and just having the love. Yet if we really look at our past, we have no evidence that there will ever be an end to the conflict because conflict keeps happening over and over again, no matter how much better we get at maintaining the love. It's true that we both learn and grow from the conflict, and in this respect the conflict is a blessing. But we have no reason to believe the conflict will ever disappear. Are we working towards a fantasy? Can two people ever achieve peace and love in a relationship? Another way of phrasing my question is: Must all relationships end eventually because relationships by nature involve conflict? Can a committed relationship evolve into a state of pure love and sharing?*

You have posed a very valid question that I am sure many others might also have. Most relationships eventually end in a conflict, or as a result of conflict, because one or the other partner has not taken responsibility for their own feelings and thoughts that the relationship is mirroring. If the relationship withstands the many seasons of purification, it naturally can grow into a stronger bond. However, to expect conflict to end is a hope created by the mind, which wants to reach a certain goal. If you drop your need to always be right, or to want the conflict to end, and instead look inside to see what the conflict is showing you about your own ego-mind, you can move from your head into your heart, and surrendering to love will happen naturally. Drop your need to have no conflict and accept the conflict just as you accept the love. If you accept one but deny the other, you are in trouble. You either accept both or drop both.

Each relationship has a history of unlived and unfinished business from this or previous lives that needs to be completed. Conflict provides the opportunity for issues to come to the surface so they can be seen, dealt with, and completed. Conflict helps us grow and evolve. It's rare to have a relationship without conflict. Every disagreement wakes us up and tells us when we've dozed off from the truth of our heart. Usually, when you are in your thoughts and focussed on your own needs and desires, you miss seeing what is happening within your partner. So you get a wake-up call through a conflict to remind you to return to your heart. Unless both of you are alert and present in your heart, you are bound to clash because you both need to be awoken to the present.

If you are present, even disharmony is harmony because you aren't trying to fix something or someone. Instead, you are keeping your focus on what you are learning. So there is no problem in disagreements or arguments if you keep your heart open and continue learning. What's most important is that you don't blame the other but look inside and become aware of your own unconscious. Everyone is a complex universe, and if you aren't doing your inner work, you won't see your own lessons within the relationship.

Generally, people don't see their own lessons within the relationship because they remain focused on blaming or trying to change the other instead of looking inside and becoming more conscious of themselves. Unless you find your own truth, you will remain insecure and eventually suffocate yourself and your partner. For a relationship to last, both partners need to commit to being honest with each other, take responsibility for their own growth, and give each other space to grow.

Love is not different from anything else in life. You may feel love one moment and not the next. This not only relates to the love you feel for others but also to the love you receive from them. No person can express love all the time; it is not possible by the very nature of things. There are times when you are focused on doing other things, such as working, taking care of your children, reading, meditating, etc. This doesn't mean, however, that your heart is closed and that you stop loving. Everything in nature moves in waves. Sometimes you feel excited and cheerful, and at other times, sad and depressed. One moment you feel love, but the next moment it may be gone. Then, it may come back again, just like a wave in the ocean.

We long for love because love nourishes our soul like food nourishes our body. But we need to remember that just as it is impossible to eat non-stop without taking breaks to digest the food, it is impossible to feel love all the time without needing breaks in between. The breaks are necessary to digest and assimilate feelings. They are like the gaps between the incoming and outgoing breaths. They create a feeling of emptiness or void inside. We need to welcome this emptiness because this emptiness is our true being. Unfortunately, due to lack of understanding and our discomfort with the feeling of being alone with our inner emptiness, we want to keep the feeling of love permanent.

The difficulty arises when, through your fear and lack of understanding, you try to manipulate the other and hold on to them so you don't feel alone. Love is a living, breathing organism. If you try to make love permanent, you will kill its breath and its aliveness. If you want love to last, you will have to surrender to its rhythms. Plastic flowers don't fade; real ones do. Real flowers bloom and start fading as soon as they appear. Eventually they die, but before they do, they leave seeds for new flowers to appear. If you try to make love permanent, you will kill its beauty and fragrance. One of the attributes of maturity is the understanding that nothing in life is permanent. If both of you can surrender to life and accept its rhythms, you will create fertile soil in which your love and relationship can grow, and your life together will become easier and more enjoyable. Conflict will end if you drop your need to always be right and instead surrender to the love you feel in your heart.

*So each relationship is going to have its own dynamics?*

Absolutely! It is impossible to find two people who are exactly the same. Everyone has a different conditioning and personal history. The way we relate to each person will be different. Each relationship mirrors and reveals a different part of our personality. Some people need to have many relationships, while others continue to grow together within one long-term relationship. One is not necessarily better than the other. It all depends on the individuals. Sometimes it is necessary to have multiple relationships that can mirror the same pattern you keep repeating with every person so you can finally understand and take responsibility for what is happening. The moment you see and take responsibility for your own feelings and behavior patterns and disidentify from your ego-mind, you grow into greater consciousness and move into the truth of your heart and being. This in turn transforms you and the dynamics of your relationship.

*How can I know if I am supposed to stay in a relationship and look further into myself with the person I'm with, or when it's right to call it quits?*

Your intuition will tell you if there is any potential to grow in your current relationship or if it's time to move apart. You cannot know this through the mind alone. If you go into your center and surrender to your intuition and inner knowing, you will know what to do. If you stay in the relationship because of your weakness or neediness, you and the relationship have no room to grow. But if you stay because of your strength and your trust that more growth is possible, then you and your partner can continue to grow through the ups and downs of the relationship.

Unless both you and your partner are committed to taking responsibility for your own healing and learning, your relationship doesn't have much chance of succeeding and being a lasting one. So first, ask yourself: "Am I staying in this relationship because I have something to learn, or am I staying because I don't accept that the relationship is over? Am I refusing to separate out of fear of being alone, or am I afraid of what others might think? Am I sabotaging myself by staying in the relationship or am I sabotaging the relationship by not wanting to work through my behavior patterns and let go of my ego?"

We can learn to trust existence by learning to trust ourselves. Intuitively we always know if or when a relationship has stopped serving its purpose. Existence always gives us more opportunities to grow in each relationship. Our challenges always provide a rich soil for growth. The challenges we face in our relationships are not always easy, but when looked at more deeply, they help us see our unconscious patterns and provide opportunities for us to become more loving and compassionate.

# 4 Thought: The Third Ingredient for Health

In this chapter we will look deeper into the nature of thought and try to understand how it creates the ego-mind. We will also look at how silence, not thought, is the key to ultimate health and wholeness; and, how to move from our thoughts to the still silent center of our being, so we can heal into consciousness.

Many people are already aware of the power that their thoughts have in causing illness and unhappiness or in creating health and happiness, and many books have been written about the power of positive thinking regarding health and worldly success.

We spend 99.9 percent of our lives thinking. It is beyond doubt that our physical, psychological, and spiritual health is profoundly affected by what kinds of thoughts we think. Although it is critical to move from negative thoughts that create pain and suffering to positive thoughts that induce healing, positive thinking alone is not enough to achieve inner wholeness and find out who we truly are. Even if we try to focus on positive thoughts, sooner or later the negative ones are bound to follow because one polarity cannot exist without the other.

The power of positive thinking is based on the assumption that health and happiness are merely a lack of pain and illness and are a result of fulfilled physical, mental, emotional, and material desires. Though it's true that negative thoughts create unhappiness, stress, and dis-ease, and that positive thoughts are vital for physical and psychological health or worldly success, all thoughts take us out of the silence of consciousness in the present, the only place where we are undivided and whole. Ultimately, it is the consciousness within the silent stillness of our being, not thought, that is the key and primary ingredient for health, spiritual transformation, and a fulfilled life.

## SILENCE:
## THE KEY TO ULTIMATE HEALTH

Silence is beyond all thoughts (positive and negative). Just as with negative thoughts, positive thoughts also take us out of the silent stillness of our being and prevent our consciousness from being fully present in the Now. Only by abandoning both positive and negative thoughts can we become conscious of the true health and wholeness that reside within silence. Thoughts can change our physical and emotional reality, but they cannot change the silent presence of our being. Our being is ageless, timeless, is never born and never dies.

Because it is impossible to describe silence, consciousness, and the presence of being, in this chapter I will concentrate on discussing the nature of thought, and why I call it the third ingredient for health. I will also give some suggestions for how to work with thought so that it can lead you to experience the silent presence of your being.

## FROM SILENCE TO SOUND

Although the Bible says: "In the beginning was the Word," in reality, in the beginning was Silence. Thought, just like sound, light, and all existing matter, arises out of silent emptiness and returns back into it. In reality, the first thing that comes into existence from within the silence, before any "word" can be uttered, is sound. Everything in creation, including every cell in our body, is in constant movement. This movement generates the different sound vibrations that, if heard all at once, unify into the sound AUM, or OM. In the East, they have depicted this sound with the symbol ॐ. It is possible for us to hear this universal sound in a moment of absolute stillness of the mind or in deep meditation, but, because we are full of thoughts and our energy and attention are scattered in many directions, we don't hear it.

The "word" or thought is secondary to sound and silence because without sounds and the silent gaps between them, we cannot make out words or thoughts. Before learning to speak and think, the child first learns to make sounds. All animals communicate through sounds. Humans too communicate through sounds, which used in different combinations create different languages. We adopted the idea that the "word" is the beginning of creation because in our forgetfulness of the original silence, which is the source of our being and everything in creation, we identified with language.

In reality, pure silence doesn't exist except within the still void where all movements cease. What may appear to us as silence is not silence but only the absence of the sounds that we are accustomed to hearing internally or externally. For example, if you are used to living on a noisy street, then go away for the weekend to the country, you become aware of the silence relative to the city noise. Or if you live in the country and are used to the sounds of the birds and crickets, and suddenly those sounds stop, you immediately become aware of the silence all around. In moments like these, you are aware only of the outer sounds and silence but not the sounds and silence that exist within you.

While looking inside or sitting in meditation you become aware of your inner sounds, and realize that in spite of the outer sounds or silence, the inner noise of your incessant thoughts continues. When the noise generated by thinking stops, you suddenly become aware of the true silence and wholeness of your being. Spiritually speaking, we define this kind of silence as *no-mind.* In a way, *healing into consciousness is a journey back from thought to sound and then to silence.* The deeper you move into your inner silence, the higher you move in consciousness and into the ultimate health of your being.

## FROM SOUND TO THOUGHT

Thoughts, words, and sounds are closely interconnected. We can describe thoughts as *inner sounds,* and words as *outer sounds.* The interplay of thoughts and sounds creates the mind. Thoughts and sounds (the mind) radiate from our bodies like radio waves projected from a tower. They can easily travel far distances and affect not only our health and well-being but also the health and well-being of others. Some thoughts and sounds create positive and uplifting emotions that heal and bring peace, while others generate negative emotions that lead to illness and destruction.

By using the power of intent, many cultures and religions have for millennia harnessed the energy of sounds and thoughts to either heal or destroy. For example, people use prayer and chant mantras to bring on good health, love, wealth, protection, wisdom, and spiritual awakening. They also use thoughts and sounds to cast spells, to sicken, control, kill, and dominate others. Today, sounds and noise created by humans such as traffic, computers, TV, music, and conversation dominate our lives more than the sounds of nature. To heal and find our inner silence, we need to become aware of how we use sounds and thoughts and take responsibility for what we think and listen to.

## FROM THOUGHT TO CONSCIOUSNESS

The evolution of both our own and the universe's consciousness depends on thought. Thoughts are tools that allow us to communicate verbally or telepathically and to function in both the material and spiritual dimensions. We use thoughts to speak, contemplate, interpret our feelings and experiences, create, or materialize our ideas and visions into reality. Thoughts are always present inside and outside of us, even while we are asleep.

We become conscious of our thoughts through awareness. What helps us become aware of thoughts is our ability to witness and observe them. Without observation and awareness, thoughts stay in the unconscious and we remain oblivious of their existence. Our ability to observe thoughts helps us to eventually disidentify from them and understand that we are not our thoughts. Through disidentification, we come to our inner center and become conscious of our silent presence. All our "aha" experiences and realizations of truth arise out of consciousness, not out of thought.

We use the same thoughts (or words) whether we communicate consciously or unconsciously. I like to call thoughts used with awareness *conscious thoughts,* and thoughts used without awareness *unconscious thoughts* or *thought-forms.* Unconscious thoughts are mechanical and have no awareness. They are created through beliefs and conditionings. Unconscious thoughts are linear and only focus on one side of reality, i.e. black or white, past or future, good or bad, right or wrong. When we look at contradictory thoughts from both sides of the duality, our thoughts become contemplative thoughts. Contemplative thoughts consider things from both sides simultaneously. Through contemplation, we are able to understand the impermanent and contradictory nature of positive and negative thoughts and eventually disidentify from them.

We disidentify from thoughts and become conscious of our true reality when we observe all thoughts without qualifying them as positive or negative, good or bad. At first it takes effort to remain aware of your thoughts, but with practice your ability to watch them strengthens, and eventually it becomes effortless. The more aware you become of your thoughts, the more your consciousness grows and expands. In other words, through observation unconscious thoughts become conscious thoughts.

As your consciousness evolves, what may be meaningful for you at one stage in the journey becomes meaningless in the next stage. For example, someone may think that his career is the most important thing in his life. However, after experiencing health problems or the loss of a loved one, his career may lose its meaning. Through this gradual progression and change in focus, awareness of ourselves and life increases, and we slowly become more conscious of life's true purpose.

## THOUGHTS AND EMOTIONS ARE ONE

Thoughts and emotions are one and inseparable. Thoughts trigger emotions – and emotions trigger thoughts. Though we always experience thoughts and emotions in the present, they only exist in relation to linear time (past or future). Thoughts by themselves are neutral. What qualifies thoughts as positive or negative and gives them power and meaning is the kind of emotional energy we attach to them. Through thoughts we interpret and express our emotions. For example, the only difference between white and black magic is the emotional energy attached to the thoughts. When our thoughts are positive, we feel good and we become a creative force, and when our thoughts are negative, and when we feel jealous, angry, or competitive we become a destructive force.

If you are identified with a thought, you are also identified with its associated emotion. If you want to change the way you feel, you need to change the way you think. This is where the power of positive thinking comes in. When you change your thoughts to positive, you also change the way you feel. We can only truly change our thinking through the transformative power of awareness. Only through awareness can we see and understand that something needs changing and how to change it. To become aware of your thoughts and emotions and know what to do with them, you need to learn to witness them.

For example, if as a child you were criticized when you failed to understand or do something, and you felt hurt and inadequate, as an adult, the same feelings of hurt and inadequacy will be triggered when someone criticizes you. To be free of any kind of emotional reaction, look inside and observe how your thoughts and emotions are interconnected – how a thought triggers an emotional reaction, and how an emotion triggers a thought. Also watch how you get identified with both. If you remain an observer to all your thoughts, emotions, and reactions, you can become conscious of their origin and, through understanding how they affect your life and well-being, can let them go. Through an ongoing process of *observation, understanding, disidentification, and letting go,* your witnessing awareness will strengthen and your consciousness will become more centered in the Now.

# FIVE CHARACTERISTICS OF THOUGHT

To help you strengthen your witnessing awareness and move out of the ongoing traffic of contradictory thoughts and emotions, it is helpful to understand five important characteristics of thought:

*First:* **The Movement of Thought Is Linear**
Life cannot exist without movement. Life is energy moving between two points; past and future, but it always happens in the Now. All matter, including thoughts and emotions, exists within the dimension of time, either in the past or in the future, and continually moves around the unmoving still center in the Now. The Now is the unchanging dimension of the timeless present, where past and future are irrelevant and, in fact, don't exist. The Now is like the zero point on a linear scale of negative and positive numbers. If one side of the scale is positive, the other is negative; if one side is in the past, the other is in the future. Thoughts move back and forth along this line, from positive to negative, from

past to future, from good to bad, from love to hate, from pain to pleasure, from illness to health, from life to death.

When you identify with one or the other side of the scale, you stay in the linear dimension of time created by the contradictory thoughts. But when you disidentify from both sides, you become conscious of the timeless dimension of the present in the Now. To be in the Now you need to jump out of the linear movement of thoughts. To see and transcend the linear movement of thought, your awareness must always be rooted in the present moment.

If your awareness is not rooted in the present moment, your attention will go where your thoughts go and you'll stay identified in their contradictory reality. You can jump out of the linear movement of thoughts by watching and accepting all thoughts without judgment and discrimination. Accepting only some thoughts and rejecting others will keep you within their contradictory nature, maintaining and perpetuating all of your problems. Only by keeping your awareness in the present can you become conscious of the linear contradictory movement of thoughts and transcend the illusion of time, space, life, and death that thoughts create.

*Second:* **The Movement of Thought Is Infinite**
Thoughts arise out of emptiness and move into emptiness. They can pass through air, liquid, and solid matter and can travel anywhere within the universe. For example, you may be thinking about someone and that person suddenly shows up or calls you. Or, you may be feeling that you need something, and existence miraculously provides exactly what you need.

There are literally zillions of thoughts floating around us all the time. Thoughts move like rays of sunlight and can travel within the universe infinitely. We can pick up thoughts that have traveled to us from other galaxies and send our thoughts to other galaxies. A single thought can be dispersed in many directions simultaneously and reach many people at the same time. This principle has been used both negatively and positively on a mass scale, both to condition and enslave people to social, religious, and political ideologies and to help liberate them from their limiting beliefs and conditioning. The kind of thoughts each person attracts and uses depend upon his or her level of consciousness.

### *Third:* **Thoughts Move Through Breath**

Our body is a container that can attract, hold, and release thoughts. Thoughts circulate through breath and movement of energy. We receive and send thoughts as we breathe in and out. One person's exhalation and thought can become another person's inhalation and thought. What is my thought one moment can be yours the next. We release thoughts out of the body through exhalation, and we bring thoughts into the body through inhalation.

For example, when you are on a busy street, in a crowded shopping mall, or in an office with many people, by the end of the day you feel stressed and fatigued. This would not be the case if you had spent a day in nature. When you are in nature and close to the earth, you inhale and exhale pure energy with no thought attached to it. Nature rejuvenates us by flushing out all the muddled thoughts from our energy and body and brings us into the present. When we are with people, we continually inhale and exhale each other's energies and thoughts, even though we are not aware of it.

Because thoughts move from one person's breath to another's, no thought is original or can be anyone's personal property. We all grow and evolve by working with and experiencing the same thoughts and emotions. By holding your breath, you hold expression and circulation of your thoughts and emotions and suppress them in your body. By suppressing the thoughts and emotions in the body, you also suppress your spiritual growth and transformation.

### *Fourth:* **Thoughts Cannot be Dissected or Analyzed**

We cannot dissect or analyze thoughts because they have no substance, and they continually contradict each other, moving between two polarities from positive to negative, from negative to positive. In my practice, I frequently meet people who have tried to solve their problems through years of counseling, psychoanalysis, or positive affirmations, but their problems persist. This happens because it is impossible to come out of thoughts by analyzing them. To analyze one thought you need to use another thought. This keeps you locked in the infinite movement of their contradictory dual nature. When you analyze one thought, its exact opposite will also need to be analyzed simultaneously. And, if contradictory thoughts are analyzed simultaneously, you would feel helpless and stuck, unable to move anywhere and create any change. It's impossible to disidentify from thoughts by using more thoughts. The only way to be thought-free is to watch them as an observer. This is why watching your breath is crucial if you want to disidentify from your thoughts and be present in your being.

### *Fifth:* Thoughts Cannot Be Counted

Thoughts are like the grains of sand on a beach or in a desert, or like dust particles in the air. They are infinite in number and can never be counted. This is why we can never "get rid" of thoughts. Thoughts are as much a part of our existence as breath. They continually appear and disappear whether we are aware of them or not. We either can be lost in them and let them run our lives or use them as tools to help us heal and evolve.

# THE FOUR STAGES OF HEALING INTO CONSCIOUSNESS

The process of healing into consciousness can be divided into four stages: *contemplation, introspection, intuition, and disidentification.* While contemplation and introspection bring forth flowering of the linear mind (logic), intuition and disidentification (witnessing) bring forth flowering of consciousness. In other words, *consciousness evolves on the foundation of the mind, intuition, and witnessing aware-ness.* Say, for example, you have been trying to keep a relationship alive by compromising in spite of your intuition telling you otherwise. As a result you feel depressed, depleted, and frustrated. You finally leave this relationship and start another, but the same thing happens again. After several relationships like this, you think that your life is a recurring circle of pain and suffering. You can either remain a victim and blame the other person, yourself, and fate, or you can ask yourself: *What is my contribution and responsibility in repeating the same pattern and attracting similar kind of relationships?*

To understand those reasons, you eventually look inside. Through introspection you begin to realize that you have been mechanically attracting these relationships because you needed to see something about yourself and learn to trust and follow your intuition. As a result, next time around you listen to your intuition and avoid repeating the same mistakes. However, the underlying reason why you went on attracting similar relationships remains.

Some get to this point and stop here. Intellectually, they may trace the cause of the pattern back to their parents and childhood experiences, but the original thought and emotional imprints continue to remain trapped in the body. To erase the imprints and break the old behavior pattern, you must take responsibility for going deeper into the unconscious hidden in your body and release the suppressed thought-forms and emotions trapped there. Through my healing method I have found that the simplest way to release the suppressed thought-forms and emotions from the body is through out-loud expression. With expression the energy of the suppressed thoughts and emotions is freed, opening space for your awareness to come in and help you release the unconscious pattern. Once you release the pattern that was controlling your behavior you can take charge of how you want to create your life using the strength and clarity of your consciousness.

# ELEVEN PRACTICAL WAYS OF MOVING BEYOND THOUGHTS

To move beyond thoughts into presence and consciousness in the Now, experiment with the following eleven exercises. Use each exercise at least three times to find the one that is easiest for you to practice. You can practice with one or two exercises at the same time if you like, but I don't recommend using more than two or three at a time. It is important to stay focused and avoid confusion. You can practice with each exercise for three weeks or longer. Practicing it for three months will help you go even deeper into the mystery of your being.

You can stop practicing with the method once you have gained the needed experience, insight and understanding, and the method no longer serves you. Then, experiment with the other methods in the same way. An ongoing practice using any of these exercises will help strengthen your witnessing awareness and your ability to center in your being will increase.

## 1. Witness Every Thought

As a regular practice, take ten minutes a day to sit and watch your thoughts. Do nothing else but watch your thoughts as they come and go. Accept and welcome every thought without judging, criticizing, or denying it. After three weeks (or longer if necessary), and once you become aware of your thoughts in your sitting practice, begin watching them during all your activities throughout the day.

Witnessing your thoughts will help you become aware of how they continually change and affect the way you feel. Through observation you will also recognize that many of the thoughts you are watching are a part of a greater collection of thoughts that you and everyone else are unconsciously and mechanically following. For example, you may think you should treat others with kindness, even when their harmful actions give you a clear intuitive message that you need to stand up for yourself. The thought to be kind may seem like your thought, but in reality, if you look deeper, you will discover that it's based on a collective moral conditioning that you are involuntarily following. As a consequence of this collective thought, you compromise your own truth and the development of your own inner strength and consciousness.

## 2. Abandon All Negative Thoughts

Before you can completely move beyond thoughts and heal into consciousness, you must first change your negative and pessimistic outlook on life. This takes time and effort. Like a gauge on a thermometer, your thoughts indicate where you are on your healing journey. The more negative and judgmental your thoughts are, the less aware and trusting you are of existence. The more positive and creative your thoughts are, the more conscious and trusting you are that existence is a friendly and a caring place.

Our experiences of illness, physical pain, loss, and emotional suffering generate a myriad of negative thoughts life after life. As a result, we get accustomed to living with negative thoughts and form a dominantly negative outlook on life. When your outlook on life is negative, you attract what you project – negativity. Negative thoughts trigger negative emotions and create a cloud of depression in and around you. To change the way you feel you need to change the way you think. When you change your negative thoughts into positive ones, your emotions and state of being also change.

Whenever you become aware of a negative thought, immediately neutralize its energy by abandoning it. To help you abandon thoughts, remind yourself that the thought is separate from you and has nothing to do with your being. Seeing it this way neither suppresses the thought nor feeds it. If you cannot abandon the negative thought easily, examine it – as you would any object – and ask yourself in what way is this thought benefitting you. Upon close examination you will see that negative thoughts sabotage your well-being and joy and keep you feeling miserable. Realizing this makes letting go of thoughts naturally easier.

To abandon a negative thought, remind yourself that you are

not what you think or feel. When you simply abandon your negative thoughts without judgment and repression, you automatically experience self-acceptance and inner relaxation. Abandoning negative thoughts not only helps with your own healing process, but it also influences the health of those around you.

If you practice with this exercise diligently and with your totality, after three months you will be able to break the pattern of negative thinking that keeps you trapped in a negative and depressed emotional state and you will begin to enjoy life instead of dreading it.

### 3. Write Down Every Thought that Passes through Your Mind

For fifteen minutes every day, write down every thought that passes through your mind without editing, judging, or ignoring any thought. Keep your awareness on your breath so your thoughts don't run faster than your speed of writing. As you do this, you will see that your thoughts continually change and contradict each other. While writing, keep reminding yourself that you are not your thoughts but are the witness who observes the thoughts. This practice will help you to move beyond your thoughts and strengthen your witnessing awareness.

### 4. Count Every Thought

Take time to sit in silence. Close your eyes and begin counting your thoughts. Each time you see a thought, count it. Don't fight with your thoughts; simply count them without judging them as good or bad. As you count, you will quickly see that it's impossible to count all the thoughts because they move faster than you can count them. If you continue with this practice, over time you may notice that at first the number of thoughts increases instead of decreasing. This is a good sign, as it indicates that your awareness of the thoughts is growing.

During the practice and throughout the day, keep reminding yourself that you are not your thoughts, but the witness that observes and counts them. With time and practice, more distance will be created between your consciousness and the thoughts, and you will notice more gaps between the thoughts. These gaps will help you to recognize that you are not your thoughts and your identification with them will gradually begin to drop. Continue practicing with this exercise until you notice that when you try to count the thoughts, they magically stop and your consciousness is no longer clouded by them.

## 5. Accept Every Thought and Let It Go

Each time a thought comes into your consciousness, look at it with a welcoming attitude, accept it, and let it go. Don't judge or analyze the thought, just accept it and let it go. When you try to analyze or judge thoughts as good or bad, you fuel them with your energy and, therefore, have a harder time letting them go. As you go on accepting your thoughts, remind yourself that you are not the thoughts but are the witnessing awareness that observes them. If you continue watching all your thoughts with acceptance, you will be free of their influences and they will no longer disturb you. With each practice of acceptance and letting go, you'll see that although thoughts always come and go, your inner silence always remains unchanged. From emptiness thoughts come and into emptiness they go. So say "hello" when you see them, and "good-bye" as you let them go.

## 6. Watch Your Every Judgment and Let It Go

Most of us are familiar with how quickly we judge ourselves, others, and life. Judgment is one of our biggest enemies because it closes the door of our heart and suppresses our innocence and intelligence. All judgments are thoughts that are projected onto reality and have nothing to do with truth. With this exercise, each time you see yourself making a judgment, stop immediately and let the judgment go. Even if at times you may be right, let the judgment go anyway and keep your mind and heart open. Use your breath to help you let go of your judgment and with each exhalation say to yourself, "I let go of my judgment." If you practice with this exercise for three months, you will feel a deep cleansing and purification in your energy and a sense of transformation in your life and relationship with others.

### 7. Let Go of Your Beliefs and Focus Your Attention on Your Inner Silence

To heal into consciousness, we need to let go of all the beliefs that make up our many personalities. In a sense, we have as many personalities as we have beliefs: about ourselves, about others, and the world. Letting go of your beliefs and personalities is like peeling away the many layers of an onion. It takes time and effort.

We often try to repress and avoid looking at parts of ourselves that we believe are "wrong," or parts that we don't like and judge as bad or evil. By denying one part of your personality, you create another personality and become more artificial, and by trying to avoid your shadow side you become more inauthentic and hypocritical.

Instead of trying to substitute one belief with another, an easy way to see and let go of your personalities and belief patterns is to focus your attention on your inner silence instead. If it is difficult at first to recognize your inner silence, try to focus on the outer silence. Sit in your room where you are not disturbed, or find a beautiful place in nature and focus your attention on the silence that's around you. Once you have a sense of the outer silence, bring your attention inside and focus on your inner silence.

As you focus on your inner silence, try to look at yourself from outside and see the way you normally behave when you act with a particular personality. Watch the kind of thoughts you think when you are in that personality. When you see your belief and behavior pattern clearly, tell yourself that you are not that belief or that personality, then let it go. When you keep focusing your attention on your inner silence, disidentification with that personality and belief will happen effortlessly. Even if you find this exercise difficult at first, don't quit right away. If you persevere, your connection to your inner silence and your understanding of yourself will increase, and you will find it to be greatly rewarding.

## 8. Let Go of Your Pain by Focusing Your Attention on Your Inner Silence

You can also try the above exercise of focusing your attention on your inner silence when you experience pain. Most of your physical and emotional pain is a result of your suppressed thoughts and emotions. If you try to fix your pain with medication alone, you may be only suppressing its cause and sooner or later the pain may resurface with even greater intensity.

When you feel physical or emotional pain, instead of focusing your attention on the pain, focus it on your inner silence. When focusing on the inner silence, pay attention to what kind of thoughts and emotions are surfacing and let them go while you remain a witness to them. By letting go of the thoughts and emotions you normally hold on to and focusing on your inner silence, you allow your energy to move freely; this also relieves your body of the accumulated stress caused by the suppressed thoughts and emotions.

*(Note: this exercise is not a substitute for medical attention. However, if your doctor finds no medical problems that cause the pain, this and the following exercise will be of great help.)*

## 9. Let Go of Your Thoughts by Expressing them Out Loud

The thoughts and emotions are not in our head alone – they are suppressed everywhere in our body and grow like weeds in a garden. Everything we feel, think and hold on to is stored in our body, layer upon layer. The layers of suppressed thoughts and emotions take us out of balance and cause our physical pain and suffering. To restore physical, mental, emotional and spiritual health and wholeness you need to purify your body of the suppressed thoughts and emotions. One very powerful way to do this is through open and honest expression. This requires courage and understanding. Expressing your thoughts and emotions out loud honestly and openly will not only clear your energy of inner turmoil but will also help you become more true and authentic to yourself and others.

101

You can practice this exercise privately or when communicating with others. To do it privately, allocate some time when you are alone and can comfortably express out loud whatever thoughts and emotions are coming up. Don't judge and criticize what you are saying, and don't let your mind stop you no matter how silly it may appear in the beginning. It's like singing in the shower. If you give it a fair try, with time you'll begin to experience more peace and understanding of yourself and others. If you express your thoughts and emotions out loud, not only will it help you become more conscious and truthful when communicating with others, it will also open your heart, free your blocked energy, and improve your physical and emotional health.

## 10. Ask People What They Think of You and Let Go of Your Attachment to What You Hear

This method can be difficult to practice because it involves other people. But if you can do it, particularly with your intimate friends and relationships, you and the people around you will greatly benefit from it.

Start by asking people to honestly tell you what they think of you. Most people you ask will have difficulty telling you their negative opinion because of their fear to hurt your feelings. If you are prepared to hear their opinion and persist in asking, some people might share their feelings and opinions honestly. As you listen to what they are saying, watch how their opinions (positive or negative) affect you, and the thoughts and emotions that get stirred inside of you in reaction. Then, without any judgment of yourself or the other, let go of your attachment to whatever you are thinking or feeling and simply remain a witness.

For example, when someone says they like you, you may immediately feel good about yourself. If they point out things that they dislike about you, you may immediately feel upset, with your inner peace disturbed. Watch both your positive and negative reactions, reminding yourself that you are neither of your reactions but simply the witness who is observing everything. If you continue to witness both the positive and negative reactions, you will realize how dependent you are on other people's opinions and their acceptance or rejection of you. Compassionately remind yourself that everyone is living in a mad world of contradictory thoughts and emotions, and be accepting of yourself and others. If you can understand that your happiness and unhappiness have nothing to do with other people's opinions of you, a distance will be created between your thoughts and your awareness, and it will be easier for you to become conscious of your true Self and live more fearlessly from your heart and being.

**11. To See and Understand Your Behavior Patterns, Contemplate the Following Questions:**

*Why do I struggle with myself, others, or life?*
*How would my life be if I let go of struggling?*
*How would my life be different if I was to always watch*
     *my thoughts and emotions?*
*How can I find my being and live consciously?*

Choose one question that resonates with you most. Sit silently and take some time to contemplate it – for at least twenty minutes or longer if you need more time for clarity. When you see and understand something new about yourself, write it down. Do this for three days in a row. Then, for the following five days, mentally reconnect to this new awareness just before you go to sleep at night, and let yourself drift into sleep with it. In the morning, just before you get out of bed, reconnect with the same awareness and understanding, and keep your focus on the new awareness throughout the day. When you are finished working with one question, repeat the same routine with the other questions.

# QUESTIONS AND ANSWERS
## ABOUT THOUGHT

*I understand the idea of needing to be present. At first, it feels like a thought and I struggle to be present. Sometimes, however, I feel I am present and actually know what it means. How does my thought "be present" relate to actually being present?*

When you hear that you need to be present, your mind immediately thinks that you should *do* something to be present. When you *try* to be present, you become confused, anxious, and begin to struggle. Then you get exhausted, and for a moment your mind stops, and you feel peaceful. A knowing arises inside you that recognizes what it's like to be present.

Observe and understand how the thought "be present" arises. Perhaps you have heard that you need to be present so many times that you have become identified with the thought itself. If you try to be present without awareness, you will feel stressed and anxious. Observe that when you are present, there is no thought that says, "be present," or any other thought. So my suggestion is whenever you see a thought or a desire, simply watch your breath. Then, suddenly, without any effort, you will experience being present.

*So my thought "be present," is not very different from my thought "I am not good enough?"*

That's right. Any thought you are identified with takes you out of the present. It doesn't matter if your thoughts are negative or positive.

*Why do we even need thoughts if all we're supposed to do with them is witness them?*

We need thoughts to put our energy into motion. Life cannot exist without movement, and without life evolution and growth in consciousness would also be impossible. Thoughts can create or destroy. Negative and fearful thoughts generate negative movement of energy, positive and courageous thoughts propel it into positive and creative action. Both positive and negative action is necessary for awareness of stillness and silence to arise.

What fuels thoughts into negative and destructive action are negative emotions of jealousy, competitiveness, greed, possessiveness, fear, selfishness, and the need for power. What fuels thoughts into positive and creative action are positive emotions of love, kindness, longing for peace and creativity, and longing to share and be one with others.

There are two kinds of action: one that arises out of the ego-mind and the other that arises out of awareness. Action that arises out of ego-mind alone is an *unconscious action,* and the action that arises out of awareness is *conscious action.* Conscious action is spontaneous and effortless, while unconscious action requires effort. Conscious action still uses thoughts to propel the energy forward to materialize something, but the person acting consciously does not identify with the outcome. When you identify with the outcome, you act unconsciously from your ego-mind. When you are not identified with the outcome, you simply learn the needed lessons from your experiences and remain open to move on with life and other opportunities it offers.

*You say that all kinds of thoughts float around us all the time, and that we attract the thoughts that we resonate with based on our level of consciousness. Does this mean that Einstein attracted and channeled the thought about the theory of relativity?*

There is much wisdom in the universe, but it can only be channeled into a physical reality through the right vehicle. Until the right person is present with appropriate quality of mind, awareness, and past life experiences and training, the universe's vast store of wisdom will remain unavailable to humanity. Each person has a magnetic field that is created by their psychological and emotional makeup and level of awareness. This magnetic field attracts, as well as rejects, the many thoughts floating in the universe.

There are ordinary, everyday, utilitarian thoughts that everyone uses. Then there are destructive thoughts that are used by some, and benevolent thoughts that are used by others. There are also *wisdom-thoughts*, which represent universal truths that are used by very few.

We naturally attract the kind of thoughts that will help our consciousness evolve and reject those we don't need or aren't ready to accept. How this happens is determined by the level of consciousness in our body – in other words, by the chakra and the energy body in which our awareness is centered.

If you focus your awareness on a certain problem (scientific or spiritual), you naturally open yourself to attract the thoughts that will reveal the answers. Scientists like Einstein, Edison, Newton, Bell, and many others like them were the right vehicles to receive the universal wisdom-thoughts. They then passed on this knowledge to benefit others and helped the entire collective evolve to a new level. Other people like Hitler and Napoleon attracted destructive thoughts, which brought more suffering and pain to the collective.

All scientific and spiritual "discoveries" not only aid the evolution of humanity into higher consciousness, they also help the person who channels them to learn what he or she needs to learn for their personal growth and evolution. In other words, as the vehicle for the theory of relativity, Einstein personally lived and evolved in a way that wouldn't have been possible for him otherwise.

*They say, "You are what you think." Does being identified with a thought mean that you actually become it?*

106

All your thoughts and emotions are part of your energy and identity. When you are identified with your thoughts, you believe they are you. On one occasion, I worked with a client who had the thought, "I am a devil," trapped in his heart chakra and his third eye. He believed and acted as though he was evil and tried to instill fear in others. He attracted this thought because he lacked self-esteem, self-love, self-power, and self-knowledge. He was also more vulnerable to attracting this thought because he was a habitual drug and alcohol user. Although he was identified with this thought, his being was, and always will be, free of this or any other thought or behavior.

*Is pain a thought? Do I feel pain first and then think it's painful, or do I think first and then feel pain? What exactly is the relationship between thoughts and pain?*

Pain and thoughts are closely interrelated. A thought can arise out of experiencing pain, and pain can indicate a presence of thought. If I pinch you, you will first feel the pain and then think that it was painful. But if you are experiencing a chronic or intense pain in some part of your body without an outside cause, you are most likely suppressing a thought in that location.

The body is like a reservoir where many thought-forms are stored. Most of the time, we are not aware of what they are. When the same thought is repeatedly suppressed, it will eventually cause pain. Suppressed thoughts can also cause illnesses like cancer, MS, asthma, and many others. In fact, most of our pain is a result of mental and emotional suppression, and resistance to what is actually happening in and around us. The more we suppress and resist what is true and natural, the more we suffer.

Treat your pain as a friend who is trying to show and teach you something about yourself. We rarely take advantage of the messages hidden in our pain. When we finally accept the pain and understand its lessons, we help to release it from our body and energy and heal into consciousness.

*I have heard you and Osho say: "I talk spontaneously and I am not attached to what is being said." Is that the best way to speak, to just let the words be expressed? If you are just saying what comes to you, then you may say that you are not responsible for what you just said. At what point do you take responsibility for what you say?*

Mystics are the most misunderstood people because they speak from "no-mind" and you hear and interpret their words with your limited logical and conditioned mind. They are also misunderstood because you take their words out of the context in which they were spoken. Everything said in a certain context applies to that context alone and might be in exact opposition to what would be true in another context. If life is viewed through logical mind alone, all of life can be said to be contradictory and meaningless.

One can take responsibility only for what one says if the words arise out of consciousness. It's impossible to take responsibility for what you say otherwise. If you speak with awareness, you don't need to remember what you have said because you respond to every new circumstance spontaneously. In life, what was true one moment may no longer be true in the next. If you stay attached to the ideas that were true in a certain context in the past, then you cannot be open to living and learning what the next moment brings you. Life always moves in a flux. No moment can be exactly like the previous or the next one. Each new moment can easily contradict the one before. Viewed in this way, even life and death, which appear contradictory, are not contradictory. If you are present in the Now, you will not find any contradictions in life, only complementaries. But if you live through logic and conditioning, everything will appear to be contradictory.

Living from the mind means living subjectively. Living from awareness means living objectively. If I speak from awareness of the objective reality and you listen with your subjectivity, you project your conditionings and beliefs onto objective reality. Only a person who lives with awareness can see life objectively and take responsibility for what he or she says. The way we listen and the way our body responds to objective truth is different from the way our body reacts to subjective truth. The person who is aware of the objective truth is simultaneously also aware of their subjectivity and their inability to communicate the truth fully.

It's impossible to describe neither the objective nor the subjective truth with words. I use words to describe parts of what I have come to know and understand through experience, but the words are always limited and can never express the full truth. If between now and the next moment I have a new experience and understanding, then the way I would communicate it would reflect my expanded consciousness.

If you simply repeat something you have read or heard as truth without having experienced it yourself, even if you say all the right things you can never be a knower of truth and take responsibility for what you say. But if you say something out of your awareness and experience, you have full authority over what you say and, therefore, also will be responsible for what you say.

The nature of existence is paradoxical – it always contradicts logic. If I used logic, I would remember everything I said because logic uses memory. I don't speak from memory, and therefore I'm not attached to the words. But I do take full responsibility for what I say in the moment because I speak through awareness. When you talk from the conditioned mind – which is full of beliefs – you cannot really take any responsibility for what you say because you don't speak from experience and don't understand or mean what you are saying.

If I speak from my inner knowing, and you listen from your inner knowing, there will be no misunderstanding and no contradiction because we will be communicating through objective knowing. If I speak with awareness and I'm in tune with my inner wisdom, and you are listening with awareness and are in tune with your inner wisdom, then we are both in tune with the same objective consciousness that prevails within the universe. With such understanding, the question of responsibility does not even arise.

109

*Can learning a new language help expand my consciousness?*

Our consciousness can definitely expand by learning a new language because each language reflects the collective energy and world-view of the people who speak it. My grandmother used to encourage me to learn foreign languages by telling me, "You are as many people as the number of languages you speak." I realized the truth of her words each time I learned a new language and observed how my consciousness changed and expanded. We learn our mother tongue mechanically, but it takes an aware effort to learn a new language. Traveling to foreign countries and learning other languages can help us expand our consciousness and break through our limiting beliefs and conditionings.

*I try to understand myself and my mind by contemplating a lot, but I still feel stuck and unhappy. Once in a while I feel the sky opens, and I am free from my mind and happy with life. But most of the time, life is a struggle. How can I come out of the struggle?*

You cannot become conscious simply by contemplating. Contemplation is a good first step to help you understand yourself, but it cannot help you experience and know your inner truth. You truly become a knower of who you are when you experience yourself as no-mind. Truth can only be known in the absence of the ego-mind. The birth of consciousness is the death of the ego-mind. If you can understand that everything in the outside world is a projection of what is happening inside your mind, then you may be able to relax into life and accept what is happening around you without blaming yourself or others. This is the only way to come out of struggle.

Your struggles are helping you to look inside and find your truth. You prevent your healing into consciousness by trying to avoid the discomfort that struggle brings. Instead of struggling with your mind, just go inside and find your inner emptiness. But this is difficult because it's painful for your ego to accept that you are pure silent emptiness.

As long as you continue to remain a somebody, you will continue to struggle and suffer.

Your ego-mind is like the bark of a tree. For a tree to survive and mature it needs the bark to protect it from the outside elements. When the tree has matured and begins to die, its bark starts to peel off. Don't struggle with the bark and try to pull it off forcibly. As long as the tree is growing, the bark needs to stay attached to the tree. Accept your bark. When it is no longer needed, it will fall off on its own.

Don't fight the mind with the mind. Look at how your ego stays alive by you needing to be in control. To break your mind's pattern of needing to stay in control, be a Zorba once in a while. Go "crazy" and risk losing your head by behaving completely differently from the way you would normally behave. This will help you break through your fears that keep you in need of control. To come out of the mind's struggle and act with maturity and responsibility you must learn to act with awareness.

# 5 THE JOURNEY HOME: MOVING THROUGH THE SEVEN BODIES

In this chapter we will explore how our healing journey into consciousness takes us from our original unconscious state of being in stillness and oneness with existence into a conscious state of being in stillness and oneness with it; as we travel the paradoxical journey of the endless cycle of creation and stillness.

The first part of the chapter describes how energy manifests into a physical form by descending through a vortex of six intangible energy bodies, and the role the human body plays in transforming the unconscious energy (darkness) into conscious energy (light), as it ascends back through the seven chakras and bodies.

The second part of the chapter describes the obstacles we must face and move through while purifying our energy of unconsciousness as we transform it into consciousness. We will also explore the dimension of beyond enlightenment and the key roles that witnessing, acceptance, and non-judgmental self-observation play in our spiritual evolution.

Mystics throughout the ages have taught us that nirvana or enlightenment is the ultimate liberation from pain and suffering. And although they have insisted that it is right Here and Now within us, we usually think of it as something we have never known and need to achieve through some form of doing or searching. Mystics have also acknowledged that although nirvana is our true nature, we can't truly know it until we search for it and experience it for ourselves. Unfortunately, we try to understand this paradox with our mind alone. As a result, we search outside of ourselves for the experience rather than looking within. In essence, our spiritual work is an internal journey of simply remembering that we already are what we are searching for and we are already at home – in fact, we are the home. To experience and know this truth is to relax into our being.

## THE ABSOLUTE: OUR ORIGINAL HOME

Both mystics and scientists agree that beneath the visible veil of our separate physical reality, everything within the Universe exists as a unified whole or oneness. While scientists have come to understand and describe this oneness through their intellects, the mystics have come to understand and know it through meditation and personal experience.

Our original home is where our physical and non-physical realities unite. We have called this unity *God, Allah, Brahma, Great Spirit, Tao, Source, Beloved, Universe, Existence,* and *Presence.* Buddha described it as *emptiness* or *nothingness,* and Zen describes it as *isness, suchness,* or the *original face.* Scientists have described it as the *zero point energy* or a *quantum vacuum sea* within which everything floats. I like to call it the *Absolute.* The Absolute is not Christian, Buddhist, Jewish, Hindu, or whatever beliefs we create around it. The Absolute is fundamentally unknowable, indescribable, intangible, and inseparable from all that is. To grasp this intellectually is to have a kind of understanding about God, but to experience it is to become God.

Although it is impossible to describe it, those who have experienced it agree that within the Absolute, there is no concept of a separate "I" or "self." Everything within it always exists in the present moment without beginning or end. The Absolute is within everything in existence, manifest or unmanifest, and it contains the life force of all past, present, and future creation.

Everything that manifests into a physical reality can only exist within a limited realm of time and space, which in itself is ultimately part of the timeless and limitless Absolute. Even the minutest particle within the Absolute, like the tiny seed of a plant, has an inexhaustible power that can create countless galaxies. To experience the power of the Absolute is to know God and experience the pure joy of creation.

The Absolute is an infinitely empty and yet full space. It appears as dark because of its depth and density. What makes the Absolute visible is the light that occasionally arises from within its emptiness.

Everything visible and invisible within the emptiness of the Absolute exists through different energetic frequencies and sounds. Ultimately, all frequencies unify into an unmoving state of *zero frequency* or *vacuum*. In other words, all seven sound vibrations or notes unify into *silence*; all thought frequencies (positive and negative) unify into no-thought or *no-mind*; and all seven colors of the rainbow unify into *pure space* that appears dark when it is invisible and as light when it is visible. This is the meaning of "all is one, and is God."

As the human intellect is only a part of the Absolute, it is impossible to comprehend the emptiness or oneness of the Absolute, or what is beyond time and space, with the intellect alone. The Absolute can only be *known* through experience.

Like two sides of the same coin, the Absolute can be divided into two major parts: unconscious energy, which absorbs all colors and sounds and appears as darkness; and conscious energy, which reflects all colors and sounds and appears as light. Unconscious energy has no self-awareness and contains *dormant power* with the potential to create, while conscious energy is aware of itself and has the *active power* to create. All conscious energies were once unconscious. They became conscious through the development of self-awareness. Before unconscious energy is transformed into consciousness, it receives nourishment from other conscious energies in the same way that life on Earth receives nourishment from the Sun.

When unconscious energy transforms into conscious energy, a part of the darkness within the Absolute becomes visible or known. All the suns, stars, and galaxies reveal a part of the infinite darkness. It is like turning on a light switch in a dark room. The moment you turn on the light, the darkness disappears and you see all the furniture and space that is in the room. However, even within the things in the room, such as furniture, there remains more darkness. It is like having rooms within rooms; lighting up one room reveals another. This goes on infinitely. As more darkness transforms into light, more of the Absolute becomes visible and known and the universe appears to expand.

As the Absolute or the universe goes on expanding, the interplay of conscious energy and unconscious energy continually changes, but its unmoving center, which is an empty void, always remains the same for both. There is no difference between the center of physical reality and the centre of non-physical reality. In every cell and atom, within all that exists within the universe – the centre is the same. Our being and the being of the universe exist within this single unmoving center. And we can experience this center of stillness by observing it in a place very near to us – between our incoming and outgoing breaths, inhaling and exhaling as we go about our daily lives. We can, in other words, observe the Absolute manifesting itself through us simply by observing it through the *witnessing awareness* that is at the very core of our being.

The witnessing awareness observes everything: the incoming breath, the outgoing breath, the constant stillness or gap between the two, and all experiences of creation and destruction, births and deaths, both within and without. The witnessing awareness is the thread between the physical world of time and space and the realm of the Absolute that exists in the Now beyond time and space.

Whatever the level of consciousness or unconsciousness within us, and within anything in existence, everything revolves around the unmoving center of the Absolute. Stillness and rest are necessary after each moment of destruction for the seed of creation to germinate. Living the ongoing cycle of life and death, stillness and creation, consciousness and unconsciousness, is the essence of existence.

The Absolute creates and expands infinitely, for no particular reason other than the Joy of creation. The Joy of creation is ecstasy. The longing to experience this Joy is in the heart of all creation. Joy makes creation and expansion possible because Joy not only arises from creation but fuels it. The Absolute's longing to create and expand is also our longing and is the purpose of all life. You have experienced this many times in your own life when in a moment of silent stillness an idea suddenly pops into your mind. As you recognize its creative potential, you feel a rush of excitement and joy. When you manifest your creative ideas in the world, you use your life force and create a meaning for your life. This fulfills your innate existential longing to experience the Joy of creation and expansion.

## THE BEGINNING OF LIFE

Nobody knows exactly when and how the first life form emerged, but new life forms continually appear and disappear within the boundless belly of the Absolute. Just as there are countless animal and human wombs that continually create life on Earth, there are infinite *cosmic wombs* that endlessly create a myriad of life forms and galaxies within the universe. Scientists call these cosmic wombs *black holes.* When the energy within the black hole develops and builds to a certain pressure, it creates a kind of atomic explosion that ejects the energy at great speed and force. This explosion, which is commonly known as the Big Bang, splits the primordial energy into many particle-beings or souls, in the same way that a wide slow river shatters into innumerable droplets as it goes over a waterfall. This division into countless particle-beings creates an illusion that each particle is separate from the whole and exists on its own. The relative differences (size, shape, etc.) and movements (speed, direction, etc.) of these particle-beings to each other create the illusion of movement that we perceive as time and space.

When it first emerges, each particle-being is enveloped in a bubble-like protective shell that scientists have referred to as a *primordial bubble.* The energy in the bubble is unconscious but holds within itself the seed of immense creativity and consciousness. This bubble protects the unconscious energy or life force from prematurely dissolving back into the cosmic sea of unconsciousness within the Absolute. The shell of the primordial bubble is like a shell that protects the seed of a plant from deteriorating and dissolving back into the earth before it can germinate.

At first, the primordial bubbles (souls) simply float within the emptiness of the Absolute like soap bubbles in the air, empty of imprints of any physical experience. Then, these countless bubbles or souls journeying within the universe incarnate into different physical forms. Through experiences in physical forms, each soul begins to form distinct patterns or imprints within its own energy-bubble. These patterns or imprints then shape that soul's essence and personality. In its endless journey of countless experiences, each soul develops its own unique essence, purpose, and direction but always remaining within the Absolute and under the influence of its greater will. After a long process of evolution, the unconscious energy of the soul transforms into conscious energy and now the self-aware soul or being dissolves back into its original source – the Absolute. How all this happens is part of the miraculous and will always remain within the unknowable mystery of the Absolute.

## LEAVING HOME: THE DESCENDING JOURNEY TROUGH THE SEVEN BODIES/CHAKRAS

Before the primordial being or soul incarnates into a human form, it evolves by experiencing life in less advanced forms, i.e. rocks, vegetation, animals, etc. After the first experience of awareness of the surrounding world, which usually happens in an animal incarnation, the soul is ready to incarnate into a human body to begin its *active journey into consciousness*. As a result of human incarnation, it experiences life for the first time, using thoughts and expressing feelings through language. As a human, the soul also for the first time becomes aware of death and identifies with the body's instinctual fears around survival.

The life force and its essence move into a human body through a three-dimensional, concentric, cone-like vortex. This vortex contains seven micro vortices or chakras that are separate yet interwoven. *(For the locations of the chakras, see page 121. For information about their purpose in our spiritual development, see Chapter 6.)* They simultaneously exist within both the horizontal (past and future) and vertical (here and now) dimensions. Although movement and change happen simultaneously within all the vortices, they all share the same unmoving still and silent center.

Depending on the direction from which we look at a moving vortex, the energy waves entering the vortex will either appear to be *ascending* and uncoiling as they slow down and open into the void, or *descending* as they spiral down and rush into its center. The vortex will also appear to move in either a clockwise or counter-clockwise direction depending on the perspective.

Seen from one perspective, the vortex appears to be moving inward to the center of the vortex; seen from another perspective, it appears to be drawn away from the axis, expanding infinitely outward. All movements – descending and ascending, vertical and horizontal, clockwise and counter-clockwise, past and future – of the human energy vortices in each chakra revolve around and merge into an unmoving vertical axis or center in the physical body, which simultaneously is also the center of the Absolute.

The photos on the next page illustrate a galactic vortex, a black hole vortex, a spiral vortex, and a tornado vortex. If you look at these photos, you can see that although the vortices initially appear separate from the

Galactic Vortex

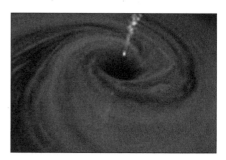

Black Hole Vortex

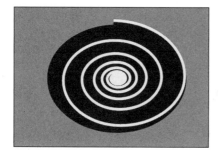

Spiral Vortex

Tornado Vortex

whole, they are still a part of it and ultimately merge into it. Although it is impossible to describe this through words, I will attempt to describe this miraculous phenomena using linear logic.

When the life force incarnates into a physical body, it moves, or "descends," into the Earth's gravity through a cone-like macro vortex. As the life force passes through the macro vortex, it separates into seven cycles or micro vortices that revolve around the same unmoving central axis, or zero-point energy. Each cycle, or micro vortex, has its own frequency, color, sound, and level of consciousness.

These seven energy vortices have also been described as the seven *energy bodies* or *chakras*. The "closer" the body is to the Absolute, the higher its frequency. The "farther" away from the Absolute, the lower the frequency, progressively becoming more dense and defined. Eventually it solidifies into matter – the physical body. Each energy body has its own center within the vertical axis of the physical body, which corresponds to a chakra point in the physical body. All seven bodies and chakras are interconnected and merge into each other as they revolve around the same unmoving central axis of the main vertical vortex.

The first cycle of the vortex through which our life force descends is the *enlightenment body* (the Higher Self) or the *nirvanic body*. This body contains the memory of our oneness with the Absolute and our potential for self-realized consciousness. Its corresponding chakra point in the physical body is the seventh or crown chakra at the top of the head.

The second cycle of the vortex through which our life force descends is traditionally known as the *cosmic body*. I like to call this body the *wisdom body* because it knows intuitively that it (the soul) is not really separate from the Absolute. This body corresponds to the third eye,

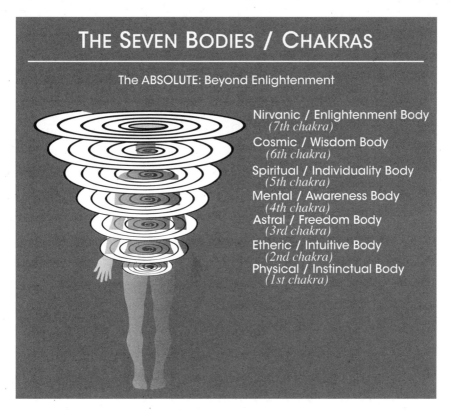

THE SEVEN BODIES / CHAKRAS

The ABSOLUTE: Beyond Enlightenment

Nirvanic / Enlightenment Body
*(7th chakra)*
Cosmic / Wisdom Body
*(6th chakra)*
Spiritual / Individuality Body
*(5th chakra)*
Mental / Awareness Body
*(4th chakra)*
Astral / Freedom Body
*(3rd chakra)*
Etheric / Intuitive Body
*(2nd chakra)*
Physical / Instinctual Body
*(1st chakra)*

or the sixth chakra in the physical body at the forehead, between the eyebrows.

The third body of the vortex through which our life force descends has been traditionally called the *spiritual body*. I prefer to call it the *individuality body* because this body contains the unique individual spirit and essence we have developed on our journey as a result of our different physical incarnations. This body corresponds to the throat, or the fifth chakra in the physical body.

The fourth cycle of the vortex through which our life force descends has been called the *mental body*. I choose to call it the *awareness body* because it is through awareness that we bridge and transform the unconscious mind into conscious mind. The awareness body is in the middle of the "lower" three and the "higher" three energy bodies and acts as a point of unification between them. The awareness body corresponds to the heart, or the fourth chakra in the physical body.

The fifth cycle of the vortex through which our life force descends is known as the *astral body*. I call it the *freedom body* because in this body we are not yet confined to the physical reality of time and space. The freedom body corresponds to the solar plexus, or the third chakra in the physical body. As the life force continues to move further down into the bottom of the vortex, the awareness of the higher bodies is pushed into the subconscious and our original state of oneness with the Absolute is forgotten.

The sixth cycle of the vortex through which our life force descends is known as the *etheric body*. I call it the *intuitive body* because its essence is intuition (gut feeling). The intuitive body corresponds to the navel, or the second chakra in the physical body, also known as the *hara*. The hara is our life center because the life force enters the physical body through the navel chakra of the mother's body and is connected to the developing fetus through the umbilical cord.

From the hara, the life force (also known as *kundalini* energy) moves to the base of the spine in the physical body and coils up there in the first chakra – the root or sex center. I like to call the physical body the *instinctual body* because it contains the blueprint of physical survival and procreation. The physical body instinctively knows how to recognize danger, heal itself, and when to eat or sleep.

Although the life force is now contained and somewhat restricted within the denser frequencies of the physical body, the other bodies continue to exist and function within their own dimension and reality. The awareness of the multidimensional reality of the other bodies remains dormant until we actively and consciously begin our ascending journey back to the original home. Our spiritual work, therefore, is to help uncoil our kundalini energy and encourage it to move from the root chakra to the crown and gradually transform it into consciousness in each chakra. In this process of evolution and transformation, it is our task as humans to ultimately surrender the protective shell of our ego-mind and release our conscious energy back into the Absolute. This process of ascension is the journey of healing into consciousness.

You can get a glimpse of the different bodies and their frequencies by experimenting with making sounds in each of your chakras, starting from the first and going upwards. Close your eyes, look inside, and while making a sound, bring your awareness into the first chakra. As you move higher through the chakras, you will notice that the frequency of the sound changes from lower to higher.

## THE PURPOSE OF THE HUMAN BODY

We have long imagined God in our own image because on some level we have recognized that we embody both the unconsciousness and the consciousness of existence and its mysterious ability to create. The Absolute created the human body so it could transform its own energy from unconsciousness into consciousness and thereby evolve and expand. This makes the human body one of the most sophisticated cosmic laboratories ever created, not only on this planet but in the whole of existence. On our planet, only humans have the ability to create and manifest things into a physical reality. Even whales and dolphins, which are recognized to have consciousness, do not have this ability.

The same unknowable intelligence that created the human body also created the seven energy centers designed to function as transformation chambers. As the life force ascends through these centers, an alchemical transformation from unconsciousness into consciousness occurs. Each one of our body's cells is like a microcosmic Absolute with their own micro centers containing both unconscious and conscious energies. Each cell houses the potential of enlightened consciousness, just as a seed contains within its shell the fragrance of the potential flower.

The human body is similar to a prism in that it divides the life force into seven colors and sound vibrations or tones. On our ascending journey, these colors and tones are not clearly defined and look like a dark grayish mass. As a result of our active and intentional spiritual work of transforming our unconsciousness (the dark grayish mass) into the light of consciousness, they once again begin to separate into seven distinct sound vibrations and color rays. We at times may see these color rays when we look inside in meditation. When our witnessing awareness is fully present in the entire body, the separate color rays reunite and turn into the white light of consciousness. In this way, as a result of each person's spiritual work and transformation, parts of the unconscious darkness of the Absolute continue to endlessly transform into the light of consciousness.

The potential of every person's enlightenment lies dormant within their life force at the bottom of the spine until it is ready to ascend and grow like a sprouting seedling. With its upward movement through the body and each chakra or transformation chamber, the energy gradually transforms from darkness (unconsciousness) into light (consciousness). If you look at the human energy vortex on page 121 you can see how the life force that was once condensed at the bottom of the spine slowly opens and expands as it moves up through the seven chakras and bodies. Altogether, the complete transformation of the soul from unconsciousness into consciousness takes many incarnations in different human forms. How long it takes depends on each soul's unique journey.

Upon physical death of the enlightened person, the now fully conscious energy merges with the Absolute, outgrowing its need to be protected by the shell of the ego-mind and body. From here on, the soul is free from the gravitational field of the Earth and the confines of the physical body and is at liberty to travel wherever the Absolute wills it to be.

Like humans, planet Earth has her own life force and consciousness. Her energy field is like an enormous laboratory where millions of souls gravitate to participate in her, and their own, evolution into consciousness. Within the cosmic void of the Absolute, the Earth is like a mother who provides nourishment and shelter to those who are part of her journey. We feel energized, elevated, and peaceful when we are in tune with her. But like a mother's womb, she also restricts us within her field of gravity. Just as we need to leave our mother's womb and eventually leave our home to continue with our own life, it is our challenge to break free from the protective sphere of mother earth if we are to continue our journey within the universe.

As part of breaking free from the force field of mother earth, our challenge and spiritual work is also to break free from the force field of the collective unconsciousness of all humans who inhabit the Earth. To liberate our soul from the pain and suffering created by us humans, we need to always remember our true purpose for being here – the transformation of our unconscious energy into consciousness.

## THE ASCENDING JOURNEY HOME:
## THE JOURNEY OF HEALING INTO CONSCIOUSNESS

Paradoxically, the ascending journey into light is simultaneously a descending journey into darkness. If we wish to rise higher in consciousness, we must simultaneously go deeper into the unconscious that is hidden within our energy and body. When consciousness is absent in the body, we behave mechanically and without awareness. We heal into consciousness as we become aware of the unconscious within our energy and body.

Although consciousness is present in all the chakras in varying degrees, we primarily function out of the chakra that has the most consciousness. The chakra that has the most consciousness becomes the center of gravity, and our life begins to revolve around it and its qualities. However, no matter which chakra is the center of gravity, to completely heal into consciousness we must become fully conscious in the entire body.

Consciousness evolves as a result of energy movements in the body. We experience transformation of unconsciousness into consciousness when the energy moves back and forth in each chakra and up and down between the chakras. The up-down and back-forth movements are created by contradictory thought-forms and emotions suppressed around each chakra. These need to be released and transformed through understanding and mutating the paradox of life's duality. Most people live identified with the constant back-and-forth and up-and-down movement of the contradictory thoughts and emotions and miss the many opportunities that life offers to integrate the contradictions into unmoving stillness in the center.

For example, the up-and-down movements of energy could be created by the contradictory thought-forms that move from "I love myself" or "I love you" in the fourth chakra to "I hate myself" or "I hate you" in the third or second chakra. Any identification with contradictory thoughts such as love-hate, past-future, good-bad, etc. keeps the energy in the duality of the mind and stops it from moving into the higher chakras/bodies. With observation and disidentification from the mind, the energy balances in the center of the chakra/body and consciousness moves into the higher chakras/bodies.

Once there is enough consciousness in one chakra/body, the

spiraling energy reaches a turning point and moves to the next chakra/ body. This is the *point of metamorphosis* when the unconscious energy transforms into conscious energy. At a point of transformation, consciousness has enough momentum and power to push the life force into the higher chakra where it expands into its corresponding body. This moves the center of consciousness from one chakra/body to the next until the fully conscious life force is liberated from the paradox of life's duality and life and death.

The illustration on page 121 shows how the movement from one body to the next opens and expands the scope of consciousness within the vortex's energy field. As consciousness centers in the higher bodies, the gravitation force of the lower bodies lessens. When consciousness rises to a higher frequency, the back-and-forth and up-and-down movements between contradictory thought-forms, emotions, past and future, consciousness and unconsciousness, slow down in the same way that the arc of a pendulum slows before coming to rest. And with the slowing down of movement, consciousness begins to root in the stillness of the unmoving center of the being.

When the life force moves through all the chakras simultaneously, all seven bodies suddenly light up as if in an explosion. You see your entire body turn into light and experience what is known as enlightenment. With this experience, your consciousness merges with the cosmic consciousness, and you realize that the whole universe is an inexhaustibly powerful and endless expression of Joy. You also realize that you and everything within the universe is made of the same Joy. After the intensity of this experience subsides, you continue to experience physical reality, but with a key difference: you no longer identify with whatever you are experiencing but simply remain a witness to it. You now truly understand that all experiences, the ego-mind, and physical death are only moment-to-moment, temporary happenings in your eternal journey within the universe.

127

# THE SEVEN BODIES

In the Eastern tradition, the fully developed consciousness of each body is symbolized by flowers of four, six, ten, twelve, sixteen, two, and a thousand petals. The blossoming process takes time and spiritual effort. With each lesson lived and learned, another petal of the flower of consciousness opens. With the blossoming of the flower in each chakra, consciousness roots in that chakra/body and begins to sprout and develop in the next. With each flowering and movement into a higher chakra and body, we transcend our fears in the lower chakras/bodies and open to the unknown reality of the higher chakras/bodies. This flowering cannot be forced. It happens naturally and in its own time. We only have the power to do our best to become more conscious and continue learning our lessons, while patiently and gracefully waiting for the flowers to open.

Although we always exist in all seven bodies simultaneously, we live most of our lives rarely becoming aware of them or experiencing them. This is because our awareness is focused mainly on the outside physical world and only very rarely moves into the body. Enlightenment, or transformation from unconsciousness into consciousness, is not possible unless awareness is fully present in the entire body. Understanding the purpose each body plays in the ascending journey makes it easier for us to become aware of and pass through them consciously. Below, the bodies and their functions are discussed in ascending order.

*1st Body:* **Physical Body**
The first body on our ascending journey is the physical or *instinctual body.* The physical body is the shelter where the seed of consciousness germinates and grows to eventually open into a one-thousand-petal flower. The physical body has the ability to reproduce and the instinct to temporarily sustain itself while the soul within it evolves into consciousness. Instinct tells us when the body needs water, food, or rest. Instinct also knows how to process and assimilate nutrition, regenerate

cells, heal wounds, and lastly, kill to eat in order to survive. All memories and experiences of our soul's history, both in human and non-human forms, as well as the blueprint of our potential future, are imprinted in our body's cells.

As children, we first see and identify with the physical body before we see and identify with our thoughts and emotions. If our awareness remains focused on the physical body alone, our existence will not be very different from that of animals, and our life will primarily revolve around sex, food, and survival. Through physical pain and emotional suffering, our attention moves into the next body where our unconscious energy needs to be transformed into consciousness. By looking into the meaning and messages that pain, illness and suffering bring, we become aware that our existence extends beyond just the physical body. To ground and center our consciousness in the physical body, we must recognize and transcend our identification with the body's survival instinct.

## *2nd Body:* **Intuitive Body**

The second body that we pass through on our ascending journey is the *intuitive* or *etheric body*. The instinctual and intuitive bodies are closely interconnected and coexist within the same survival mechanism of the physical body. The intuitive body is inherent in both animals and humans, and we often refer to it as the "gut instinct." Through the intuitive body, we know how to adapt to our environment, relate to each other, distinguish between benevolent and harmful energies, and protect ourselves against potential harm.

If consciousness develops without the obstructions of social conditionings and interference from the ego-mind, we trust our intuition and easily make important life decisions. If we are used to following the mind instead of trusting our intuition, we remain preoccupied with our desires and survival fears and are unable to grow higher in consciousness. When we are fully conscious of and learn to trust our instinct, our consciousness is ready to move into and evolve in the next body.

129

*3rd Body:* **Freedom Body**

With the blossoming of trust in the intuitive body, the center of consciousness moves into and begins developing in the *freedom* or *astral body.* Here we begin to awaken to a dimension beyond the physical. The freedom body has the power or free will to choose how and where to direct the life force. It is not tangible and can freely and easily pass through anything physical. Ghosts, for example, are seen in their freedom body and can therefore appear and disappear at will.

If we are in tune with the freedom body, we can see events and people in a different reality from how they normally appear and present themselves. We spontaneously experience the freedom body in dreams when we see ourselves fly, see past lives or future events, or receive messages from our guides. We often become conscious of the freedom body when people or circumstances infringe upon our free will. We experience this as inner discomfort and uneasiness. We can also experience the freedom body in meditation when we feel a sense of weightlessness and expansion (a feeling of moving out of the physical body's limits).

With the centering of consciousness in the freedom body, we become aware of our inner power and our ability to shape and influence the world around us. Unfortunately, most people don't use the power of their freedom body because of the fear, insecurity, and doubt suppressed in the lower bodies. Although our inner power and freedom are often restricted by people of social, religious, and political authority, we need to remember that they can never be taken away. Our work in the freedom body is to learn self-confidence, self-respect, self-trust, and courage. When we have learned and integrated these lessons, we understand, respect, and honor the free will in ourselves and in others.

*4th Body:* **Awareness Body**

Once consciousness is centered in the freedom body, the energy moves to develop in the fourth body, the *awareness* or *mental body.* The awareness body is like a thread that connects the three lower with the three higher bodies. Ascending through it is the pivotal halfway mark between our animal-like existence in the lower chakras and godlike potential in the higher ones. This body, like thought or language, is unique to humans. The awareness body functions independently from all the other bodies and provides us with the ability to observe and witness. It can easily move into lower and higher bodies and everywhere within the physical body. The awareness body uses thought to communicate what it observes, and unlike the other bodies that can be seen clairvoy-antly, the awareness body can only be heard clairaudiently.

It is impossible to become conscious of something without becoming aware of it first. The awareness body helps us see and transform our unconsciousness into consciousness in all the seven bodies and is closely related with the experience of love. Love, in its irrationality, takes us out of the set behavior patterns and conditionings of the ego-mind, and even if for just brief moments, breaks down the illusion of separation. Love helps us surrender and merge in oneness with other beings, ultimately giving us an opportunity of becoming aware of our inner longing to reunite with Existence. Through love and awareness of oneness, we develop acceptance, understanding, and caring for each other. Love takes us out of our mind's limiting beliefs and conditionings, and our perception of being separate from each other and existence begins to break down. Through awareness, we recognize that love is the very nature of existence and always rises from within us effortlessly and spontaneously. Awareness of love opens us to higher dimensions of consciousness and truth and shifts our focus away from need and towards giving.

If our ability to self-observe and witness grows in proportion with our physical body, by the time we reach youth we become more lov-ing, caring, and compassionate towards ourselves and others. On the other hand, if the development of self-observation and awareness is hindered, the survival instinct overshadows feelings of unconditional love and caring for others. Instead, lust, insecurities, and attachments become disguised as love. A disguised "love" is selfish and manipulative; it doesn't know how to give but uses others to fulfill its own needs.

With lack of self-awareness and experience of unconditional love, a person stays self-centered, feels ill will towards others, and is more concerned with taking from others than giving. The awareness body helps us witness and surrender our attachments to things and people and assists us in learning to love ourselves and others unconditionally. Unconditional love is aware that it needs to give freedom to others instead of trying to possess, manipulate, or control them.

### 5th Body: **Individuality Body**

The *individuality body*, commonly referred to as the *spiritual body*, is the closest to the two highest bodies. The function of the individuality body is to pull the frequencies of the lower bodies up and bring our energy inwards. The quality of the individuality body is self-sufficiency. The individuality body counterbalances the gravitational force of the survival instinct, fears, and outside influences and helps consciousness to move into and operate in the higher realms. Through experiencing the individuality body, awareness of our spirit and unique essence begins to grow, and our longing to create and manifest our dreams and visions into physical reality intensifies.

In the individuality body, we are able to face our fears and the ego-mind with more courage and take more responsibility for our actions. The individuality body helps to move our thoughts and emotions from negative to positive and to direct our energy towards creation instead of destruction.

The development of consciousness in the individuality body will stagnate if we follow our social and religious conditionings or become too concerned about other people's opinions. When we fully realize that we alone are responsible for how we live and create our lives, consciousness is free to move into the wisdom body where we begin to explore the realm of the mysterious.

### 6th Body: **Wisdom Body**

The *wisdom body*, which is also known as the *cosmic body*, is the doorway between the known physical reality and the unknown cosmic reality. The wisdom body holds the mystical and esoteric knowledge of cosmic truth and of the divine unity of everything in existence. In the wisdom body we don't think about truth, we *know* the truth. The wisdom body enables us to experience bliss and divinity. Through experiencing bliss and divinity, our identification with the material world, thoughts, and emotions breaks down and we recognize our immortality.

In the wisdom body, we transcend the dualities of the positive-negative mind and the male-female polarities, and for the first time experience the oneness of our being with existence. Before consciousness begins to function in this body, we only intellectually understand that we are not our physical body, thoughts, or emotions. But with the experience of the *am-ness* of our being, we truly come to *know* it. In the wisdom body, we realize that the same being or *am-ness* also exists within everyone and everything, here on Earth and in the rest of the universe.

As consciousness develops in the wisdom body, we also begin to experience our psychic abilities. If we become attached to these abilities or misuse them to manipulate others and the world around us, we are thrown back into the lower bodies and delay our enlightenment and liberation from the ego-mind.

Developing our wisdom body is both a blessing and a curse. It is a blessing because it liberates us from suffering. And it is a curse because, as the greater force of the Absolute begins to pull our energy up, it simultaneously becomes more difficult for us to function in the lower-vibration frequencies of the physical world, and to contend with its limitations and the projections of others who are still struggling in their lower bodies. It also becomes difficult for others to understand and relate to us. Many true masters and teachers willfully keep their consciousness centered in the wisdom body, delaying their complete and final liberation because of their compassion and desire to help others on their healing journey. Once consciousness moves into the seventh body, it becomes more and more difficult to stay in and cope with physical reality.

*7th Body:* **Enlightenment Body**

In the *enlightenment body*, we lose our identity as a separate soul and experience true oneness with boundless existence. We melt into it and merge with it. In the process of moving into the seventh body our fear of death and the unknown intensifies. If we are able to witness our mind and its fear of disappearing into the unknown, we can easily move into the seventh body and surrender our will to the Will of the Absolute.

During the "Big Bang" moment of enlightenment, our life force rushes from the root chakra to the crown, blasting it open and completely transforming every cell in the body from darkness into light. Based on my own experience, I would like to describe this state as an explosion of *Cosmic Joy*. In the East this experience has been illustrated as the blossoming of a one-thousand-petaled lotus. With enlightenment the fear of death and the unknown evaporate, and only celebration of the soul's final liberation remains.

In the process of our spiritual work we glimpse moments of mini-enlightenments, known as *satoris* in the Zen tradition. These moments happen when our witnessing awareness is fully present in the gaps between thoughts. The ultimate experience of enlightenment is a gift from existence, and it cannot be willed. After this experience, the soul can either leave the body or continue its existence within it. As a result of enlightenment, the soul not only becomes a light unto itself but is also able to help others in their evolution and liberation from pain and suffering. The last step of the soul's dissolution into the nothingness of the Absolute happens with the death of the physical body.

**Beyond Enlightenment**

If enlightenment is the lighting of the individual flame, then returning to the Absolute – *beyond enlightenment* – extinguishes the still separate flame and merges it back into the vast sea of the Absolute. Before the candle is lit we are in an empty space, but unconscious of it; after it is lit, we are still in the same empty space, but conscious of it. Buddha used the word *nirvana* to describe this state. This has also been described as the state of *super-super consciousness* – a state of *omniscient presence.*

This final liberation into the state of beyond enlightenment happens at the time of physical death when the fully conscious life force is freed from the limitations of the physical body, empty of all thoughts, emotions, and the perception of being a separate soul or a being.

The extinguishing of the flame symbolizes the individual soul's reunification with the Absolute. In this state, the being completely surrenders itself into the Absolute and only a pure consciousness remains. At this point, consciousness has a choice to exist as light or be in a state of invisible empty presence.

Just like appearing and disappearing stars, planets, and suns, consciousness can be lit again at will, when the Absolute needs its light. The now fully conscious omniscient presence has the power to create and manifest new stars or planets, new species or even a new galaxy, so that consciousness can continue to evolve and expand further into infinity. Such creation and manifestation is not much different from how we create and manifest our visions and dreams here on Earth. The play between consciousness and unconsciousness, creation and destruction, life and death, goes on eternally within the infinite emptiness of the Absolute.

## STUMBLING BLOCKS ALONG THE HEALING JOURNEY

There are many stumbling blocks that we must face and pass through as our consciousness grows through the seven cycles of our development: *infancy, toddler, child, teenager, youth, adult,* and *old age.* The stumbling blocks are connected to the survival instinct, society, familial and religious conditionings, personal beliefs, fears, desires, judgments, jealousy, envy, misuse of power, mental and emotional suppressions, identification and attachment to people and things, emotional and psychological wounds from current and past lives, and so on.

For example, if the root chakra is damaged through moral conditioning or sexual abuse, it will affect the intuitive, freedom, and awareness bodies and block the movement of energy and development of consciousness in the higher chakras.

If the energy flow is blocked in the lower chakras with sexual inhibitions, suppressed emotions like anger, hatred, shame, or resentment, no matter how hard you try to cultivate love and compassion, the suppressed thoughts and emotions will undermine your ability to feel unconditional love and compassion. On the surface you may try to be loving but deep inside the unresolved unconscious blocks will continue to sabotage the purity of your energy.

To avoid working through these stumbling blocks, many people turn to food, cigarettes, alcohol, drugs, and sex. Even though these may give temporary relief, an experience of bliss or a glimpse of an altered state of consciousness, the experience will be short-lived and eventually, with habitual use, will undermine the growth of consciousness.

Transforming unconsciousness into consciousness is not an easy task and has no shortcuts. It is the challenge of every spiritual seeker not only to break through their own unconscious but also through the collective unconscious that keeps ninety percent of humanity trapped in the lower chakras of mundane existence. Being trapped in the lower chakras is like being stuck in quicksand. If you don't consciously seek liberation and transformation, you remain a victim of habit and continue to suffer. Each of the seven bodies has its own challenges and blessings.

To find the treasure of eternal life, you must persevere in your ongoing spiritual work and break out of your unconscious habits. Many people are able to reach the awareness body, but they get stuck there because of identification with their emotions and their attachments to people and things. Only a small number of people reach their individuality body and begin to search for their own unique truth. From the higher elevation of the individuality body, it is easier to see the world and the influence of the collective unconscious on one's personal development. To move higher from this body into the wisdom body, you need to become more aware so that what subtly remains unconscious within your energy can be seen.

The path from the individuality body to the wisdom body is narrower and more difficult to travel because now you are left to your own devices. You now know that you cannot live with the values of the collective, and yet it becomes more difficult not to be influenced by its weight and gravity. It's also more difficult to detect the subtle tricks that your ego-mind plays to stay alive. To see the subtleties of the mind and break through them, most people need guidance from someone who has passed through the tricks of their own ego-mind and can guide others through theirs. If you manage to pass through the wisdom body without getting identified with your psychic abilities, you can easily transcend this body and be liberated from the confines of the material reality.

After reaching the enlightenment body you will have one last chance of returning to another physical incarnation, if you so choose. It is the last chance, for two reasons. The first is that living in the lower vibrations of physical reality is very limiting and difficult for a soul with advanced consciousness. The second is that after millions of years of evolution, when the soul has reached the highest possible state of consciousness on this planet, existence needs this evolved consciousness to continue creating and expanding itself elsewhere in the universe.

## PURIFYING THE SEVEN BODIES

Now that we are aware of the seven bodies and how our journey of healing into consciousness moves through them, and we are aware of the stumbling blocks along the way, usually related to the unconscious parts still remaining in our energy, we must humbly remember that in spite of those encouraging glimpses of enlightenment, on-going purification is still required before our ascending journey into full consciousness is complete.

To heal into consciousness, the energy in all the bodies must be purified from all negative thoughts and emotions. The purification process in the first six bodies involves a conscious effort of clearing the mental, emotional, and spiritual wounds suppressed in the energy and the physical body and remaining a witness to what is. Reaching the seventh body is a gift from existence and can only be experienced as a result of complete surrender of the ego-mind.

All illness, pain, suffering and unhappiness are only symptoms indicating that the ascension of consciousness through the seven bodies is impeded. The purification process involves lessons that we absolutely must learn. Learning our lessons and releasing the negative thoughts and emotions from our body allows the energy to move upwards through the seven chakras and bodies without restriction.

Unless we purify our physical body of negative thoughts, emotions and fears, it is impossible to be aware of the other bodies because it is through the physical body that we relate with and ascend through the other bodies. By purifying the physical body of the suppressed thoughts and emotions, we become more present and conscious in all the other bodies.

To purify the physical body, you must first cultivate and strengthen your ability to witness and disidentify from your thoughts, emotions, and the body's survival instinct. As I mentioned in Chapter 1, *witnessing is the detached, unidentified, and non-judgmental observation of what is.* In other words, it is an alert watchfulness without mental or emotional engagement. Just as we have an inherent ability to read, we also have an inherent ability to witness. However, like reading, this ability needs to be trained with dedicated and sincere practice before it can become effortless.

You can strengthen your ability to witness through meditation and breath awareness. Breath awareness is a simple watching of the incoming and outgoing breaths and the gaps between them. In existence, inhalation is life, movement, and action. Exhalation is death, letting go, and surrender. And the gap between inhalation and exhalation is the stillness of the being. In the gap, you jump out of the linear movement of the mind and its reality of time and space and enter the timeless vertical reality of divinity. Through this gap, you can also connect to, and become aware of, all seven bodies and find your way back home.

Without the gaps between the incoming and the outgoing breaths it would be impossible to even see the difference between the incoming and the outgoing breaths. What sees the breath coming in and going out is the witnessing awareness that is always in the gap between the two. The gap is the reference point similar to the zero point on a scale of positive and negative numbers. It is impossible to divide the numbers into positive or negative without the reference point, which is the zero.

With a disciplined meditation practice, the awareness of the gap and the stillness of the being gradually strengthens and, in the process, purifies the energy in each body of the contradictory thoughts and emotions. The deeper your awareness can reach into the unconscious energy hidden in the lower chakras of the physical body and allow the energy to move, the more conscious you become of the higher bodies.

## COMPLETING THE ASCENDING JOURNEY AT DEATH

You can complete your ascending journey through the seven bodies and heal into consciousness while alive or at the moment of death. In either case, the journey is the same – your energy must pass through all the seven chakras and bodies.

Moving through the seven bodies at death is like moving through a tunnel. It can be a blissful or a nightmarish experience, depending on your ability to remain a detached witness to your thoughts, fears, and experiences. The unknown may feel overwhelming and your fears might lead you to doubt that you may survive. If you can keep your witnessing awareness focused in your navel (second chakra) while passing through the darkness, and remember that you are not what you see, feel, or experience, you will be able to disidentify from your mind's fears, desires, and attachments, and your journey into light will be guaranteed.

If you become afraid and decide to stop or go back, you will miss the opportunity to reach liberation from your ego-mind and will have to wait for another chance in the next incarnation. With enough trust and courage, you will grow accustomed to the vastness of the unknown and see that it is not as scary as it at first seemed. With the movement of the life force from one body to the next, your consciousness and understanding of yourself and true reality will increase. If you continue to remain a witness, as you come closer to the end in the seventh chakra, you will literally begin to see light. The *Tibetan Book of the Dead* describes the process of death in great depth, and I highly recommend it to anyone who wants to make his or her death a conscious experience.

If you are unable to stay alert and aware when the life force begins to move through the chakras/bodies, or continue to struggle with death and submit to fear of the unknown, you will not be able to surrender to existence and will fall back into unconsciousness. In your next life, you will continue your development from whichever body your consciousness managed to reach at the time of death.

Each incarnation gives us many opportunities to continue our growth and evolution. In between incarnations, you may choose to rest in the unmoving belly of the Absolute and assimilate the lessons of your most recent life until you are ready to come back into another physical form. Or, you may choose to be quickly reborn and continue your healing journey into consciousness in a new body. What you choose would depend on how attached you are to your physical body and the world, and how desperate to be back in it. The process of movement, rest, and transformation is ongoing. We reincarnate into a physical body again and again until we have completed our journey of healing into consciousness and no longer have any fear of being anywhere within the vast mystery of this endless universe.

# QUESTIONS AND ANSWERS
# ABOUT THE SEVEN BODIES AND CHAKRAS

*You have said that the navel chakra is our center, but you also said that the center moves from one chakra to the next. Can you please clarify?*

There are seven main energy centers or chakras in the physical body. They all merge into one vertical center that moves through the middle of the body, starting from the bottom of the spine to the top of the head. The life force revolves around this unmoving central axes, spiraling up from one chakra to the next. Some teachers emphasize either the navel or the heart as the center, and some focus on the third eye as an important center. In truth, each chakra is a center with its own unique qualities, and your consciousness is usually centered in the chakra where your attention and awareness are focused.

When I refer to the center, I usually mean the meeting place of your *life center,* in the navel chakra, with the central axis that runs through all the chakras. The second chakra is the center through which we incarnate into a physical body and upon which our physical growth and worldly existence depend. The primary function of the life center is to sustain the physical body. This center can also be called the *world center.* Everything that we do in life depends on this center. Without the life center, physical and spiritual growth would be impossible.

You evolve spiritually when your attention and awareness are no longer focused on survival but on love. When you feel that love, peace, and unity are more important than material gain and survival, your heart becomes the new center – the *spiritual center.* This center represents our humanity.

When independence, creativity, and freedom from emotional attachments grow to be your focus, the center of consciousness moves

141

to the throat chakra. We can call this center the *individuality center.*

When mysticism, consciousness, and finding who you are become your focus, then the center of consciousness moves to the third eye. We can call this center the *wisdom center.*

When experiencing and transcendence of fear of death becomes your focus, the center of consciousness moves into the seventh chakra in the crown. We can call this center the *cosmic center.*

But remember, regardless of which center your consciousness is focused in, for enlightenment to happen your witnessing awareness needs to be fully present in the whole body and in all the chakras simultaneously. When all the chakras are open and the life force swiftly moves through them with great force, suddenly reaching the crown, it is difficult to prevent the energy from moving out of the body. If you have not practiced grounding your awareness in the second chakra in the navel (the life center), the intensity of the movement may not allow the life force to remain in the body, and death of the physical body may result. To keep the life force in the physical body while experiencing such a rapid and powerful energy movement, it's necessary to willfully focus and anchor your awareness into the second chakra.

*How do I know which chakra I am working on right now?*

To know which chakra you are working on look at what kinds of thoughts preoccupy you. There are specific lessons that need to be learned in each chakra and your thoughts will reflect the lessons you are presently learning.

If your thoughts and attention are primarily focused on sex then you are working through the first chakra. If your thoughts and emotions are primarily focused on your survival needs, then your consciousness is developing in the second chakra. In this chakra, you may be working on learning to trust that you will be taken care of without needing to lie and manipulate others to get your needs met.

If you are focused on comparing yourself with others and feeling

142

inferior or superior, your consciousness is developing in the third chakra. In the third chakra, you struggle with your desire to be first and win no matter what, and you feel the need to always be in control. To be fully centered in this chakra and move to the fourth chakra, you need to learn to find your own authentic power.

If your thoughts are primarily focused on your need to share and love yourself and others, your consciousness is developing in the fourth chakra. Here, you desire love, strive to release your anger, jealousy, and competitiveness, and try to love and forgive yourself and others. You work on recognizing and understanding others' needs and learn respect and consideration. You also learn to share, give, and receive.

If your thoughts revolve around needing to live your individual freedom and be able to express yourself and your creativity by speaking your truth and finding justice, then your consciousness is developing in the fifth chakra.

If your thoughts primarily revolve around searching for truth, meditating, and wanting to discover your inner truth, then you are working in and developing your sixth chakra.

If you are focused on surrendering your will to the will of God or existence, and you seek self-realization and liberation above all else, you are moving into the seventh chakra. But, regardless of which chakra your awareness is focused on, you develop in all of the chakras simultaneously but in different proportions.

Every lifetime offers its primary and secondary lessons that we must learn in order to continue our evolution in consciousness. Regardless of how developed your consciousness is, if you have any unfinished lessons in the lower chakras, you will eventually need to go back and complete them.

For example, your consciousness may be centered in the fifth chakra and focused on developing individuality, but you may also need to complete your unfinished lessons in the third chakra about fully letting go of your jealousy and competitiveness with others. Once a lesson is learned and consciousness is integrated you move through the chakras with much less time and effort in your next lifetime. This ongoing learning process is the essence of our healing journey into consciousness.

*Do all the bodies need to be empty of suppressed thoughts and emotions before we can experience our inner nothingness or nirvana?*

If you fully surrender your ego-mind and remain a witness to what is, you can experience nirvana or nothingness at any moment. So, it is not a matter of the bodies being completely empty of thoughts and emotions; in life that is impossible. To recognize the truth and be in the Now, your awareness simply needs to be in your being.

By their nature, the seven bodies are only different manifestations of existence. We don't recognize this because our attention is usually focused on our thoughts, emotions, desires, and fears instead of on our inner presence. We are in nirvana when we are fully conscious of the emptiness of our being. We exist in nirvana all the time but remain unaware of it because we avoid emptiness.

For example, even though you asked this question and are hearing what I am saying, you are struggling to understand it with your mind because unconsciously, something inside you is saying: "I am not ready to experience emptiness yet, I haven't lived yet, how can I abandon everything and become a nobody? I don't want to disappear into the unknown emptiness and be extinguished." You are afraid to surrender your fears, attachments, and unlived desires that make up your identity. Many say that they want to be free of suffering, but they are afraid and don't want to let go of their ego-mind identity. Try to understand your fears and why you are holding on to them.

Trying to grasp the concept of emptiness overwhelms the mind. The mind cannot accept that you are emptiness because in emptiness it can no longer have a purpose. The mind tells you that you will be lost within the emptiness, so you cling to your identity. To experience nirvana or your inner emptiness, you need to see, understand, and dis-identify from your fears and thoughts. Don't try to understand what

144

I am saying intellectually. Instead, try to observe what is happening inside you when you hear (read) these words. See what kind of thoughts or emotions are coming up, and how they disturb your inner silence and peace. In your watchful awareness, you will have a glimpse of your inner emptiness and will see your thoughts and emotions as temporary clouds just passing by. This will give you the courage to trust your inner emptiness and begin experiencing and enjoying the divine bliss of the unknown.

*How does my inner emptiness relate to my being?*

All of us experience our inner emptiness at times but miss recognizing it as our being. When we feel emptiness, instead of feeling it and going deeper into it we usually try to stuff it with food, or try to divert our attention from it with work, sex, TV, etc. Instead of avoiding the emptiness, just close your eyes, look inside, and try to feel it. Remember that whenever you experience emptiness, what you are experiencing is a moment of no-mind. Understand that this emptiness is your own being and make friends with it. Stay present, watch your breath, and keep feeling and welcoming the emptiness. Allow it to grow and expand.

The deeper you move inside and invite the emptiness, the more you will begin to feel that it is actually not really empty, but full. It is full of peace, full of joy, full of love. These feelings have nothing to do with anything external. They are the blissful and divine qualities of your own being and existence that we call God.

*Does living my individuality mean that I am living my truth?*

Your truth is more than your individuality. Your individuality is based on the quality of your ego-mind, and your truth is based on no-mind. In this sense, your truth and my truth are not different, but my individuality and your individuality are different because the history of our travels is different. The emptiness of my being is the same as the emptiness of your being, but we manifest our energies differently based on our individual ego-minds. So don't confuse living your individuality with living your truth. Our individuality allows us to fly with our own wings, but our truth is the open sky where we all fly together.

# 6

## DEVELOPING AND HEALING THE EGO-MIND INTO CONSCIOUSNESS IN THE SEVEN CHAKRAS

In Chapter 2, I discussed the ego's overall purpose and development. Now let's explore in greater detail how the developing ego-mind helps to expand consciousness as it evolves in the seven chakras or energy centers in the physical body. In this chapter we will examine:

a) The function of ego-mind and consciousness in each chakra.
b) How it would look if the ego-mind and consciousness had developed naturally from childhood.
c) What prevents the ego-mind and consciousness from developing naturally in childhood.
d) What is needed to help develop the ego-mind and heal it into consciousness.

I have mapped the developing ego-mind and consciousness through the seven chakras in a linear fashion. But, just as with the seven stages of the ego's development, its healing into consciousness is not linear. The ego-mind evolves and heals in each chakra through living and learning the needed spiritual lessons.

Each one of us is a mystery, and our paths are as unique as we are. We all come with our own past history and potential and continue our evolution from where we left off in our previous life. The age and maturity of our soul will determine the lessons we have come to learn this time around.

*1st Chakra (the Root):*
**Foundation of Life**
The function of the first chakra, which is located at the bottom of the spine around the tailbone *(see Illustration on page 121 for the position of all the chakras),* is to ensure the procreation of the species and the healthy sustenance of the physical body. The first chakra is the foundation of life. Each person's life force or kundalini energy coils up in the first chakra at the base of the spine from where it begins its journey upwards.

Although some literature refers to the first chakra as the survival chakra and the second as the center of sexuality, in my experience both personally and in my healing work, I have found that in fact they are very closely interconnected and in a way merge into one another. I like to describe the first chakra as the sex center because while experiencing sexual pleasure we don't concern ourselves with survival worries. Actually, procreation of life comes through sex (the first chakra), and instinct to survive comes through the belly (the second chakra). Once our body comes into existence through sex, its survival in our mother's womb depends on the umbilical cord located around the second chakra through which we receive nourishment and sustenance. When the life force or the kundalini energy moves from the first into the second chakra, we feel our connection to life and the world and our need to survive within it.

*The ego-mind and consciousness develop naturally* in the first chakra if the child is allowed to explore his or her body freely and without condemnation. Children like to cuddle with their mother, father, and siblings to feel their warmth and explore their bodies. They do this by touching, smelling, putting things into their mouths, and playing with their own and others' bodies. When the child starts to explore his own body, and then other's bodies, he discovers that his existence is separate from theirs, and the seed of separate self-identity or ego-mind and consciousness begin to sprout.

A child's first chakra will develop naturally if parents and society don't condemn the child and judge his explorations as "dirty" and "shameful" but instead are open, understanding, and supportive of the child's innocent explorations. If the child is allowed to freely explore his body and sexuality, and is guided without blame or criticism, he will learn to satisfy his curiosity and develop trust in himself. By the time he reaches puberty, he will have a solid and balanced emotional foundation and will naturally develop a healthy approach to his and other people's sexuality. Instead of being preoccupied with suppressed sexual thoughts, he will begin exploring his intuition, individuality, and creativity. He will be excited about learning and expanding his intellect through the exploration of science, literature, art, and music.

*The ego-mind and consciousness don't develop naturally* in the first chakras of most people because parents, society, and religions have condemned our body and sexuality. When parents and society impose their conditionings and inhibitions on the child, they cripple the child's emotional and mental development as well as the development of his consciousness in the higher chakras. Instead of focusing on creativity and the search for his or her own gifts, the child's mind stays preoccupied with unexplored physical desires, suppressed emotional needs, and unlived sexual thoughts. The child learns to fear pleasure and punishment. In order to fit in and be accepted, he also learns to control himself, lie to and manipulate others in the same way he was controlled, lied to, and manipulated. Later in life, he struggles with poor self-esteem and feels unable to freely manifest his innate power, creativity, and unique gifts.

*To heal the wounded ego-mind in the first chakra,* contemplate your attitude and views about sex. Do you feel overly preoccupied and disturbed with sexual thoughts? Do you feel at ease with your body and sexuality or do you feel ashamed of and need to hide your body? Can you freely express your physical needs, or do you expect others to know and fulfill your needs?

Once you understand how your sexuality was formed and molded in your early years, take action to heal your wounds around your sexual inhibitions or perversions. If you want to grow higher in consciousness, it is imperative that you break through the sexual taboos and conditionings imposed upon your natural energy by your parents, society, and any religious ideologies you've come to believe and adopt.

Unless you break through the sexual taboos and freely explore your sexuality, it will be very difficult for you to experience true love. Without breaking through all your conditionings and inhibitions about sex, your innate natural energy will remain distorted by repressed sexual thoughts and your psychological development will remain infantile.

One way to break through your sexual inhibitions and conditionings is to stay present and witness your thoughts, emotions, and inhibitions during sex. If you watch and understand their origins, it will be much easier to disidentify from them and let them go. Stay committed to feeling and understanding your mental and emotional blocks regarding sex and sexual enjoyment. Give yourself permission to explore and enjoy your body and sexuality as well as your partner's body and sexuality in spite of your inhibitions. Watch any fears that may arise. During sex, keep your awareness focused on your breath and body sensations instead of your fears and thoughts. Then, gradually begin by consciously letting go of your inhibitions, and have the courage to freely express them to your partner. Breaking through sexual fears, taboos, and conditionings is not easy, but it is crucial if you want to heal your wounded ego and grow into greater consciousness.

*2nd Chakra (the Hara):*
**Ensuring the Survival of the Physical Body**
The function of the second chakra, which is located about two inches

below the navel, is to ensure the body's survival. The survival instinct is the body's built-in intelligence, which is present both in animals and humans. The intelligence that helps the body know how to survive is part of the cosmic intelligence, which is independent of the ego-mind. If you cut your finger, the body's intelligence will close and heal the cut without any action on your part. The body's survival instinct continues to function regardless of how developed the ego-mind and consciousness is. Even those who have transcended the ego-mind and disidentified from the body must abide by the body's survival instinct for as long as the body is alive, but with one difference – they are conscious of it and are not identified with it.

*The ego-mind and consciousness develop naturally* in the second chakra if the child receives abundant physical nourishment through food and bodily comforts through comfortable and secure shelter. When the child's survival needs are taken care of the child begins to develop a sense of security about its survival in the world.

Children, just like newborn animals, are attached to their parents for nourishment and safety. The child who receives the needed love and nourishment through his mother's milk and feels that he is secure in his home, grows up feeling that life supports him. He doesn't struggle to survive or stop himself from living fully. If the second chakra develops naturally, the child develops trust and views the world as a safe, friendly, and supportive place.

*The ego-mind and consciousness don't develop naturally* in the second chakra if the child doesn't receive sufficient physical care and nourishment. He grows up believing that everything in life is scarce and begins to project that belief onto the world. Instead of developing trust, he learns to fear and doubt himself, others, and existence. He becomes timid and incapable of expressing his true feelings and learns to suppress his needs and vulnerability. He fears he will not be taken care of, or that he will be punished if he acts contrary to what is expected of

151

him. He grows up fearful of making mistakes, agonizes over success and failure and other people's opinions.

Because the first and second chakras are so close to each other, lack of nourishment and natural development in either will force the child to grow up insecure and either be overly concerned with sex and survival or depressed and care little for his life. As an adult, he will be afraid to live and to die, unable to take risks, to accept and enjoy his body, to enjoy pleasure, and experience true love and abundance. He will feel ungrounded, alienated from others and the earth, lonely, frustrated, angry, and envious of those who are enjoying themselves. He will be critical and judgmental of himself and others. He will be unable to accept, trust, and love himself and others and have difficulty experiencing intimacy. He or she may develop health problems related to digestion, sexual/reproductive dysfunction, elimination, kidney and urinary tract problems, and may experience physical pain in the lower back and abdomen. In fact, most of our psychological and many other physical problems are associated with a wounded and undeveloped ego-mind in the first and second chakras.

*To heal the wounded ego-mind in the second chakra,* whenever you feel fears around survival or an insecurity about yourself, bring your awareness and breath into your second chakra at the navel. Remind yourself that this fear and insecurity is connected with your body's survival instinct and has nothing to do with the survival of your being. Remember that your being is here eternally and can never die. As you keep practicing this, you will gradually heal and strengthen your ego-mind in the second chakra and will develop trust that existence indeed takes care of you. Trust is essential if you are to evolve higher in consciousness because without trust you cannot surrender to life.

*To heal the wounded ego in the first and second chakras, I recommend two very powerful and transformative active meditations: the Osho Dynamic and Kundalini meditations. I have used them personally and in my healing practice for many years with remarkable results. To help accelerate purification and healing of the ego-mind in all the chakras, I've also devised a self-healing version of my method – DHM (Dalian Healing Method). This light-speed technique will help to quickly open blocked energy in the body and release the suppressed thoughts and emotions that undermine growth in consciousness. The Osho Active Meditations[1] and the Self-healing DHM are best done with a pre-recorded CD. (All the meditations suggested in this chapter are described in the e-book* Healing into Consciousness with Active Meditation & Visualization *available at www.madadalian.com.)*

*3rd Chakra (Solar Plexus):*
## Developing Self-Power and Decision-Making Ability
The function of the third chakra, which is located in the solar plexus, is to develop awareness of self-power and learn to create needed boundaries. This is the ego's adolescence. Like a growing animal that learns to recognize its power and starts to defend itself and its territory, the developing ego-mind and consciousness of a teenager begins to recognize his or her own independence and power. He begins to develop the courage to make his own decisions and defends himself against outside intrusions and impositions. He begins to distinguish friends from enemies, and learns to set boundaries to protect himself from harm.

*The ego-mind and consciousness develop naturally* in the third chakra if parents and society don't suppress the child's emerging sense of self-power and freedom of choice and instead encourage and help the child to make his own decisions and learn from his mistakes. Parents are often

---

1   In today's highly stressful modern world, where we must tackle multiple tasks with daily information overload, passive sitting is challenging, and in most cases almost impossible to practice. To help the contemporary seeker solve this problem, Osho, the twentieth century mystic, created new active meditation techniques. Not only are the active meditations fast and effective, they are also fun to practice. For further details, visit www.madadalian.com

concerned that if they don't impose their will, their child will be out of control and impossible to discipline. In fact, the opposite is true. The more attempts made to suppress and control a child's emerging sense of self-power and independence, the more he will rebel and challenge parental authority later on.

Allowing children the freedom to express and assert their individuality does not mean that as a parent you do not guide your children. It is your responsibility to guide your children because you have more life experience, but you also need to simultaneously listen to your children so you don't suppress their growing sense of self-worth and trust in their own power and decision-making ability.

If the child is allowed to freely express and experience his or her own power and freedom of choice, the parent will actually be helping their child to develop a sense of responsibility for themselves and their actions. A child who grows in freedom will not feel the need to rebel in reaction later on, see himself as a victim, or withdraw from life.

As a result of experiencing his own power and freedom of choice, the child will discover that there are consequences to his actions, and he will inevitably begin making wiser choices. He will recognize that he is not separate from others but rather part of a greater whole. This will help him to mature psychologically and he will start growing out of his selfishness and self-centered neediness. His intelligence and self-esteem will develop naturally, and his psychological maturity will follow his maturing body. By the time he reaches puberty and is ready to face the world, he will have developed his ability to make decisions and take responsibility for his own actions.

*The ego-mind and consciousness don't develop naturally* in the third chakra when the child's inner power and freedom of choice are suppressed. Generation after generation, most parents unfortunately and unconsciously suppress their children's emerging sense of inner power and decision-making ability. We crush our children's developing sense of individuality so they can fit into the society.

For example, my daughter, questioning her parenting skills, called me for advice about my then two-year-old granddaughter Majaii. They were in the park, and she watched as an older child approached Majaii and proceeded to empty the bucket she had filled with sand. He then threw the empty bucket back into the sandbox waiting for her reaction. Majaii looked at the boy, picked up her empty bucket, and started filling it up again. When the bucket was full, the other child picked it up and emptied it again. After a third round of the same, Majaii picked up her empty bucket and pushed the boy away. At this point, my daughter jumped to intervene and told Majaii to be "nice." By doing so, she unconsciously suppressed her daughter's growing sense of self-power, self-respect, and personal boundaries, and indirectly sent a message to the other child that his behavior was acceptable and had no consequences.

An undeveloped third chakra causes a child to grow up emotionally immature. Part of this immaturity may manifest as fearful behavior patterns, such as anxieties and phobias that will need to be overcome later in life. Parents who want to set an example for their children and help them grow into wholeness first need to heal their own wounded egos and reclaim their own sense of boundaries, self-respect, and inner power. The parent whose ego-mind is healed in the third chakra is equipped to guide the child through third-chakra development without wounding her; the wounded and unconscious parent will inevitably wound the child the same way he or she was wounded.

Most people who have a damaged third chakra are often afraid to make decisions and look for others' approval before making them. Decisions made out of insecurity and conditioned reaction, instead of inner strength and freedom of choice, produce two different inner and outer outcomes. Agreeing or disagreeing to do something based on fear, insecurity, and conditioning is a reaction and not a response to life. Reactions that stem from the wounded ego-mind cause stress, unhappiness, and an unfulfilled feeling inside.

Actions that arise out of the wounded ego-mind don't bear any fruit on the outside and don't benefit oneself or others. On the other hand, actions that arise from the freedom of choice, inner power, and clarity of the healthy ego-mind create a feeling of happiness and wholeness inside and bring blessings to others and the world. A healthy ego-mind responds to situations rather than reacts and can freely change its decision and direction at any time when circumstances change. The healthy ego-mind, like the captain who steers his ship in whatever direction he chooses, can focus its actions in the direction the inner being needs and wants to go.

*To heal the wounded ego into consciousness in the third chakra*, we need to develop the courage to risk acting in spite of our fears and conditionings. To do this, take some time to look inside and make a list of all the fears that prevent you from freely expressing and acting upon what your being needs and longs to live. Understand that these fears are part of your wounded ego-mind and stem from your childhood conditionings and life experiences. Remind yourself that you are now old enough to know that your freedom and existence do not depend on anyone's acceptance or rejection of you. Feel that you have the power and intelligence inside yourself to support what your spirit needs to do. Risk taking action in spite of your fears and trust that even if you make a mistake or fail, you will learn an important lesson that in the end will only make you stronger and more conscious.

If you practice risk-taking and expressing your inner truth sincerely and authentically, you will help to transform your wounded ego into a healthy ego and can begin the development of your consciousness in the fourth chakra.

Healing the wounded ego in the third chakra will help you to develop self-respect and confidence in your abilities to chart your own path. With a healthy ego in the third chakra you can easily stand up for yourself and make conscious decisions about how you want to live your own life. With the power to create your own reality, you will stop struggling inside and outside and will begin to experience inner peace and belonging. This will help your life force and consciousness to begin developing in your heart.

*To heal the wounded ego-mind in the third chakra with practical self-help methods that generate quick results, I once again recommend practicing the Osho Dynamic and Kundalini active meditations alongside the Self-healing DHM. In addition, you can also practice the No-Yes active meditation* (described in the e-book mentioned on page 153).

*4th Chakra (the Heart):*
**Transforming Instinctual Lust into Unconditional Love**
The function of the fourth chakra, which is located behind the sternum of the chest near the heart, is to transform the body's need for survival and the instinctual lust for self-gratification into unconditional love. Unconditional love lifts the ego-mind from the lower into the higher chakras and transforms the life force into greater consciousness.

With maturity of the physical body, the ego's purpose of protecting the body becomes secondary and the need for spiritual evolution comes to the forefront. The ego-mind is now ready to pass through the transformation chamber of the heart, which nurtures the seed of unconditional love and compassion.

The heart is the bridge between the three lower instinctual chakras and the three higher spiritual chakras. As consciousness develops in the heart chakra it sets in motion the evolution of the spirit. Until we begin to develop the heart chakra we cannot become truly spiritual. In the heart chakra, the ego-mind learns to share and give unconditionally; compassion towards self and others begins to transform the wounded ego-mind, and as it becomes healthier, it becomes more attuned to the higher realms of existence and consciousness.

In the heart chakra, the ego-mind begins to purify from the consequences of all its unconscious actions (karma), which have been arising from its instinctual survival needs. As a result, true conscience begins to arise. With true conscience, the spirit experiences pain and guilt regarding its unconscious actions and attempts to correct them. The pain associated with guilt allows the ego-mind and consciousness to evolve to a greater understanding and acceptance of oneself and others.

When the ego-mind passes through the purification chamber of the heart chakra, it realizes that it is not different from others, that others also experience similar feelings of sadness, pain, fear and insecurity. This realization helps the developing ego to understand that mistakes, pain and suffering are necessary for the evolution of consciousness.

This emerging understanding and unconditional love crumble the wounded ego, and acceptance, forgiveness, and trust begin to replace the negative emotions of anger, jealousy, competitiveness, insecurity, and mistrust. Consciousness now takes the front seat, and it becomes easier to distinguish between the ego's instinctual lust, which arises out of the body's need to survive and reproduce, and unconditional feelings of love that arise out of spiritual awareness and understanding of oneness with others and the universe. With increased consciousness, the spirit gradually learns to trust and surrender to life and begins to recognize that the ego-mind is an illusion that separates the being from everything else in existence.

*The ego-mind and consciousness develop naturally* in the fourth chakra when the child experiences unconditional love and acceptance from his parents. If this natural development occurs, by the time the child is a young adult, he will be able to discriminate between unconditional spiritual love and conditional instinctual lust. He will feel confident and content within himself and will grow to become a loving, trusting, tolerant and caring human. He will be emotionally balanced and responsible, and he will not need to exploit and manipulate others to have his needs met. He will develop honesty and dignity. He will know when he is being manipulated and will have no difficulty setting boundaries. He will not need to seek love and recognition from others because he will love and recognize himself. His love will be unconditional and he will have no difficulty in surrendering to love.

*The ego-mind and consciousness don't develop naturally* in the fourth chakra if the child doesn't experience unconditional love and acceptance from his parents, caretakers, and society. Without being loved and accepted, the child's consciousness doesn't mature with the maturity of the body and he grows to become an emotionally wounded and needy adult. A lack of experience in the form of unconditional love will perpetuate his self-centered emotions in the instinctual chakras and will distort his perception of love. This will force him to suffer the consequences of his selfishness, resentment, self-pity, and hatred of himself and others. To find respite from his negative emotions, he may fall victim to food, cigarettes, alcohol, sex or drug addictions.

Trapped in an emotionally juvenile state, his ego-mind will force him to either manipulate and exploit others, or to be manipulated and exploited by them. Manipulative behavior will keep him emotionally and mentally confused and will create more suffering for himself and others. He will not trust himself and others and will be afraid of intimacy and commitment. He will not be able to discriminate between lust and love and will sabotage his own happiness by not being able to let go of control and surrender to love. Unless he consciously heals his wounded ego and begins to unconditionally love himself and others, he will continue to suffer the wounded ego's pain.

*To heal from wounded ego-mind into consciousness in the fourth chakra,* you need to embrace all your pain and suffering and understand that whatever emotions others trigger in you only mirrors what you need to see and heal inside yourself. You need to forgive those who you think have hurt you, and you need to forgive yourself for hurting others.

Many people are unable to experience true love and intimacy because they are afraid to surrender the identification with their wounds. For example, if someone is feeling wounded because they have been abandoned, neglected, or abused, they derive their identity from the wound itself. They continue to hope that someone will come and heal their wounds by giving them the love they want and need. But because others have their own wounds to heal and may be expecting the same from them, they will continue to experience disappointment after disappointment.

Unless you stop blaming others for your wounds and take full responsibility for transforming your wounded ego into a healthy ego you cannot experience true love and trust; nor can you understand that existence has already taken care of you by giving you your life. Look inside and recognize that if you don't yet know how to trust and surrender, you won't be able to experience a quantum leap in consciousness.

To transform your wounded ego into a healthy ego, allow all your thoughts and emotions to come to the surface and be expressed without control, judgment, or blame. Take a risk to surrender to love and forgiveness. If you feel like crying, laughing, or expressing your sadness or joy, allow yourself to do so. Learning to trust what you feel and giving yourself permission to express it openly, honestly, and without shame will help to open your wounds and heal whatever pain you are feeling in your heart. A simple truthful expression can release you from the burden of your suppressed mental and emotional suffering and pain and will transform your wounds into more awareness and health.

As you do your healing work, it is crucial to remind yourself that your wounds are there to teach you something about yourself. By remaining a detached observer to your feelings and thoughts, you will see the lessons you need to learn. Once you become conscious of the lessons, your attachment and investment in your wounded ego will drop naturally.

Be courageous and remind yourself as often as possible that you need to face your fears and feel your pain if you want to transform your ego-mind into consciousness. Through courage and observation, you will be able to heal and transform your pain into acceptance and compassion for yourself and others.

When you understand that your wounds are caused by your own ignorance, and that you alone are responsible for your healing, something inside you will relax. You will begin to see and understand the difference between your desires and emotions, and the unconditional spiritual love that arises out of the purity and innocence of your heart.

The presence of a spiritual teacher or a master can also be of great help and benefit. A master is a guide who knows and understands your pain and with his or her unconditional love and wisdom can guide you through the dark night of your unconscious. Support groups can also assist in healing the wounded ego-mind to some degree, but they don't help to transcend it. Being with a guide who has transcended his or her own ego-mind into consciousness inspires trust that you can go deeper into your inner darkness without feeling overwhelmed with fear. A true guide will encourage you to keep going until there is nothing left for you to hang on to, not even him or her.

The East, which is more heart oriented, is well aware of the blessings created by the energy field of an awakened being and they take advantage of it. They understand that the energy field of such a person provides the needed nourishment for their wounded ego to heal and transform in ways that otherwise might be difficult or in many cases impossible. A true guide creates an environment of unconditional love, acceptance, and trust, which allows the wounded ego to heal more easily than if you were struggling through it alone. The West, which is more mind oriented, unfortunately does not understand and misses this blessing.

Once you pass through healing your wounded ego-mind in the fourth chakra, you understand the pain of others and compassion naturally and effortlessly arises from within your being. This is how Christ-like love-consciousness is born. Through unconditional love in the fourth chakra, your wounded ego transforms into a healthy ego and your old self-identity dissolves.

Once your wounded ego begins to dissolve, you understand that you have only been hypnotized into believing that love is scarce. You see that unlike lust, which is only limited to gratification of your transitory physical senses, spiritual love is limitless and abundantly available within you and the universe. This realization naturally helps you feel appreciation and gratitude towards everything in existence and allows you to give of yourself unconditionally and with joy.

*To heal the wounded ego in the heart chakra, in addition to the Osho Dynamic and Kundalini meditations and Self-healing DHM, I recommend the Osho Nadabrahma, as well as a meditation beloved to many seekers known as Atisha's Heart Meditation (see e-book).*

*5th Chakra (Throat):*
## Developing Individuality and Freedom of Expression
The function of the fifth chakra, which is located at the base of the throat, is to nourish the healthy ego by developing individuality, freedom of expression, and creativity. Through free expression, the healthy ego begins to discriminate between right and wrong, conscious and unconscious action, and breaks out of its old beliefs, behavior patterns and social conditionings. For the healthy ego, honesty and integrity become more important than the survival fears and power struggles that drive the wounded ego to compromises and keep the life force and consciousness restricted and undeveloped.

In the fifth chakra, consciousness threatens the wounded ego's survival by forcing it to do activities such as facing fears, taking risks, meditating, fasting, and confronting the collective conditionings. The healthy ego turns inward to seek answers and find its own truth. By actively pursuing healthy and positive goals and new ways of being that contradict fear-based social beliefs and conditionings, the healthy ego harnesses the energy that comes through awareness to pursue its existential need for creativity and self-knowledge.

Thanks to increased awareness, the healthy ego is able to distinguish truth from lies and becomes more concerned with finding and living its true purpose than with fulfilling other people's needs and expectations. The healthy ego has strength and courage to face the collective unconscious and fearlessly express and manifest its own truth in the world. Instead of feeling wounded by the collective, it becomes instrumental in shaping the collective and helping it move out of its old beliefs.

*The ego-mind and consciousness develop naturally* in the fifth chakra if the child is encouraged to express him- or herself without fear of being ridiculed or criticized. A child encouraged this way will grow up learning to act in spite of his or her fears and will not worry about other people's opinions. She will take responsibility for her views and actions and her communication will be sincere and truthful. Her mind will be positive and she will understand the virtues of honesty and integrity. She will say what she means and mean what she says, and will have a sense of purpose in life which is greater than mere survival. She will be courageous and creative and her imagination will develop without restriction. As an adult, she will search to find her own truth and will be able to discriminate between what is stifling and what is beneficial for her personal development. She will be able to distinguish truth from lies and will learn to accomplish life's goals without struggle. She will learn to communicate clearly and fearlessly and to see the situations of others with empathy. She will be psychologically mature by early adulthood and diligent with her spiritual work from an early age. She will be able to accept life, herself and others without compromising her own truth, and instead of being influenced by the collective she will influence the collective and help it move into higher consciousness.

*The ego-mind and consciousness don't develop naturally* in the fifth chakra if the child has been forced to behave according to his or her parents' and society's expectations. The child will grow up fearing authority and living a hypocritical life. He will learn to lie and hide his true feelings and opinions to fit in. He will struggle internally and externally, will be self-loathing and critical of himself and others, and will not be able to live his soul's potential. He may be afraid to look inside, find his own truth, and speak it freely. He may be unwilling to confront the collective and will instead live fearfully, identified with his conditioned beliefs. He will also inevitably learn to suppress others' truth and freedom of expression in the same way his were suppressed.

Ninety-nine percent of humanity does not develop naturally in the fifth chakra because of our social and religious conditionings and belief systems. These systems teach us to conform instead of confront, and because of our need to survive and be liked we hardly recognize that we are lied to, criticized, controlled and manipulated. As a result, we fear everyone in authority and have difficulty standing up against those egos who like to hold political, religious, and economic power over us. People in power who have a vested interest in ruling teach us to view our differences in ideologies, cultures, religions, and gender, as a competitive threat. In our schools we don't teach our children to explore and discover the truth of their own beings. Instead, we condition them to adopt a false identity that will prepare them to conform to the expectations of those in power.

No society or organized religion can ever help an individual to grow in consciousness and liberate him from his ego-mind because society functions through the laws of average consciousness rooted in the first three chakras. Society's role is to create and sustain rules that will allow masses of people to live together. Conscious and fearless people are dangerous to society and the status quo because they propagate honesty, independence, self-sufficiency, individuality, and fearlessness.

People who don't want their power and position shaken have always crucified those who shine their light on the collective unconscious because their light reveals for more and more people how they have been lied to, used, and manipulated. Our history is full of examples of our intolerance of those who shake our old foundations and beliefs and point our awareness towards truth. Jesus was crucified, Socrates and Osho were poisoned, Buddha is thought to have been poisoned in his old age, the tenth-century Sufi mystic Al-Hillaj Mansoor was beheaded, Martin Luther King Jr. was assassinated – and the list could go on and on. Many people have paid the price with their own lives for trying to live with dignity and honesty and help evolve humanity to higher consciousness. We listen to their message and adopt their views only after we crucify them and they are no longer a living threat.

If you honestly look at yourself you can see how, through your own fears, beliefs, and need for power and prestige, you do the same with those around you. You don't recognize that by judging and condemning, or feeling threatened and envious of those who appear smarter or better off than you are, you sabotage your own well-being, robbing yourself of your potential for success, love, and happiness.

Not living and expressing your inner truth may cause ailments of the throat like thyroid imbalances, chronic tonsillitis, neck and shoulder pain and inflammation, and illnesses such as MS, fibromyalgia, tumors, and even cancer. Every time you don't give voice to your inner truth, regardless of whether it's positive or negative, you add another layer of suppressed thoughts and emotions to your throat and body. To improve your physical and emotional health and allow your consciousness to evolve, take the risks necessary to face and let go of your fears of making mistakes and express your inner truth without reacting or holding back. (See exercise *Let Go of Your Thoughts by Expressing Them Out Loud* on page 101.)

*To heal the wounded ego into consciousness in the fifth chakra*, a committed effort to look inside is necessary so you can become aware of what's truly happening in your mind, heart, and body. Once you are conscious of your inner world, give yourself permission to express what you think and feel in spite of your fears. Remember, it is entirely your responsibility to live and express your life's truth. If you don't express it, the potential for your growth into higher consciousness will remain dormant and unlived. Gather courage to express and live your inner truth if you want to break out of your conditionings and behavior patterns.

To help you understand your fears and why it is important to express yourself freely, ask yourself: *Why can't I allow myself to say what I feel and think? What will happen if I truthfully express what I feel and think? What can I do to free myself from fear to express what I truly feel?* Then, act upon the answers that come right away. Action puts your energy into motion and helps you break your habit of repression.

To live your truth, you must be willing to face both your own and the collective unconscious and say: "I am going to live according to my own truth, light, and wisdom and not according to my wounded ego-mind or anyone else's beliefs and conditionings." This may feel like a difficult task in the beginning because, compared to the small light of consciousness that burns inside you, the weight and power of the collective unconscious seems overwhelming. But if you persevere and continue taking risks to be true to yourself regardless of the outside consequences, you will gradually find your inner strength and develop courage and trust in yourself and existence. By risking honesty and exposure you discover the purity, simplicity, and power of your being and begin enjoying living your life more freely and fully. Simply express what you think and feel without judging or blaming yourself or others. Understand that everyone and everything is here to help you grow in consciousness and find your being.

To heal the wounded ego-mind in the fifth chakra, feel your vulnerability and let go of your pattern of procrastinating or holding yourself back from doing what you know you need and want to do and say. You may need to express that you feel hurt and insecure, angry and frustrated, or that you feel yourself to be special and better than others. Expressing yourself honestly will bring you to your authentic inner wisdom and strength.

Try to remember: *How did your throat and your being feel when you wanted and needed to say something and held back? How did it feel when you spoke up?* Experiment with what happens in your energy when you express and when you suppress your true thoughts and feelings. Expression will increase your awareness of the many layers of the unconscious and will help free your body of the layers of suppressed thoughts and emotions that keep your consciousness undeveloped.

As you practice taking risks and freely expressing yourself, I recommend that you simultaneously practice meditating. Taking risks will help you understand why you are suppressing yourself, and meditation will help you disidentify from your fears and find your inner center.

*To heal the ego-mind into consciousness in the fifth chakra, in addition to the meditations and the Self-healing DHM mentioned earlier, experiment with the Osho Gibberish, Chakra Breathing, and Chakra Sounds meditations* (see e-book mentioned on page 153).

*6th Chakra (Third Eye):*
**Developing Wisdom and Intelligence and Discovering Your Being**
The function of the sixth chakra, which is located in the forehead between the eyebrows and is linked to the pineal gland (also known as the "mystery" gland), is to reveal and expand the psychic knowing that makes understanding, intelligence, and wisdom possible. With the opening of the third eye, extrasensory perception begins to develop, and the ego-mind discovers its ability to use thought to move energy and manifest ideas into reality. Here, the ego-mind literally begins to see or hear different states of reality that exist beyond the limited physical reality, and the door to the cosmic reality (both conscious and unconscious) opens.

If one's focus is on spiritual growth and transformation of the ego-mind into consciousness, one develops awareness and learns to trust and discriminate between intuitive inner knowing and the intellectual knowledge of the mind. Through acceptance of what is arises trust, and surrender of the individual will of the ego-mind to the will of existence becomes possible. With surrender of the individual will, the soul for the first time glimpses its eternal presence or "am-ness." This experience crumbles the ego's identification with the body-mind-emotion system and sets into motion its final extinction. With extinction of the ego-mind there arises a true knowing that one's being is not separate from existence, and that the same "am-ness," "is-ness," or "such-ness" also exists within everyone and everything in the universe.

*The ego-mind and consciousness develop naturally* in the sixth chakra if the child is encouraged to trust himself, develop his intuitive inner knowing, and form an accepting and life-affirming attitude towards all of his experiences. With a positive attitude towards life, he will grow saying "yes" to himself, others, and whatever life brings him. He will trust and use his intuition and inner knowing to make his decisions instead of relying on his mind and other people's opinions. He will grow to recognize and trust his own inner wisdom and will pay attention to the information received through his telepathic ability, dreams, psychic visions, and extrasensory perceptions (clairvoyantly, clairaudiently, and intuitively). By trusting and developing these abilities, he will grow in intelligence and understanding and learn to surrender to and trust the mystery of life and existence.

*The ego-mind and consciousness don't develop naturally* in the sixth chakra if the child has been mocked, laughed at, and ridiculed for his or her extrasensory perceptions and has been judged, disapproved of, and criticized for openly expressing his or her opinions and perceptions. For example, many children see or hear entities that don't have a physical form and they become afraid. If the child is told it's only his or her imagination, the child will doubt, suppress, or even try to forget about her extrasensory abilities in order to be accepted and fit in. Her fear will remain suppressed in her body, and she will grow up feeling insecure about herself and afraid of both the non-physical and physical realities. In the long run, this will not only sabotage the flowering of her wisdom but will also sabotage the benefits others could have gained from her extrasensory perceptions and abilities.

*To heal the ego-mind into consciousness in the sixth chakra,* you must learn to discriminate between your mind and inner knowing, and trust your intuition and unique gifts and abilities. You must begin surrendering your ego-mind, with the understanding that it is only a finite mechanism that allows you to function in the material world of time and space, beyond which it cannot exist. When it comes to truly knowing the mysteries of your being and the universe, the mind becomes useless and obsolete because true knowing always arises out of experience, not out of the mind.

To heal the ego-mind in the sixth chakra, you must transcend the mind (both negative and positive) and know that you are pure consciousness with no beginning and end. To transcend the ego-mind in the sixth chakra, you must remain a witness to all your thoughts, emotions, and experiences and understand that they, including your body, are transitory. You transcend the mind when you stay rooted within your witnessing consciousness that sees everything coming and going.

**Signs of the third eye opening:**
When the door to the cosmic unconscious opens in the sixth chakra, memories and experiences of past lives, including animal lives, that have been hidden in your unconscious begin to emerge. With trust and understanding you recognize these memories as part of your soul's journey and realize how your past lives have shaped your spirit and essence and created your current reality. With experience of your eternal existence, you understand that you are not limited to this life alone but have always been and will continue to be in the universe forever. This experience and understanding give you enough confidence and trust to eventually completely surrender your ego-mind and be liberated from the fears of life and death.

When your third eye begins to open, you may start to feel pressure in your forehead, and your eyes may begin to roll upwards. You may begin to see and hear things that are not physically visible and may feel unusually sensitive to different energies inside and outside of yourself. With the deepening of your meditation, you will feel and see pulsating waves of light arising from inside your body and opening like a sun as they reach the third eye. The blackness that you used to see inside when you would close your eyes will begin looking grey.

As the light waves move through your body, they begin to expose the remaining parts of your unconscious energy so you can continue healing and transforming them into consciousness. If you feel doubt or don't understand your experiences, just remember to witness whatever is happening without identification, fear, or judgment. Simply observe your doubting mind and your experience in the way you would observe any other experience, and let it go.

In this stage of development, the ego-mind becomes extremely subtle and difficult to detect. As your third eye continues to open, you will experience parts of your old ego-identity crumbling and may have an experience of no-mind. The ego-mind will put up its last fight by trying to trick you into identifying with the experience and make you believe you now know the truth. You may start to think you are now enlightened and are wiser and more spiritual than others who are still searching. You may start to think you have nothing more to learn and may imitate the socially perceived idea of how an enlightened person should behave. You may try to artificially humble yourself while the mind attempts to come in from the back door. If you see that you are *trying* to be modest, understand that this is another form of conditioned thought and let it go. When you see the ego-mind becoming stronger, don't judge or suppress it but live it openly and authentically. If you try to suppress your mind, you will delay your final transformation into enlightenment. Be true to yourself and remember that one more step needs to be taken to fully surrender your need for recognition, in order for your ego-mind to completely dissolve.

**Pitfalls and dangers surrounding the opening of the third eye:**
Through your spiritual work and the opening of the third eye, you may discover spiritual and psychic powers and feel you can manifest whatever you want using your will and imagination. It's important, therefore, to purify your energy of all competitive and negative thoughts and emotions so you don't run the risk of misusing this power. You need to stay mindful and conscious to recognize that ultimately all power belongs to existence, and you are simply a vehicle to manifest its will.

People who try to open their sixth chakra by force (through personal or assisted outer stimulation), before they have purified their energy of negative thoughts and emotions such as unresolved anger, resentment, jealousy, blame, or feelings of inferiority or superiority, run the risk of unconsciously manipulating and misusing this power. If the ego-mind wants power because it has a subtle wish to be special or superior to others, or wants to fulfill its hidden desires and protect its own interests, such an ego-mind is likely to misuse its power.

With the sixth chakra open, the ego recognizes the unlimited power available in the universe and in its ignorance thinks that it too has the same power and can do anything it wishes. The dangers of misusing power become apparent when the ego-mind, which has bypassed its purification process in the lower chakras, acts out of fear, anger, insecurity, or revenge. As a result, the soul suffers the consequences of the ego's actions and the life force is thrown back into the lower chakras for more purification of what remains in the unconscious. More suffering and pain become inevitable in order to make up for the missed steps in healing the wounded ego-mind and purifying the energy.

After experiencing the painful consequences of misused power, you may begin to feel guilty and afraid to use it again. If you stay identified with fear and guilt, instead of witnessing them, understanding their causes, and letting them go, you will remain stuck in the lower chakras. Every seeker needs to recognize, accept, and understand their capacity to misuse power and disidentify from it. You will be able to pass the final test and start to use your power wisely when you learn the needed lessons, forgive yourself and others for any mistakes or misused power, and begin using your power through your heart.

The sixth chakra can also open suddenly through a physical accident, near-death experience, or use of drugs. Such experiences can unexpectedly open all the chakras, allowing the kundalini energy to rush from the base of the spine into the pineal gland in the head from where a window to the cosmic reality (conscious or unconscious) opens. If the kundalini energy doesn't reach the head, but only reaches into a certain chakra, one's experience of the qualities of that chakra will intensify.

When the sixth chakra suddenly opens during an accident or a near-death experience, it happens innocently and without willful or forceful interference of the ego-mind. In that quick accidental opening of the third eye, if the person is of positive mind and can surrender his or her will to the will of existence without struggle, the life force (kundalini energy) will quickly move into and out of the seventh chakra. This will allow him or her to have an out-of-body experience and realize that even without the body they are still alive. Such a realization is similar to the one that happens through near death experience or through meditation, when one experiences expansion out of their body limits and realizes that one is pure consciousness, which is separate from the body, mind, and emotions.

When the sixth chakra opens suddenly through drug use, the ego-mind is premeditatively involved and the experience doesn't originate from one's innocence. The influence of the drug causes the kundalini energy to either move up into the sixth chakra (revealing a glimpse of cosmic consciousness), or it can stay in the lower chakras or even move below the first chakra into personal, collective, or cosmic unconscious (see Chapter 7, *Breaking through the Three Veils of Illusion*).

If the ego-mind is predominantly positive, the energy may move upwards and expand your existing consciousness into a higher state and greater light. If the ego-mind is negative, and it predominantly revolves around sex, the energy may move down and out of the first chakra into the cosmic unconscious, and you may become frightened of disappearing into the dark bottomless abyss. Without a guide or a strong witnessing awareness you may be traumatized, lose your common sense, or even go mad. This is why drugs are considered unhealthy and dangerous.

If you have been meditating and can maintain your witnessing awareness and know how to center your energy in your body, you may be able to understand the experience and learn a very valuable spiritual lesson. If your witnessing awareness is not enough, however, you may come out of the experience feeling depleted and even more confused than before. With repeated drug use, the logical common-sense mind – which you need in order to take responsibility for your actions

– will gradually deteriorate, and you will find it increasingly difficult to gain control over your life. People in this situation may find themselves medicated or placed in a mental institution.

All of humanity's psychological problems, including schizophrenia and other mental illnesses, are related to malfunctioning of the sixth chakra and a lack of witnessing awareness. To heal your psychological problems you need to go back into your unconscious and do the needed healing work missed in the lower chakras. This can be a long process and patience is required. First you need to strengthen your body through exercise and healthy eating and gradually come off all mood altering medications – which only weaken the body, dull the sensory perceptions, and prevent consciousness from developing. Then you must purify your body by releasing the suppressed thoughts and emotions blocking your energy (see the exercise called *Purify the Body of Suppressed Thoughts and Emotions through Expression* on page 200). Finally, you must move towards strengthening your witnessing awareness through meditation and self-awareness (see the exercise called *Look at Everything with Self-Awareness* on page 196).

*To heal the ego-mind into consciousness in the sixth chakra, in addition to the active meditations and the Self-healing DHM mentioned in the previous chakra sections you can also practice the Osho Gourishankar meditation and Looking at the Tip of the Nose exercise (see e-book).*

### *7th Chakra (the Crown):* **Dissolving the Ego**
The function of the seventh chakra, which is located on top of the head, is to act as a transition point between the limited physical reality and the boundless cosmic reality. The ego-mind begins to develop with the emergence of a separate self-identity in the first chakra and ends with its dissolution into the sea of universal consciousness in the seventh chakra. The seventh chakra is the portal of ultimate liberation from the ego-mind and symbolizes its final death. In the sixth chakra, we

become conscious that the universe is unknowable, and in the seventh, we enter into it. The seventh chakra facilitates the transition of the life force from material reality of time and space into the timeless reality of ever-evolving consciousness. Through the seventh chakra we unify with the will of existence and merge into the mysterious unknown. The seventh chakra can never be tampered with or corrupted.

To move from the sixth to the seventh chakra we must surrender our attachment to being special and recognize that the idea "I am special" is just another passing thought, which comes one moment and is gone the next. The story of Jesus vividly illustrates this crucial turning point. First he becomes aware of his powers and uses them to heal others. Then he thinks of himself as special (the only begotten son of God). With the thought of being the only begotten son of God, his ego-mind reaches the peak of its development. Unwilling to compromise his wisdom and inner knowing, he is tortured and nailed to the cross. On the cross, he shows his humanity and questions God: *Why have you forsaken me?* At this moment, he recognizes his ego-mind and fully surrenders it by saying: "If this is thy will, let it be done." As I see it, Jesus on the cross quickly moves from the sixth to the seventh chakra and experiences the death of his ego-mind, when he fully surrenders to the will of God. His complete trust and surrender leads to his awakening and liberation.

If you are to take the leap and surrender your ego-mind the way Jesus did, you will need a strong witnessing awareness and a willingness to face your fear of death and surrender your personal will to the will of existence. To surrender your fear of death, trust is absolutely essential because with the opening seventh chakra you begin to feel as if you can no longer hold on to anything. Your individual self-identity becomes vague and everything you thought you knew feels false, everything you thought was real no longer seems real, and you realize you don't really know anything.

To pass through the seventh chakra and heal into consciousness, you must completely let go of your fear of death and understand that the fear of death is only your ego's fear of disappearing. To surrender your ego-mind you must remain a witness to the mind and the fear, and anchor your awareness in your center. You can also use the guidance and presence of a master to help you find the courage to surrender the ego and welcome the unknown. A master is someone who has passed through the seventh chakra and knows how to guide you through the pitfalls of the mind and its fear of death. He or she can help you remain centered and a witness to it. A master will teach you, far in advance, about the need to develop trust, witnessing, and surrender, so you don't miss the opportunity when the door to the cosmic reality opens. With the disappearance of the ego-mind, your now-conscious life force is freed from the wheel of *dharma* (life and death), and you are ready to embody and live the Joy that permeates existence.

Liberation from the ego-mind can happen either while you are alive, or at the time of physical death. How you die is a reflection of how you have lived and prepared yourself. If you have lived fearlessly and consciously, your death will be the ultimate liberation of your being and a cause for celebration.

Osho exemplified the process of conscious dying. He knew of and prepared for his death six months before it happened. He made his final arrangements and gave his last instructions. Three months before his death, he stopped eating solid foods to make the transition out of his body easier. According to his physician, Osho behaved as if he was just saying goodbye before going away for the weekend. He died joyfully and fully conscious, just as he had lived. He gracefully released his energy and consciousness into the cosmos, like a flower scenting the air with its fragrance. His death became a blessing and an example for all those who were around him. For weeks after his passing, I and many others who were there at the time of his death rode on the wave of bliss that he left behind. I felt his Joy of finally being liberated from the confines of his physical body and merging with existence. If you die consciously as Osho did, you will die peacefully and joyously while witnessing your own death, and your death will be a blessing for others.

If you have lived unconsciously and fearfully and have struggled with life, you will also struggle in death and create pain and sorrow for those around you. When my father was dying, he became frightened as he approached death. He struggled and tried to hang on to life until the very last minute. Though he was a creative, intelligent, and kind man, he struggled with regrets about not having fully lived his heart's longings. He regressed from an eighty-four-year-old man to a needy nine-year-old boy. He moaned all night looking for someone to save him from death.

Right after he stopped breathing, I felt his energy move up into his heart chakra and then his throat. Although I was happy that he managed to reach the throat chakra, I felt compelled to help him to move higher. When I touched his third eye and then his crown chakra, his energy quickly moved up and out of his body. However, the vastness of the unknown was shocking for him. His consciousness was not prepared for an experience of such magnitude, and his sudden freedom literally created a windstorm that wreaked havoc all around, breaking branches from trees and stirring dust in the air. I tried to calm his frightened spirit by telepathically talking to him and singing ancient Eastern mantras to help center his energy and consciousness. Several hours later, he finally settled into his new state of being and, like a bird on the wings, started to enjoy his newly found freedom within the infinite vastness of the sky.

Below, I include some advice for those who find themselves nearing the end of their lives and want to use physical death as a chance to die consciously and be liberated from their ego-mind.

### Physical signs of experiencing death and leaving the body:

Two or three weeks before your death, you may notice physical signs that you are about to leave your body. (You may also feel some of these symptoms when someone close to you is nearing their death, or when your life force begins to move higher into the sixth or seventh chakra, i.e. in meditation.) You will feel energy movement like a vortex opening in your second chakra. As your life force starts to gradually move away from your body, it will feel like a spiraling whirlpool of energy. This sensation will gradually intensify, reaching its peak on the day of your physical death. You cannot control or stop this movement. You may feel uncomfortable and nauseous. If you do throw up, don't worry; it is a way for the body to cleanse itself. At a time like this, it is of utmost importance to be alert and aware and to simply watch the sensations in the body as an observer. Don't try to suppress the feeling of movement and opening with your mind, medication, or food. Instead, stop eating solid foods and make a commitment to stay alert and remain a witness to your death, no matter what is happening in your body.

Even though you may have been working and striving for liberation throughout your lifetime, at the time of physical death you may feel overwhelmed with fear of the unknown. Your ego-mind will know that it is disappearing and your fear of the unknown will try to prevent you from surrendering the ego. Be brave and face your fear of death and the unknown no matter how hard it may seem. Remind yourself that you are not the one who is dying. Accept the body's death and let go of all your worldly attachments. Welcome the vast unknown space that your consciousness is being pulled into. Remind yourself that the death of your body is an opportunity to consciously surrender your ego-mind and fully heal into consciousness.

If you don't remain alert, watchful, and conscious during death, and if you try to cling to what you are leaving behind, you will fall back into unconsciousness. If you die unconsciously, you will be reborn into another body unconsciously.

Think of the opportunity to awaken at death as a train that you must catch without a preset timetable. Something inside you knows that you need to get on the train, although you have no idea when it will arrive or where it will take you. When the train finally arrives, it stops on the platform for a short time, giving you a few moments to get on. If you don't get on out of fear of the unknown destination, it will leave without you. You will then have to wait for the next train and no one knows when it will arrive. Fortunately, existence is very compassionate and keeps sending new trains our way, so we can eventually get on one. As your consciousness and ability to be alert, watchful, and present strengthens, your fear of death and the unknown subside, and your patience, excitement, and preparedness to catch the next train increase.

### Completing unfinished business:

If you have been meditating, are alert and aware of yourself, you will know when to begin preparing for your death. Six months before you die, you will have an inner knowing that you are approaching death and can use these six months to complete any unfinished business. Look back at your entire life and see how you have lived it. Finish your unfinished business with people. Express what you have held back on. Don't leave anything left unsaid. If there are things you have done and regret, forgive yourself and ask for forgiveness from others.

You don't have to wait for death to do these things. If you can begin living this way, your life will be more fulfilling and meaningful and a blessing to yourself and others.

### Transcending the fear of death while still alive:

Even if we don't think or speak about death, sooner or later every one of us will die. Although physical death gives us an opportunity to transcend death and be transformed into an enlightened consciousness, we don't have to be dying for this to happen.

On our journey of healing into consciousness, we pass through many moments of death and rebirth. Throughout our life, we must remain alert and aware to recognize these moments and the opportunities and gifts they bring. Surrendering our separate will to the will of existence allows us to also surrender our fear of death without struggle.

You can work with your fear of death by re-experiencing any one of your deaths from a previous life and passing through it again consciously. The memories of all your lives and deaths are in the cells of your body. Once you access them and relive them, you can understand that you have lived and died many times before and realize that your fear of death and the unknown are an illusion. With this understanding, you will begin to live life more fully and joyously. (For more on transcending the fear of death, see Chapter 7, "Breaking through the Three Veils of Illusion."

## The gift:

Once you surrender to the will of existence and experience your oneness with the universe, all the qualities that religions try to teach will arise naturally. You will resonate with Buddha and Christ consciousness. You will know that whatever happens in the world and the universe also happens in you. You can truly love your neighbor as yourself, and do unto others as you would have them do unto you. Your wisdom will echo the ultimate truth of existence that both darkness and light, good and evil, are a part of you as much as they are a part of everyone and everything. You will feel grateful to your friends, as well as your enemies, for contributing to your growth. You will forgive yourself and others for mistakes and shortcomings, and your compassion will become a tremendous healing force. You will feel self-sufficient, peaceful, silent, joyful, and completely blissful in your aloneness. You will know that everything in life is impermanent and know that the journey is the only permanence and is in itself the goal. You will transcend the fear and illusion of death and can live your life moment to moment without holding anything back. You will realize that what your ego-mind created was very insignificant compared to what existence creates through your being. True justice, humility, loyalty, devotion, love, compassion, and duty to help others will become your lifestyle. You become a *Bodhisattva*, who in the Buddhist tradition is one who helps others to find liberation out of suffering.

All the meditations suggested for the first six chakras are good preparation for the opening of the seventh chakra.

*To work with the seventh chakra and the fear of death, you can also practice with the guided visualizations Entering Empty Space and Transcending the Fear of Death and the Unknown described in the e-book*

179

Healing into Consciousness with Active Meditation & Visualization. (*The recording of the guided visualization Transcending the Fear of Death and the Unknown is available at www.madadalian.com*).

## QUESTIONS AND ANSWERS
## ABOUT HEALING THE EGO IN THE SEVEN CHAKRAS

*I've been doing my healing work for a while now, but I feel an undercurrent of tension, and sometimes an agony, below the surface. Every once in a while I feel it so strongly that it makes me question if I am ever going to get it ... I know that I want to know myself and find the truth. I know I am after something that the masters have called enlightenment, but how am I supposed to get it? I am becoming more aware and seeing many things about myself, but how does enlightenment apply to this? What am I supposed to do to get it? How long am I supposed to be doing this work? How does enlightenment feel? Am I even going to get it after all the trouble I am going through? It seems like a frustrating, arduous, and endless task. Can you comment?*

Until you understand that you cannot experience enlightenment by desiring it – or by doing something with your mind – you will continue to suffer the frustration and the agony created by the mind itself. When you think that enlightenment is the end of suffering and try to achieve it through effort, you fail to see how effort produced by the mind is the cause of suffering. In this way, effort keeps you away from experiencing enlightenment. The ego-mind cannot understand that effort is the cause of suffering because the mind cannot exist without effort. Yes, enlightenment brings an end to agony and suffering created by the ego-mind, but it happens through letting go and surrendering the desires of the mind. In surrender, you understand there is nothing for you to do except to be present Here and Now and let things happen on their own while you simply respond to and flow with whatever is happening. The difficulty arises when you don't truly understand what it means to surrender the mind. You think surrendering the mind means to stop thinking and become a zombie or a piece of flotsam on the ocean, with no say about anything in life.

The key to surrendering the mind is to accept the mind and disidentify from it. What creates the difficulty and keeps you in agony is your identification with the desire of the mind that once you are enlightened, all your problems and your suffering will evaporate. For enlightenment to happen, you need to let go of the desired outcome while surrendering to what is and doing whatever is necessary to heal into consciousness without grudge or complaint.

Another important key to coming out of the agony and suffering of the mind is to make your commitment to knowing yourself one hundred percent. Partial effort or quitting halfway will yield partial results and will not reveal the gift. This doesn't mean, however, that you shouldn't be playful. It is good to be playful, but be total in whatever you are doing and put all of your energies into your search. Totality and sense of humor are essential principles that apply in the success of both the spiritual and the material worlds.

Most people normally hold back from putting one hundred percent of themselves into their work, relationships, as well as their search for enlightenment. You hold back from laughing and crying totally because of your fears. You are afraid of success and failure, afraid of pleasure and pain, and afraid of life and death. By holding back you live and manifest only a small percentage of your inexhaustible energy and potential. You allow negative thoughts to sabotage your greatness. Thoughts such as: "How can I survive without money? How long can I keep doing this spiritual work and not worry about my bills?" Or "What will happen to me if I let go and surrender?" sabotage your inner power. You give power to your insecurities by not trusting and jumping into life totally.

When your energy is only half lived, you undermine the possibility of reaching the destination you seek spiritually as well as materially.

There might also be an undercurrent of fear in your mind, which believes that once you become enlightened you will lose the pleasures this world can offer. This is simply a misconception. In enlightenment, you don't lose any part of your worldly existence. On the contrary, you begin living your life more fully, without agony and inner tension.

Regardless of how frustrating it gets, if you continue looking in, meditating, and doing whatever it takes to become more conscious, you will reach a point of no return and something inside you will feel lighter and freer. Then, even if you continue feeling the frustration of the mind at times, you simultaneously feel that you are not as lost as you were before you started your healing journey consciously.

To help your mind relax, change your hostile attitude towards your mind. Instead of saying: "Oh no, here's that thought and feeling again!" say, "Okay, I see the thought, I see my frustration, and I know that it will pass. I trust that existence knows when it's the right time for me to wake up and it will give me the gift when I'm ready." This kind of attitude will bring you closer to your being, which is always peaceful. Keep reminding yourself that everything in life is transitory. Watch your thoughts when you feel happy, and watch them when you feel sad or frustrated. Remember, just as the positive thoughts and feelings pass, the negative thoughts and feelings also pass.

In life, every experience of a peak always follows the experience of a valley and we go back and forth between them. In fact, the higher the peaks the deeper the valleys. On the peaks, we glimpse the big picture and realize how far we have come. We feel good about ourselves and feel that our journey is becoming easier, lighter, and more exciting. The moment our ego-mind becomes identified with the peak experience and tries to make it permanent, existence suddenly brings us a valley experience and we feel disappointed or frustrated again, thinking our journey is getting worse. These back-and-forth movements are like the waves in the ocean. They move on the surface, always remaining part of the great depth of the peaceful, silent water beneath them. Until you understand that both the peaks and the valleys are inevitable and will eventually pass, and you disidentify from both sides, you will miss seeing your unmoving center, which is untouched by your thoughts, feelings, or experiences.

When you remain a witness to both the ups and the downs of life, you relax. You know that when you are experiencing a peak, a valley will soon follow. Witnessing everything allows you to let go of your attachment to any outcome and accept life with all its colors. If the moment brings a valley experience, you experience it and watch it; if it brings a peak experience, you experience and watch that too. By watching all your experiences, you come to understand that nothing is good and nothing is bad. Experience is simply that – experience. Each experience is there to reveal something and help you learn and expand your consciousness. Simply watch your frustration and your desire to reach somewhere, and let it go.

*I had an abusive childhood. In what way was it my own creation or choice?*

Nothing in life is accidental. All of our experiences have the same purpose: to help us know ourselves. If you look deeper into your unconscious, you will see that there was a reason behind the abuse. Somehow, you consciously or unconsciously attracted the experience to further the evolution of your consciousness. It's possible that you may have needed to complete a karmic relationship with your abuser, or had to pay a karmic debt. Perhaps you had abused this or some other person in your past life and now needed the experience yourself so you could understand how it feels to be abused. Or perhaps you needed to experience the abuse so you can learn to stand up for yourself and assert your inner power and individuality.

Each experience is an opportunity for us to see and understand who we truly are. To recognize our ability to hurt others, we need to feel the pain of how it feels to be hurt by others. Once we recognize our own ability to misuse power and hurt others, we will not need that experience any longer, and our healing will be complete.

*Do we bring patterns and conditionings from other lifetimes?*

All our unconscious patterns move from one life to the next until we become conscious of them and learn the lessons they contain. Each new incarnation contains the history of all our travels, both unconscious and conscious. In this way nothing in existence is ever lost. If you move deeper into your unconscious, you will see the past life patterns that you are still repeating in this life.

For example, one of the common patterns that most people carry from life to life is fear of rejection, fear of being alone, and fear of death. If you don't break out of these patterns, your consciousness cannot evolve and you will continue to suffer the anxieties created by your fears. We usually avoid breaking out of our ego-mind patterns because we don't want to face our fears. If you want to be free of pain and suffering, you need to face your fears. By facing your fears you begin to see your patterns and conditionings and liberate your consciousness.

*In my meditations, I sometimes see colors and light, or I hear sounds. I don't understand what is happening, but I am excited when it happens. Do these experiences indicate that I am coming closer to my being?*

As you move deeper into yourself you will become more sensitive and aware of what is happening in your energy. You will begin to see the colors of the chakras or hear the sounds that they represent. The experiences of seeing colors or hearing sounds would excite you because these experiences take you out of your ordinary perception of reality and make you conscious of another dimension. But remember, these experiences are still part of the mind.

Your excitement indicates that you have become identified with the experience instead of simply remaining a witness to it. If you stay attached to the memory of the experience, you will close the door to experiencing other moments and dimensions of reality. It is good that your awareness is growing, but don't stay identified with the experience. Once you have learned and understood something from the experience, let it go and move on until nothing is left except your inner silence and witnessing consciousness.

*What if I don't free myself from all my patterns before I die? Will I have to come back to another life?*

What keeps you reincarnating is your attachment to the world and your unlived desires. Just as you have many opportunities to see and break your ego-mind patterns during your life, the time of your death provides you with another opportunity to clear your slate and liberate your being from those patterns. To break your patterns, both in life and in death, you need to witness your body, mind, and emotions and see your being and consciousness as separate from them. So the choice to come back into another body or die with full awareness is always yours.

In my healing practice, I have seen many times how, when people start to re-experience a previous life's death, they become afraid, just as they were at the time of that life's death. They try to cling to life, afraid to let go of their attachment to the physical reality and disappear into the unknown. As I work with them, they begin to "tune out" or fall back into unconsciousness in the same way they did previously. When I bring their attention to their breath and ask them to stay alert and watch their mind and emotions and what is happening in their body, they suddenly realize they are actually not dying, but only feeling their energy expanding out of their body's limits. With this awareness, they immediately disidentify from the fear of death and experience the joy of expanding into the unknown. By staying alert and witnessing what is happening, they see that the unknown is not as scary as they initially thought.

185

When you re-experience a death from a past life, you understand that your consciousness is independent of your physical life. Experiencing and relaxing into the unknown will help you approach both life and death from a place of wisdom and trust that physical death isn't the end. If you don't let go of your attachment to life and your fear of the unknown, you will continue to struggle through your life as well as your death.

When death comes, no power in the world can stop it. Through fear we miss our literally once-in-a-lifetime opportunity to experience the divine beauty of ultimate liberation that death brings. If you are unwilling to face your unconscious while alive, death will expose everything you have suppressed and make you face it. Everything will be stripped away: your body and possessions, your reputation and relationships, your mental and emotional attachments, your culture and religion. If you don't let go voluntarily and with understanding, the unconscious parts of your ego-mind will be reborn and you will have to continue your journey from where you left off. So start your spiritual work without postponement. Peel away the layers of your unconscious beliefs and conditionings so you can live a conscious life and die a conscious death.

# 7 BREAKING THROUGH THE THREE VEILS OF ILLUSION

What separates our consciousness from the cosmic consciousness and keeps us in pain and suffering is a multi-layered veil of illusion. This veil is like a mirage, and though it is intangible, it can be seen and felt. To liberate our consciousness from the illusion created by the veil and awaken to our true reality, we must understand and break through it. In this chapter we will look in greater detail at what constitutes the veil and how to break through it.

The veil of illusion can be divided into three layers: *personal, collective,* and *cosmic.* These layers are intertwined and represent our personal, collective, and cosmic unconscious. Each layer has its own unique characteristic and is represented by its own thought-forms, emotions, and sensory perceptions. These layers include our survival instinct, our attachments to people and the material world, our unlived desires, fantasies, fears, beliefs, conditionings, and memories of all our experiences from this and previous lives – including our plant and animal lives.

We keep ourselves chained to the illusion of the veils by believing that we are our body, thoughts, emotions, and experiences. When we refuse to let go of our identification and attachment to the illusion, we continue to suffer in its shadow. It is painful to live in the illusion

187

because no matter how hard we try, there is nothing in it that we can hold on to. By its very nature, illusion is fleeting and impermanent like a dream. When we struggle to hold on to and make permanent something that is literally a passing cloud, we strengthen the illusion and create more pain and suffering for ourselves and others.

You have lived within these veils of illusion for so long that your unconscious state has become familiar and comfortable to you. As a result, you don't even think there might be another reality than the one you are perceiving. Fortunately, in spite of this, you continue to search for peace, happiness, and enlightenment because you never stop feeling the pain of your unconsciousness and your separation from the whole. Your attachment and identification with success and failure, love and hate, poverty and riches, life and death create the illusion that pain and suffering belong to you. If you want to be free of pain and suffering, you must break through all three veils of illusion. However, intellectual understanding alone is not enough to break through them.

To break through the three veils of illusion, you must do the necessary and challenging work of peeling away the many layers of the unconscious in your energy and body. The process of peeling the layers is not easy, as there are many obstacles you must face on the way. But if you persevere, the reward of transformation into light and joy is guaranteed. The joy that liberation into consciousness brings transcends the illusion of death and any material pleasure this world can ever offer. Ultimately, the choice to stay suffering in the illusion or break free from it rests with you.

## THE THREE VEILS OF ILLUSION

### Personal Veil of Illusion

The personal veil of illusion contains each person's individual unconscious and ego-mind. Each one of us experiences our personal veil of illusion according to our own perception of reality, which itself is based on the quality of our mind, conditionings, beliefs, personality, and the past experiences of our soul's history. This layer is maintained by our self-identity and attachment to the world. It is true that our body, thoughts, emotions, experiences, personality, and profession are part of our existence, but they are all temporary and will one day evaporate into nothingness.

Our longing for love and happiness, and our search for truth and self-realization, indicate that consciously or unconsciously we yearn to break through the veil of illusion created by the mind and find something eternal. Unless we find who we truly are (the inner emptiness of our being), instead of who we think we are (our body, mind, emotions, and experiences) we will stay trapped in the personal veil of illusion.

The personal veil of illusion is maintained by thoughts and memories from current and past-life experiences that have not been resolved and completed. For example, if you had a painful experience in your childhood, such as abuse or abandonment, and were unable to freely express what you thought and felt, your unlived and unexpressed thoughts and emotions will be stored in your energy and your body's cellular memory. As an adult, you will project these suppressed thoughts and emotions onto others who had nothing to do with your childhood experiences. Your projections, which are part of your personal veil of illusion, will prevent you from seeing others as they truly are and will separate you from reality.

To break through the personal veil of illusion, you must remember that the world always mirrors back to you what you need to see to transform your unconsciousness and disidentify from your ego-mind. To do this, you must continually watch, understand, and disidentify from all your thoughts and experiences. This means disidentifying from success and failure, beauty and ugliness, inferiority and superiority, riches and poverty, depression and happiness, and so on. Identification with these things keeps you self-centered and in an illusory world created by the mind.

No one can predict when and how the breakthrough will happen.

We can only prepare the ground by purifying our energy, disidentifying from our ego-mind, and surrendering to the will of existence.

## Collective Veil of Illusion

By gradually peeling away the layers of your personal unconscious, you begin to recognize the collective veil of illusion. This veil is the unconscious of the whole of humanity and contains its entire history. The collective veil is created by our collective belief systems and our identity with being a human. This identity includes the socio-economic, national, ethnic, political, and religious beliefs and conditionings, which we think are part of who we are.

The collective veil includes many contradictory ideologies that you unconsciously follow. For example, one belief says that if you are "wronged," you should turn the other cheek. Another says that if you are "wronged," you should even the score and get an eye for an eye. So, one person learns to act out of the belief "an eye for an eye" because he is identified with his anger, pain, or inferiority and believes that if he gets revenge, it will relieve him of his pain. Another person learns to "turn the other cheek" because he is afraid to be judged as sinful and unkind if he exposes his anger or true feelings. Your identification with either one of these beliefs keeps you trapped in the collective veil of hypocrisy that casts its shadow on your inner purity.

The cloud of the collective veil of illusion overshadows our being from the moment we are born. It first infiltrates into our psyche through the influence of our family, then friends, school, the community, the country we are born in, and our religious and political beliefs. All these imprints shape our world-view very early on and become part of our behavior and lifestyle. Our social, political, religious, and economic climates change every twelve to sixteen years. Whatever was happening in the world at the time of our birth and up to our teens creates or breaks a layer in the collective unconscious.

For example, women's liberation and the sexual revolution movements caused marriages and relationships to undergo a dramatic transformation. The divorce rate increased as both men and women felt the need to find a relationship that would be more fulfilling and supportive of their individual needs. Children born during this time, whether their parents got divorced or not, were influenced by these social changes and did not form the same strong beliefs against divorce as previous generations. As an adult, they are more likely to understand that to have a good and loving relationship, both partners must support each other's personal growth and freedom, and their relationship must be a friendship between equals. If they decide to marry, they will do so with greater commitment and more awareness and respect for each other's values and individuality.

The collective veil of illusion is much older and more rigid than our personal veil, and it's harder to break through. You stay stuck in it by mechanically following your social and religious conditionings instead of finding and living with your own awareness and values. Your fears about the opinions of others keep you trapped in this veil. The collective strengthens your personal veil of illusion by either pumping your ego through flattery or idolization, or by wounding it through criticism, judgment, condemnation, and suppression. You either believe you are a "somebody," or that you are a "nobody." You are afraid to break through the collective veil of illusion because of your fears of authority, persecution, and isolation.

To break free from the collective veil of illusion, you must first recognize what your collective beliefs and conditionings are. Investigate and identify what national, religious, political, and socio-economic group you are part of. Explore what was going on in the world at the time of your birth, and understand how the collective beliefs associated with your familial, religious, and national upbringing prevent you from knowing your true Self and your oneness with all that is. Once you understand these conditionings, then have the courage to stand apart from what doesn't support your heart, individuality, and true nature.

Most of humanity lives under the influence of the collective veil of illusion unable to break out of it. It is difficult to break through this veil because the weight and gravitation field of humanity's unconscious is too heavy. The world's power structures (economic, political, and religious) have an investment in keeping the masses unconscious. It is the only way that they can keep their authority alive and dictate how everyone should live. Those in charge of these structures are afraid that if the masses break free of the collective veil, they won't be controllable and won't do what they are told. To break free of the collective veil of illusion, you must find the courage and determination to face your social and religious conditionings and stand alone in your individual truth. When you break free from the collective veil of illusion, you experience true independence and realize that your existence does not depend on anyone's approval or disapproval.

### Cosmic Veil of Illusion

The cosmic veil of illusion is the unconscious that exists within the whole universe. Our psychological fear of death and the body's survival instinct keep us behind this veil. The cosmic veil of illusion contains the history of all our incarnations in different forms – such as mineral, plant, and animal. It also contains the history of our possible existence on other planets or galactic systems before our earthly incarnation. The cosmic veil is maintained by our identification with the body's survival instinct.

We are afraid to break out of the cosmic veil of illusion because we believe (especially in the West) that we are separate from the universe and cannot survive outside of our body. We think we have only one life and are afraid to lose it. It is true that each physical body has only one life span, but we forget that our soul is deathless and will continue to exist eternally. Our body belongs to the earth and will return to the earth, but our soul belongs to the boundless universe. Forgetting this keeps us in the illusion of separation and fear of death.

To break free from the cosmic veil of illusion, you must disidentify from your fear of death and the unknown. To do this, you must understand that the root of this fear is hidden in your body. The body is programmed to survive through a built-in survival instinct, and for as long as the body is alive, it will continue to operate. By reconnecting with your essence, understanding that you are not the survival instinct, and disidentifying from it, you stop fearing the illusion of death and liberate your consciousness. As you break free from the cosmic veil of illusion, you experience your original essence and oneness with the universe, and liberate your consciousness from the illusion of separation.

## THE WORLD: OUR MIRROR IMAGE

Imagine yourself standing in the middle of a room. The walls, the ceiling, and the floor are all covered with thousands of mirrors. Each mirror reflects a face, but you can't tell which one is yours. Some faces are talking, some are singing, others are angry, sad, happy, in love, or asleep. As you look at each face, you experience a different emotion. One moment you feel happiness, the next anger, sadness, fear, hatred, or love. You feel as if you are in a madhouse and could go crazy at any moment. You struggle with the faces. You judge, blame, and criticize them. You yell at them and fight with them, but you cannot make them go away. You feel frustrated, lost, confused, and frightened. You want to escape, but you see no way out. You feel tired, depressed, and sorry for yourself. You think it's better to die and be free from this madness. You pray for help and hope that someone takes you to the exit.

Then suddenly you hear a voice: "There is a way out, come follow me!" You feel excited and hopeful that you may be able to find the exit. You follow the voice. It now says: "When you find your original face out of all the faces you see, you will find the exit!" The voice is coming from somewhere inside the room, and you don't know if you can really trust it. You begin to doubt the voice and stop looking. You fall back into the old madness and feel even more pain than before. You wish you had never started looking. You hear the voice again: "Don't struggle.

Keep looking at the faces until you find your original face!" You begin to examine the faces, but you can't tell which one is really yours. It feels like an impossible task, but you know you have no other option except to keep looking.

The voice continues to encourage you: "When you find your original face, you will end your suffering!" Though your mind is confused, your heart now trusts the voice. Somehow, you know that it speaks the truth. You stop struggling with the faces and continue searching. As you observe the faces, you realize that the moment you feel or think something, the face in the mirror reflects it back to you. You now understand that none of the faces are real – they are only projections of your own mind. You recognize that some mirrors reflect your beauty and some reflect your ugliness. Some reflect your wisdom, and some your ignorance. And sometimes you see one face masking another. You now understand that when you struggle with the faces you are only struggling with your own mind. You feel confident that you have found the way out. You relax and stop looking. You bump into a mirror. You realize that you are still in the room. You are again distracted by the reflections in the mirrors. You again feel lost and discouraged. You realize that you have not found the exit yet and wonder if you ever will.

Then, you hear the voice again: "Continue looking. You are coming closer to the exit." You are encouraged – you are not alone. You continue searching. The voice whispers next to your ear: "Destroy all the mirrors!" You start breaking the mirrors, one by one. With each mirror broken, a window opens onto an empty space. You feel more and more peaceful and the room grows emptier and quieter.

You continue breaking the mirrors until you arrive at the last one. You realize that the voice, which was guiding you, was coming from this mirror. It now says, "Break me." You hesitate. You feel so grateful to it for guiding you that you don't want to break it. The voice insists. You have no choice. You break it – you are free. There is nothing left except the empty space. You recognize it. It is your original face. You understand that there were never any walls and that you were the exit.

You see others still searching. You shout to them: "You will find the exit when you find your original face!"

## SELF-OBSERVATION: THE KEY TO BREAKING THROUGH THE THREE VEILS OF ILLUSION

Our ability to break through the veils of illusion is determined by the amount of consciousness present in our body. When consciousness is everywhere in our body, we finally break through the veils of illusion and attain the state that J. Krishnamurti described as the union of the observer and the observed. In other words, we realize that we are pure consciousness. This homecoming is the end of suffering created by our unconsciousness.

We transform our unconscious into consciousness through observation. The more you observe yourself and the reality around you, the more conscious you become. When you observe your life and pay close attention to how everything comes and goes, you will begin to recognize and understand the impermanent nature of life. When you observe your mind, emotions, and experiences, you will realize that they too are impermanent. Through observation, you gradually begin to understand the fleeting illusory nature of life and begin to recognize that what always remains constant is you, the observer.

You break through the three veils of illusion through breath awareness and self-observation. You can connect to and strengthen your ability to recognize yourself as the observer by practicing breath awareness. As I had mentioned earlier, breath awareness is the essence of meditation. With disciplined practice of self-observation and breath awareness, you can disidentify from the many layers of thoughts and emotions that prevent you from being in consciousness.

In the next section, I have given practical exercises that will help you to cultivate *breath awareness* and *self-observation*.

## How to Break Through the Personal Veil of Illusion

Below I have listed several exercises that can help you break through the personal veil of illusion. Experiment with each one for at least three weeks and find the one that is easiest to practice. You can practice with two if you like, but I don't recommend using more than two at a time. Staying focused on one or two methods will give you the most benefit. You can practice with each method for three weeks to three months. On-going disciplined practice will yield greater benefits. Alternate between methods occasionally to avoid becoming mechanical with the one you are practicing.

**Look at Everything with Self-Awareness:**
Practice looking at everything while at the same time remaining aware of yourself as the observer. We can call this technique *observation with self-awareness*. Observation with self-awareness is another way to describe what I have been referring to as *witnessing awareness*. Observation with self-awareness is the key to breaking through the veils of illusion and disidentifying from the mind. Usually, you don't have much difficulty observing what is outside of you and occasionally may observe what is inside, but you rarely observe yourself as the one who is observing. Observation with self-awareness helps you see what's inside and outside of you at the same time and remain a witness to both.

Observation with self-awareness is like a torch that illuminates the unconscious darkness both inside and outside and transforms it into conscious light. To see the world with self-awareness means to stand apart from whatever you are observing instead of being identified with it. Observation with self-awareness helps you feel safe enough to venture into the darkness of the unconscious (personal, collective, and cosmic) and disidentify from it.

If you observe everything in the outside world and at the same time remain aware of yourself as the observer, you can never be lost in any situation. You will know that you are simply a detached observer of what is happening. With self-aware observation, you simply look at everything that comes to pass without judging, blaming, or identifying with anything. The self-aware observer has no bias towards what is "good" or "bad," "right" or "wrong" – she simply observes all judgments as passing aspects of thought. Cultivating the ability to observe with self-awareness takes time and effort, but if you persevere in looking at everything with self-awareness, your consciousness of the world and yourself will gradually increase.

*To practice looking at the world with self-awareness, look inside yourself while at the same time observing what is happening outside.* If you are looking at the sky, look at yourself looking at the sky at the same time. If you are watching a movie, look at yourself watching the movie. If you are talking to someone, observe yourself talking to that person at the same time. Or, look inside yourself this very moment while you are reading. As you look in and out at the same time, observe your thoughts, feelings, reactions, and responses. You can practice looking with self-awareness at any time and in any place.

It is important to practice living your life with self-awareness. If you don't cultivate your witnessing awareness and accidentally pierce through the veils of illusion, you will be disoriented and unable to relate to people and the world. You will find it difficult to live life and adjust to your surroundings.

The three layers of illusion naturally begin to break down at the time of death. If you haven't prepared yourself to live with observation and self-awareness, you will be unable to remain conscious during the process of "dying" when your life force begins to leave the body. This will make it difficult or impossible for you to disidentify from your fear of death, and you will be forced to fall back into unconsciousness – returning to another body and going through the same wheel of life and death, pain and suffering all over again.

You can practice strengthening your ability to observe with self-awareness using the following four exercises: *Watching Your Breath; Watching Your Body; Watching Your Emotions, and Watching Your Thoughts.* These will give you the fundamental skills you need to experiment with all the other exercises in this chapter. They will help you strengthen your witnessing awareness and your ability to center and ground your energy and consciousness in your body.

## Watch Your Breath

Breath is always *the* key to experiencing and strengthening your witnessing awareness. No matter how far you have traveled on your healing journey, you will always need to watch your breath. Breath awareness is the simplest way to break through all the veils of illusion.

Practice watching your breath by simply watching how your breath comes in through the nostrils, goes down into the belly, and then goes out again through the nostrils. Focus your attention on your belly while you are watching your breath come in and out of your nostrils. Dedicate at least fifteen to twenty minutes a day to this practice. Just sit silently and watch your breath. You can also practice breath awareness any time during the day as you go about your daily activities: taking a shower, watching TV, talking on the phone, cleaning, etc. After practicing this for three weeks to three months, move to the next practice. Remember that breath is life, and breath awareness is the thread moving through all the other practices.

## Watch Your Body

Begin watching your body while you continue to watch your breath. Watch the physical sensations inside your body, such as tension, pain, heaviness, energy movements, and blockages. Watch how your hands, feet, and head move. Observe the different expressions of your face. Notice how your expressions and body movements change when your moods change. Watch your body from inside when you sit, walk, lie down, exercise, run, or whatever physical activity you are engaged in. Observe what makes your body tense and what helps it to relax.

You can watch your body anywhere and at any time. Watching your body will help you become more aware of its needs and know how to take care of it. Over time, your identification with the body will lessen, and your ability to observe with self-awareness will increase. After practicing this for three weeks to three months, move to the next exercise.

## Watch Your Emotions

Once you have gained enough awareness of your body and your breath, focus on watching your emotions. Observe how your emotions change, appearing and disappearing like waves in the ocean. As you continue to observe your emotions, you will gradually begin to see how they change from self-confidence to self-doubt, from unhappiness to happiness, from anger to love, from fear to courage. With disciplined practice, your identification with your emotions will lessen and you will start to experience the peaceful empty spaces that exist between waves of changing emotions.

Watching the emotions will be easier if you continue watching your breath at the same time. Notice how your breathing changes with different emotions and how, when there is no emotion, your breath becomes soft and natural. After practicing this for three weeks to three months, move to the next exercise.

## Watch Your Thoughts

Watching thoughts is more challenging than watching the body or emotions because thoughts are subtler, they move faster, and are harder to see. Thoughts are like dust particles that easily get into everything and hide in corners and underneath things. To be able to see your thoughts, you have to practice watching them with patience and diligence.

Allocate at least fifteen to twenty minutes a day when you can sit quietly and watch each thought as it comes and goes. Don't judge any of the thoughts as good or bad. If a judgment arises, simply observe the judgment as just another thought. You can also watch your thoughts by writing them down as they come to your mind and observing yourself writing. Pay attention to how thoughts take you out of the present moment and into the past or future. Notice how even though they continually change, the same thoughts keep reappearing over again. Don't worry about this repetition – just continue watching or writing down each thought as it comes and goes.

As you become adept at watching with self-awareness, you will begin to notice that when a certain thought arises, it immediately activates its associated emotion. One moment you may feel sad because of a certain thought, but the next moment, when that thought changes, your sadness turns into anger or happiness. With observation, you will notice that the reverse is also true: when emotion changes, the associated thought also changes. With time, as your witnessing awareness grows stronger, you will be able to see your thoughts and emotions as they arise, and they will drop away before you get identified with them. Practice with this and the previous exercises until you are able to watch your breath, body, thoughts, and emotions effortlessly. Below I include three other exercises to help you break through the personal veil of illusion.

## Purify Your Body of Suppressed Thoughts and Emotions Through Expression

As I mentioned earlier, although we commonly believe that thoughts exist only inside our head, the truth is that there are many thoughts and emotions suppressed everywhere in our body. Every thought and emotion you have ever thought and felt and held on to is stored in your body, layer upon layer. These suppressed layers of thoughts and emotions force you to stay unconscious and cause all of your pain and suffering. To release these layers from the body, practice expressing your thoughts and emotions out loud.

I can't stress enough how expressing your thoughts and emotions out loud can help to detoxify your body, bring you closer to the innocence and purity of your being and free you from all kinds of physical, mental, and emotional pain and suffering. Expression will also help you to become more conscious of yourself and others and will help you find your inner peace. This practice is similar to the exercise *Let go of the Thoughts by Expressing them Out Loud,* which I described in Chapter 4, but here we will practice it with more understanding of the following seven stages: *witnessing, accepting, expressing, surrendering, understanding, letting go,* and finally, *acting with new awareness.*

*1. Witness:*

To connect with the suppressed thoughts and emotions in the body, close your eyes and bring your breath and awareness into the center of your body around the navel. Scan the body with your witnessing awareness and observe any sensations, such as pain or tension that may be present anywhere in the body. While keeping your awareness in your center, bring your attention and breath to where you noticed tension or pain. Pay attention to the thoughts or emotions that surface as a result of your awareness and breath, focusing on that spot.

If you don't detect any pain or tension in the body, just work with whatever thought or emotion comes up in that moment. Don't judge the thought or the emotion as wrong or irrelevant. Trust whatever is there. If nothing comes up, trust that too and work with the thought that says: "Nothing is coming up, I see and feel nothing," as you move to the next step.

*2. Accept:*

Accept the thought or emotion that surfaces without any judgment. Don't struggle with anything. It will be impossible to accept what you see, think, and feel if you struggle. Accept everything, even your non-acceptance. *Remind yourself that you are not your thoughts, emotions, or whatever you are experiencing but are simply an observer.*

*3. Express:*

Next, express the thoughts and emotions that are there out loud so you can hear them. Remain a witness to what is being expressed, and watch what is happening in your body. Your thoughts may be coming from the past or projecting into the future, but they have nothing to do with your consciousness in the present moment. In the present, you are simply seeing yourself expressing what you think and feel out loud. With expression, you will soon notice that it becomes easier for you to disidentify from your thoughts and emotions and release them from your body and energy.

*4. Surrender:*
Surrender to your truth and to whatever you are experiencing without blame, shame, judgment, or justification for why you feel the way you do. Whether you are feeling anger, grief, fear, shame, guilt, love or joy, surrender to these emotions without resistance. Surrendering will lead to self-awareness and understanding.

*5. Understand:*
When you understand that all your life experiences were necessary for you to learn the lessons you needed to heal into consciousness, your unconscious energy will be transformed into conscious energy. With understanding, something deep inside you will relax and you will feel an inner opening and expansion. When you understand the deeply rooted causes of your suppressed thoughts and emotions, you will begin to take responsibility for them and will understand that how you feel or what you think have nothing to do with other people and the way you are choosing to live your life.

*6. Let go:*
Once you understand that you are responsible for all your thoughts and emotions, release your hold on them and let them go. Don't get attached to any thought, emotion, or experience. Life continuously offers us so much more to live and learn.

*7. Act with new awareness:*
Once you let go of the suppressed thoughts and emotions clouding your

body and energy, a new awareness and clarity of vision automatically arises from within your being. Now start acting with that new awareness and understanding. By acting with awareness, you break your old thought and behavior patterns and help your new understanding root in your body. Action with awareness creates a permanent shift in your energy and changes your life.

Ongoing purification of your thoughts and emotions makes your body lighter, healthier, more energetic, and youthful. You also feel more respect for yourself and others, and instead of blaming others for your problems, you begin to feel grateful to everyone for challenging you and helping you heal into consciousness. You become more aware of your being and begin to see that while your thoughts and emotions come and go, your being remains the same. With more awareness, your old thoughts and emotions cease to have the power to take you on a roller-coaster ride, keep you stuck in the past, or worried about the future. By purifying your body of suppressed thoughts and emotions, the personal veil of illusion begins to break, and you start to live each moment of your life more openly and fully.

## Listen with Your Heart

Much of what we hear filters through our ego-mind and we miss many opportunities to be present in the Now. Another way to disidentify from your thoughts and emotions and become conscious of the present is to listen with your heart instead of your mind.

To listen with your heart, bring your breath and awareness into your heart and literally listen through your heart. Keep your attention centered in your heart while you listen to whatever others are saying to you. Watch any thoughts, emotions, or feelings that arise inside you as a result, and understand that the other is simply triggering parts of your ego-mind. If you listen with your heart, your judgments of yourself and others will weaken, and you will be able to see yourself, others, and the world with more objectivity and compassion.

203

## Listen with Your Being

Once you get used to listening with your heart, start to experiment listening with your being. To listen with your being, bring your breath and awareness into your inner center, a couple of inches below your belly button, and literally listen from your belly. Listening with your being will help you develop and trust your intuition. Your intuition is much closer to your being than your heart and your mind. Your mind can be conditioned, but your intuition and inner knowing always stay pure, regardless of whether you are in tune with them or not. What you can sense and know through intuition, the mind cannot explain because intuition surpasses logic.

To listen with your being, observe what people are saying without reacting or getting involved emotionally. Observe if they are speaking from their heart, their mind, or from their inner knowing. Are they being truthful or just telling you what they think you want to hear? For example, someone might be saying nice things about you, but if you listen intuitively with your inner being, you know that they are not being truthful but only trying to flatter you. You feel that they are being nice because perhaps they want something from you or simply because they are acting out of a conditioned social behavior. On the other hand, if someone is saying something that hurts your ego, if you listen with your being, you know that they are speaking truthfully because they care about you.

Listening with your being will also help you learn to recognize when you are false and mechanical, and when you are authentic and truly in your heart. To know the difference between listening intuitively from your being and listening from your mind, you must look inside and be honest with yourself. When you pay close attention, you realize that when you listen from your being you don't react or magnify your problems. You feel peaceful and content within. When you listen with your mind, you remain in the illusion of separation created by your thoughts and emotions and you react instead of respond. When you listen and respond from your being, you are always genuinely truthful with yourself and others. Listening with your being brings you closer to your authentic self and helps you feel good about yourself and life.

## Signs of the Personal Veil Breaking

As the personal veil of illusion begins to break down, you begin to feel disillusioned by the world around you. What was meaningful and important to you before feels meaningless and unimportant. Your ambition and desires begin to drop, along with your identification with the material world. Worldly pleasures and values like money, career, status, physical beauty, and possessions seem empty and fall away. Your increasing self-awareness helps you realize that nothing lasts forever, including your body. Superficial relationships start to diminish, and you feel drawn to more authentic, meaningful, and heart-centered relationships. Sincerity, honesty, love, and kindness take precedence over any material achievement or success.

As you begin to break through the personal veil, you will feel as though you and your consciousness are expanding. You experience a longing to move beyond the familiar and restricting conditionings of your ego-mind and open yourself to the mysterious reality that exists beyond the mind.

You are close to breaking through the personal veil of illusion when you:

- Begin to see the illusion of your thoughts and desires
  more clearly.
- Are able to witness and disidentify from your thoughts
  and emotions.
- Are comfortable being alone and can take risks without
  worrying about the consequences or the outcomes.
- Don't take yourself and your problems so seriously, and can
  laugh at yourself once in a while.

- Stop judging yourself and others, and don't take anything that others say or do personally.
- Are no longer afraid to make mistakes and understand that what ever happens in life is there to help you heal into consciousness.

You will experience these at different times and in different proportions as you go on breaking the personal veil of illusion by practicing self-awareness.

## HOW TO BREAK THROUGH
## THE COLLECTIVE VEIL OF ILLUSION

To break through the collective veil of illusion experiment with the following exercises.

**Find and Live Your Individuality**

To break through the collective veil of illusion, which is the unconscious of the whole of humanity, we must find and live our individual essence and truth. The collective unconscious forces us to suppress our individuality and live behind artificial social, religious, and political masks. The more we suppress our inner truth, the more artificial and hypocritical we become. To break through the collective veil of illusion, we must find our childlike innocence and live our individuality.

The limitations and restrictions imposed by the religious and political institutions on each individual are challenging to see and break through. This challenge, however, is an essential test of your character and commitment to awaken. Without this challenge, you might not be able to recognize the need for change and the necessity to find and live your individuality.

People who have found and expressed their individuality have often been judged, criticized, and even persecuted. Individuality is dangerous to the social structure because it threatens the status quo. The collective always evolves more slowly than individuals do. Though society suppresses individuals, it paradoxically also evolves because of the courage of a few individuals who dare to live their own truth and shake old foundations.

Social and political activists like Gandhi, Martin Luther King Jr., Nelson Mandela, and many others who fought for justice and peace have changed the way the masses view the world. Scientists and inventors like Isaac Newton, Charles Darwin, Albert Einstein, Thomas Edison, Alexander Graham Bell, Nicola Tessla, the Wright brothers, Bill Gates, Steve Jobs, and many others pushed through the boundaries of the ordinary mind and in the process helped to transform the lifestyle of the whole of humanity. Writers, artists, and entertainers like Shakespeare, Oscar Wilde, Dostoyevsky, Leonardo da Vinci, Michelangelo, Van Gogh, Mozart, John Lennon, and many others dared to live their individuality, and by doing so confronted and shook up the social and religious taboos of their time, helping everyone take a step forward out of their conditioned perceptions of reality. Philosophers, scholars, and educators like Karl Marx, Friedrich Nietzsche, Sigmund Freud, Carl Jung, William Reich, Joseph Campbell, Oprah Winfrey, and many others pushed the ordinary human intellect to a new level of seeing and understanding life. And, finally, enlightened masters and mystics like the Buddha, Jesus, Lao Tzu, Bodhidharma, Socrates, Pythagoras, Rumi, Georges Gurdjieff, Osho, and other masters helped to raise humanity to a new level of consciousness – the cosmic reality of oneness, which transcends the worldly illusion of the ego. Ultimately, everyone who finds and lives their unique individuality contributes in their own way to making the world a better place for everyone.

To break through the collective veil of illusion, find your original innocence and don't hold back from living and expressing who you truly are. By trying to fit into any social, religious, or political group at the expense of your own individual truth, you miss living your own innate potential. Don't be afraid to make mistakes in the process of finding and living the gifts you have brought with you. Face your social and religious conditionings and choose to live your life courageously with your own truth and individuality, even if others disagree or disapprove. Face your fears of being alone and be a light unto yourself. Trust and follow your inner truth, even if at times it leads you to a dead end. Remember that nothing in life is accidental, including your "mistakes." Existence creates everything the way it is for your consciousness to evolve.

### Find and Live Your Innate Freedom

Freedom is our true nature and birthright, but we live under a cloak of collective hypnosis believing that we are not free. This idea comes from our conditioned mind, which is trained to fit into and comply with our man-made social, religious, and political institutions. Of course, there are certain moral and functional rules that we all must follow to make it possible for us to coexist, but these rules are *common-sense rules* that don't infringe upon our individuality. The rules and conditionings that threaten our individuality are those that impose a certain ideology that goes against our inner truth and our basic human right to live it. Humanity is forced to follow and live by *non-common-sense rules,* created by those few in authority who, because of their fear of losing their economic, political, and religious power over others, impose a fear of consequences if we don't comply with their rules. Unfortunately, those who impose and those who comply both feed into a corresponding sense of inferiority or superiority and a lack of self-awareness, empathy, and compassion for one another.

A free expression of individual consciousness is dangerous to the religious and political structures because it threatens the foundation of their survival. Survival issues, which are common to all humans and animals alike, create a blanket of collective fear around the globe, keeping us all stuck within its veil. Your fears around survival and being alone cause you to give up your innate freedom and conform not only to those who hold economic and political power over you, but also to those within your immediate relationships such as colleagues, friends, and lovers.

To find and live your innate freedom and individuality, you must break through the non-common-sense rules that threaten your consciousness and courageously explore the collective conditionings and beliefs that keep you in bondage. *Remind yourself that your being is already free and it will always stay free regardless of how much you or others suppress it.* Understanding that you are already free can help you disidentify from your survival fears and collective conditionings and live with the light of your own conscience.

To free your being from the influence of the collective veil of illusion, risk being true to yourself and take responsibility for the consequences (positive or negative) of your choices. People may criticize, judge, and reject you for not conforming to their expectations, and you may feel hurt by their comments and actions. But to break free from the collective veil of illusion, you must learn to stand alone and recognize how others' fears (those of friends, family, or communities), keep you from living your innate truth and freedom. While doing this, however, watch that you are not reacting and judging others or being self-righteous to prove your point. Simply look inside, connect with your gut feelings, and trust your intuition about what feels right. To live your freedom you must be honest with yourself and others and honor your inner truth. Even if it takes years or lifetimes, you will eventually break out of the collective veil of illusion and come to recognize that truth and freedom are inseparably one.

**Take Risks**

Everyone of us contributes to the collective veil of illusion through our personal fears. To break through the collective veil of illusion, you must have the courage to face all your fears and take risks to act in spite of them. You must feel the discomfort your fears of being different, making mistakes, failing, or being judged, rejected, and punished generate and do what you know you must do anyway, remembering that your inner core can never be touched, fail, or be punished.

When you follow your fears and stop yourself from what your being longs to live, your energy remains stagnant and you miss many opportunities to heal into consciousness. Taking risks moves your energy into action and creativity and your fear of the unknown turns into excitement. Joy and abundance are the rewards that come from jumping into and exploring the unknown. Neither spiritual transformation, nor material success is possible without taking risks. And a risk is not a risk unless you are willing to stake everything. Let go of the security of the past and your investment in the future and live your life knowing that your being can never fail.

## Live Spontaneously

To live spontaneously means to live in innocence, responding to life moment to moment without projecting anything into the past or future. When Jesus was asked who will enter the kingdom of God, he picked up a small child and said: "Those who are like this child." Children are not concerned about the past or the future. They are not concerned about how they are perceived or judged; they are always in their innocence until we corrupt them by restricting their spontaneity and conditioning them to behave in a certain way. Spontaneity is an attribute of the Now, where the mind, which is always preoccupied with past or future, is for a moment inactive.

To live spontaneously, don't inhibit your natural responses when they arise in a moment of no-thought. Allow yourself to feel and truthfully express what comes up in the moment without fear of rejection, self-criticism, or concern about other people's opinions. Watch how your mind tries to stop you from doing what you naturally feel you need to do and act in spite of what it says. Don't criticize or judge yourself when your feelings and opinions change; and don't judge and criticize others when their feelings and opinions change. Living spontaneously does not mean you will not make mistakes. Viewing your mistakes as lessons, rather than as reasons to judge yourself, will bring you closer to your authentic truth.

To live spontaneously act from your intuitive knowing instead of your fearful mind. Remember that mind can never be spontaneous because it can only exist either in the past or in the future. And I'm not saying don't use your mind; just don't let it interfere when its service is not required.

You experience happiness and joy only when you are spontaneous. To be spontaneous does not mean to be impulsive either. Impulsiveness is a reactive behavior. Spontaneity is an innocent response to every new situation. At times, your spontaneous behavior may go against other's expectations and may even seem to hurt them, but don't worry. If you behave out of innocence you will help everyone's spiritual growth. So be spontaneous and enjoy the surprises that life brings.

## SIGNS OF THE COLLECTIVE VEIL BREAKING

You begin to break free of the collective veil of illusion when you become conscious of the falsity of the collective conditionings and begin acting in spite of them. At this stage, you begin to consciously confront the artificial game created and fueled by greed and fear. You may start to feel isolated from friends, family, and the rest of the world. You may also begin to doubt if you are doing the right thing by going against the collective. But in spite of your doubt and fear of isolation, you simultaneously also feel elevated from within and supported by existence and those who are traveling in the same direction.

With time your inner strength begins to grow and you feel joyful that you are able to stand out of the density and heaviness of the collective unconscious. By firmly standing your ground and not compromising, you feel a new sense of compassion and acceptance of yourself and others, as well as the need to share your expanding consciousness. As your consciousness grows, you begin to act out of true conscience and integrity, driven by a sincere desire to make the world a better place for yourself and others. As you break through the collective veil, you assert your individuality and become a role model for others to do the same.

211

You have broken through the collective veil of illusion when you are no longer disturbed by the opinions of others and understand that although you accept everyone as they are, you are not obliged to live by their rules and fears, but rather, can live your life with your own rules and conscience.

## HOW TO BREAK THROUGH THE COSMIC VEIL OF ILLUSION

What prevents us from breaking through the cosmic veil of illusion is our fear of death. This fear can be divided into three layers: *the body's survival instinct, the psychological fear of death, and the fear of losing your essence (not existing).* To become fully conscious and break through the cosmic veil of illusion, you must understand and transcend your fear of death.

Below are some guidelines and exercises you can practice with. You can experiment with these after you have practiced with the ones described earlier, or jump straight in.

### Disidentify from the Five Senses

The body's survival instinct operates through the five physical senses (touch, taste, sight, hearing, and smell). To break through the cosmic veil of illusion, you must separate your consciousness from all your sensory perceptions.

As you go about your life, practice reminding yourself that everything you perceive and experience through your senses is not you. Remember that you are the observer who perceives and experiences everything. To understand this, give yourself a hard pinch on the arm. Feel the pain of the pinch and continue observing the pain. Watch and feel the pain until it gradually dissipates. You will notice that what remains permanent before, during, and after the pain is your witnessing awareness that observes everything coming and going. By avoiding or struggling with the pain, you stay identified with the illusion that the sensation of pain creates, and by feeling and watching the pain you disidentify from its physical sensation. Watch and disidentify from all your senses the same way. Disidentification will allow you to break out of the illusion that the physical senses create.

You can practice disidentifying from the five senses while eating, drinking, bathing, listening to music, walking, running, etc. Practicing with each one of the senses for three weeks, twenty minutes a day, will heighten your awareness of the senses and strengthen your inner witness. Below are some specific exercises for each of the senses.

*Touch:* Pick up any object and hold it in your hand. Close your eyes and feel the object. Notice its qualities: texture, density, weight, temperature, and size. Observe the sensations you feel in your hand and body. Remind yourself, *"I am not the one who is touching and feeling. I am the observer who is watching the sensation of touching."*

*Taste:* Practice eating and drinking with awareness. Observe the food or liquid as it goes into your mouth. Eat or drink very slowly. Taste it on your tongue. Feel the texture and temperature. Feel how your jaw and face move, how your teeth touch each other while you chew, how your tongue moves when you drink. Feel the taste of the food in your mouth. Remind yourself, *"I am not the one who is tasting. I am the observer who is watching the sensation of tasting."*

*Sight:* Bring your awareness into your eyes. Pick a point and focus your gaze on it. Notice everything else in your scope of vision while focusing on that point. Keep your awareness in the eyes while you look. Observe yourself looking through the eyes. Remind yourself, *"I am not the one who is looking and seeing. I am the observer who is watching the sensation of looking and seeing."*

*Hearing:* Bring your awareness and focus into your ears. Listen to the

213

sounds that are around you. Pay attention to your ears and how they pick up different sounds. Notice how your attention goes from one sound to another and try to be aware of all sounds simultaneously, while keeping your focus and awareness in your ears. Remind yourself, *"I am not the one who is hearing. I am the observer who is watching the sensation of hearing."*

*Smell:* You can practice this exercise while cooking, taking a scented bath, burning incense, or diffusing aromatherapy oils. Focus your attention and awareness on your nose. Feel the sensations that arise in your body as a result of the smells. Remind yourself, *"I am not the one who is smelling. I am the observer who is watching the sensation of smelling."*

### Disidentify from the Psychological Fear of Death

The psychological fear of death is the mind's fear of losing itself. The mind prevents us from breaking through the veils of illusion by attaching itself to the material reality. It tries to protect itself from dying by either holding on to the known past or by trying to control the unknown future. Focusing on the past or the future, the mind and your attention stay securely fastened to the illusion of time.

To disidentify from the psychological fear of death, you need to face your fear of the unknown. You usually think that when you feel fear, you should stop doing something. In truth, the fear actually gives you an opportunity to transcend the mind. What helps us to disidentify from the psychological fear of death is the strength of our spirit. When your spirit is strong enough to face death, you are psychologically ready to break through the veil of illusion the fear creates.

To help you practice disidentifying from your psychological fear of death, take some time to be by yourself and, knowing that death is inevitable, begin contemplating your death. Feel any fear or emotion that may arise with the thought of death. Look inside and see where in the body you are feeling the fear. Stay focused in that area and don't allow your mind to distract you by pulling your attention into thinking about other things. Feel the fear in your body no matter how intense it may seem. Keeping your attention on your breath, breathe into the area where you are feeling the fear. As you breathe, look at the thoughts or emotions that are coming up and tell yourself that no matter what happens, you are going to feel and face the fear. Breathe deeply into your belly and keep your focus in the belly. If you are still afraid, ask yourself: *Why am I afraid? What is the fear trying to tell me? Why do I try to escape from it?* Remind yourself that the fear is an opportunity for you to find your true Self, which can never die. Continue to feel and observe the fear until it eventually dissipates and transforms into ecstasy.

### Disidentify from the Body's Survival Instinct

To break through the cosmic veil of illusion, we must also disidentify from the body's survival instinct. The human body, just like any animal's body, is programmed to do what is necessary to survive. The body tells us when it needs food, water, and rest, and it knows how to heal itself. The different components of the body's survival instinct get activated spontaneously when needed. Instinct always responds to what the body needs to survive. Like anything physical in existence, the body has a limited lifespan and will eventually begin to break down and die. No amount of human effort can ever prevent this from happening. It is important therefore to gradually learn to disidentify from the body's survival instinct before it is ready to die, so at the time of its death we can leave it gracefully and fully conscious.

To understand the body's survival instinct, you need to first experience it. This is not always easy to do. I experienced my body's survival instinct through fasting. Fasting has been used in all religious traditions to help seekers experience, understand, and transcend the body's survival instinct. (In addition, fasting can also help you understand and disidentify from your psychological fear of death.)

Through fasting, you can, for the first time, experience true hunger and the body's compulsion to survive. When I talk about fasting, I mean total fasting – only water and a little fresh juice at the most. True hunger of the body has no relationship to our conditioned mental clock that says, "I am hungry, it's time to eat lunch." The mental clock is a habitual programmed reflex related to when we usually eat our breakfast, lunch, or dinner.

I recommend fasting to everyone because it's not only a helpful and necessary tool for spiritual transformation, but it is also very helpful in maintaining good physical health and longevity. Do your own research on how to fast and how to break a fast properly. It is good to make a decision to fast spontaneously and intuitively. Don't push yourself into fasting prematurely relying on your mind. Your own consciousness and your body will tell you when it's the right time. Trust your intuition. When you are ready, your fast will happen easily and effortlessly. Fasting with effort fuels the mind instead of putting it to rest.

Fasting produces different experiences and results for everyone. How long you need to fast before you experience your body's survival instinct will depend on the constitution, weight, and age of your body. For me, it took eighteen days before I experienced the true hunger of the body.

When you experience the true hunger of the body, don't be in a hurry to break your fast. Feel the hunger so you can understand and disassociate from your body's need to survive. This will take a little more effort on your part, but it is worth it. Don't give up if you have made it this far. Remind yourself that the experience of hunger is not you but is simply your body's need to survive. You are only the witness, not the hunger. When you see and understand this, you have broken through the body's survival instinct and the cosmic veil of illusion. This is a cause for celebration as you will now begin to live with a greater sense of freedom.

It is not absolutely necessary to fast to experience the body's survival instinct. If you never get to fast, you can still have an opportunity to experience it in times of physical danger. However, it will be difficult to disidentify from the survival instinct if you haven't done the necessary preparation work. If you can witness any dangerous situation without struggle and surrender to death, you will be able to break through the cosmic veil of illusion and be liberated from your fear of death.

## Disidentify from and Transcend Your Essence

To be completely free of the cosmic veil of illusion, we must also disidentify from our identity as a separate soul or essence. Our essence begins to develop from the first and most prominent experience we had as an animal. Our animal lives influence the development of our essence the most because as animals we begin to move freely and put our energy into action (hunt, graze, mate). With action also begins a long chain of karmic consequences – positive and negative.

All your animal lives have shaped the way you are today; the way you experience fear of death, pain, pleasure, tribal identity (belonging to a herd, pack, pod), maternal and paternal instincts, competition, domination, submission, etc. Just as there are many different kinds of behavior responses to the survival instinct among animals, there are also as many different responses to the fear of death among humans. However, because we have experienced life in many animal forms, our essence is multifaceted, and each face is reflected in our different personalities. Sometimes we are nurturing and kind, at other times fiercely competitive or protective of ourselves and our close family members, and still at other times we may be independent and self-sufficient, or plain, unconcerned about what happens around us. Each animal has its unique qualities, strengths and gifts, which Native American traditions refer to as *animal medicine.*

For example, if you had a past life as a mouse, as did my editor Jesse Carliner, you will be practical, well-organized, and pay great attention to detail. You will be curious about exploring everything, but in a cautious manner. If you were a black panther in a past life, as I was, you will have no fear of being alone or facing the unknown. You will courageously look into and explore whatever is hidden in the darkness of your unconscious and will strive to maintain your independence at all costs. Our essence dictates how we behave when our survival is at stake.

The mouse personality and the panther personality respond differently when their survival is threatened. The mouse instinctively runs and hides. The panther, on the other hand, faces the challenge and fights if necessary.

To see, understand, and disidentify from your essence, you need to go into the cosmic unconscious where the memories of all your past lives as animals are hidden. You need to remember and understand your animal lives and disidentify from their character traits and survival behavior. When you remember your animal lives, you'll recognize that their qualities are still a part of your many personalities today. You will also understand how your current attitudes towards life, death, sexuality, and power were formed. Knowing this will help you to better understand yourself and others. (I have presented some of the important animal lives that have shaped my own essence in Chapter 8, "One Spirit's Journey.")

You cannot experience your essence through the mind alone because animals live through their instinct – not the mind. The mind actually prevents you from experiencing the essence. The mind thinks you are civilized and are above your animal instinct. As a result, you judge and suppress your essence and instincts. For thousands of years, humanity has explored and experienced the cosmic unconscious through tribal dance, vision quests, and meditation.

To help you experience, understand, and disidentify from your essence, try a meditation I call Svarasa. In Sanskrit "svarasa" means both *juice or essence* as well as the *instinct of self-preservation* (see *Healing into Consciousness with Active Meditation & Visualization* e-book at, www. madadalian.com).

Experiencing your essence will help you understand that other people's essence and behavior are shaped by other animals different than your own, which will help you become more accepting, tolerant, and loving towards yourself and others. Ultimately, it's not about changing your essence but about understanding that your consciousness is separate from it. You transcend your essence when you truly know you are pure consciousness.

# SIGNS OF THE COSMIC VEIL BREAKING

As the cosmic veil begins to break, everything that you thought was "you" and "your truth," and everything you were identified with and thought to be important, begins to feel empty and meaningless. Even what you perceived to be your essence or "truth" begins to feel like an illusion. You realize that you don't know anything, and whatever you thought you knew is false. Your self-identity begins to dissolve, and you feel like a nobody. You also begin to experience yourself as emptiness or nothingness.

You may perceive these experiences as positive or negative, depending on your attitude. This could feel uncomfortable or exhilarating. If you feel uncomfortable and judge the experiences as negative, you will feel your energy shrinking and find yourself falling into depression or a lethargic state. If your goal is spiritual transformation, you will be able to welcome, watch, and pass through this process without diversion or fear. With a positive and welcoming attitude towards nothingness, you can surrender your fear of disappearing into the unknown and allow yourself to experience the sense of expansion and joy that comes with letting go.

If you always remember to remain a detached observer to whatever is happening, you will easily break through the veils of illusion. If you get afraid or excited and cannot remain a witness, you will stop the process short of completion. When you feel fear or doubt, simply understand that it is only coming from your conditioned mind, which is trying to protect itself from disappearing, and come back to watching your breath.

To break through the cosmic veil of illusion, you must be in your innocence and purity and have no shame or judgment hidden in your unconscious towards yourself and others. If you miss one opportunity to fully break through, don't worry: there will be others. Eventually, everyone awakens from the dream.

You have broken through the cosmic veil of illusion when you know that you have never been separate from existence or God. When you know your eternity, all your fears and inhibitions evaporate and the universe becomes your home. You now unconditionally embrace life with all its ups and downs, knowing that the journey is the goal. Your life becomes a light that guides others to awaken to the same truth.

## QUESTIONS AND ANSWERS ABOUT THE THREE VEILS OF ILLUSION

*My friend just came back from India and told me that he became enlightened after being touched by a teacher who gave him an energy transmission. He told me that thousands of people are becoming enlightened this way. Can you please comment?*

Enlightenment is not something that can be given or transmitted. What that teacher has done is an ancient technique of transmitting energy called *shaktipat*. When someone who is like an open vehicle to the powerhouse of universal energy touches you, especially in the area of the third eye, you receive a surge of energy into your body. This makes it possible for you to jump out of your worldly reality and have an experience of bliss or an altered state of consciousness. This experience may seem very profound, especially if you have never experienced the bliss of your being through meditation. Someone else's energy might help you have a momentary experience of bliss, but ultimately it is always your readiness to surrender that determines if shaktipat will work.

Through shaktipat, the other person's energy momentarily pierces through your ego-mind. This may give you a glimpse of no-mind, but it is not enlightenment. If you remain identified with the experience and begin to brag about it, you will only be feeding your ego-mind, or someone else's ego-mind, and doing yourself and them a great disservice.

Enlightenment cannot be given or bought. Enlightenment is a gift that only comes through the grace of existence when you are ripe and ready to fully surrender your ego-mind and remember who you truly are. To remember who you truly are, you need to be prepared to die as an ego. You can only prepare yourself to experience enlightenment through your own hard work of introspection, meditation, and self-awareness. To me, an experience of "enlightenment" through shaktipat is not much different from the experience that drugs can also offer. Both experiences depend on outside influence and can feed your ego-mind even more and stunt your spiritual development. Remember, every experience is just an experience. What remains in the end is only your memory of the past experience as you continue to experience what is in the next Here and Now.

Osho also used shaktipat, and as a result, thousands of people experienced bliss and altered states of consciousness. Eventually he stopped doing it because he felt that shaktipat robbed people of the thrill of finding the experience of bliss on their own. He discovered that shaktipat created dependency and took away people's dignity, which eventually lead to resentment.

Energy transmittance also happens indirectly as a result of any kind of energy healing work such as Reiki or massage. During my healing sessions, people have profound experiences as a result of energy rushing through their body when they release their suppressed thoughts and emotions from the body. They feel their energy and consciousness expand beyond their body limits, or at times even have an experience of no-mind – inner nothingness and oneness with the universe.

I know that their experience and awareness are extremely valuable and are a big step in their spiritual work, but I also know the dangers of me giving them the idea that they are now enlightened. Though they may have experienced an altered state of consciousness, if I make a big deal about it, their ego-mind will immediately jump on it and eventually make them suffer even more. Both Gurdjieff and Osho have said that if there are two hundred enlightened people on the planet at one time, the collective unconsciousness of humanity will be transformed. Why only two hundred people? Because preparing oneself for enlightenment and ultimate death of the ego-mind is one of the most arduous tasks possible.

Enlightenment requires one to fully and fearlessly delve into the dark night of their soul and completely surrender their mind. This requires tremendous courage, honesty, commitment, and trust. One has to work hard to face and break through the fears of the abysmal darkness of the unconscious and the unknown. Only those beings who have suffered the darkness of their ego long enough will be willing to surrender it unconditionally.

It took the Buddha many years of focused effort searching, meditating, and practicing austerities to be ready to receive the gift of enlightenment. His efforts not only rewarded him with the Joy of his personal liberation but also transformed his heart into a powerhouse of compassion that helped, and continues to help, many others on their journey.

I can understand how "transmitted" or "instant enlightenment" may appeal to the ego-mind, which thrives on needing fast results. If someone could package enlightenment in a bottle and advertise it on TV, the business of enlightenment would be most lucrative. My advice is: never sell your soul to buy enlightenment from anyone if you truly want to find it.

*I try to be aware of and watch my mind, emotions and attachments, but I feel unable to see the way out of my illusion. I feel frustrated. How do I come out of this frustration?*

To see the illusion that your thoughts and emotions create, your awareness needs to be fully grounded and present in your entire body. If your awareness is not fully in your body, you cannot know yourself or be present to your own reality. Through my work with hundreds of people,

I have come to discover that most people's awareness floats above their knees. They walk without any awareness of their feet touching the earth.

Your feet connect you with the earth. If you are not even aware of your own feet, how can you be aware of who you are? To know yourself you need to be fully grounded in your body. If your awareness is not in your body, your attempt to break through the suppressed thoughts and emotions, attachments and survival instinct will be futile because they will still be coming from the mind, which creates the suppressions and attachments in the first place.

To break through your emotions and attachments, you need to be conscious of your whole body, including your feet. By bringing your awareness into your feet, you will be more present in the Now and can break through your mind's attachments much more easily. Without becoming fully aware of your body you will continue to be frustrated. To increase your body awareness, practice bringing your breath and awareness into your body and feel the ground under your feet. Do this as often as possible. Over time, this will strengthen your inner observer and help you feel more present and grounded.

*Do we have so many suppressed thoughts and emotions because social rules don't allow us to do what we need and want?*

This is a complex question. On one hand, we need society and its rules if we are to live together as a group and learn from one another. On the other hand, these rules prevent our individual consciousness from growing and evolving higher than the collective consciousness of the group. Society needs rules because without rules there would be chaos. Everyone brings their level of consciousness and behavior patterns into the group. Some behaviors can be harmful and some beneficial to the members of the group. Each individual needs to be protected from the harmful behavior of others.

Society can only function within the law of averages, based on the level of average collective consciousness. When any person's individual consciousness moves lower or higher than the group's average consciousness, the group feels threatened. Society then needs to suppress the individual to protect its rules and maintain its law and order. If the individual's consciousness is below the average collective consciousness, and he physically harms any of its members, he is incarcerated or executed. If the individual's consciousness is above the average collective consciousness, and he tries to bring the collective consciousness higher than the average, then he too may be incarcerated or assassinated. Either way, society does not and cannot support the individual. Until the number of individuals who function at a higher level of consciousness increases, the collective consciousness cannot change and evolve.

The way the group consciousness suppresses and controls individuals is by judging them and creating doubt and guilt in their minds. If you watch closely, this is also what you do with others when you want to control them and bring them down to your level. When someone's consciousness moves higher than yours, or if someone is happier or wealthier than you, you criticize, find fault, and try to manipulate and condemn them. By doing so, you unconsciously also suppress your own possibility of growth and happiness.

To break out of the social law of averages and live your unique individuality, you need to face your selfishness and insecurities. All societies have evolved because of a few individuals who have been strong enough and have cared enough to fearlessly express their individual truth. These individuals have fought for truth, justice, and the greater good of all. They have courageously staked their own lives to help others and have become the social pillars helping to move the collective to a higher level of consciousness.

*But didn't you say that society also helps us learn and transform our unconsciousness?*

A social group is made of individual members. All members of the group individually and collectively provide the background for us to see and recognize our own strengths and weaknesses. Each member of the collective, on many levels, mirrors what is happening inside ourselves and gives us many opportunities to see what needs to change and transform inside our own unconscious.

So in a way, the group forces each individual to recognize that he has either fallen below or has risen above the average collective consciousness. Seeing himself through many mirrors (social, religious, political, and other people) the individual develops self-awareness, intelligence, personal strength, and wisdom. Once you are clear that you don't want to follow the collective but want to sing your own song, you won't need to struggle with or rebel against society, but use what it offers without becoming a slave to it. Only your own consciousness can help you become a positive and creative force that can benefit not only yourself but also the members of the society in their own process of evolution to higher consciousness.

*I feel I am rebelling against something, but I don't know what it is. Sometimes people react back and I feel insecure and confused.*

Many people confuse reaction with rebellion. There is a big difference between rebelling and reacting. Reaction arises out of fear, insecurity, and unconsciousness, and rebellion arises out of courage, strength, and consciousness. You can only rebel when you know yourself and have an understanding of what you are rebelling against. When you truly rebel, you feel clear and confident inside and have no need to force or impose your ideas upon anyone. You simply stand for what's true for you and give people total freedom to be themselves. If you have been obeying others and compromising yourself, you will sooner or later react. When you rebel, you don't suppress anything but voice your opinions freely, without needing anyone to agree with you. In rebellion, you always take full responsibility for the consequences of your choices and actions.

I've often come across people who react but think they are rebelling. If you feel confused when people react to your "rebellion," then you are not really rebelling. A true rebel sees the other person's reaction clearly, understands where it comes from, and is not disturbed by it. We also often confuse rebellion with stubbornness. Very often people stubbornly pursue their desires and justify their ego-mind by calling it rebellion. When you insist that your way is the only right way, you are not rebelling, you are simply reacting and being selfish. When you react with stubbornness, you manipulate and criticize others and try to impose your will and power over them. When you react, deep down you remain insecure and as a result need to control and dominate others or blame and judge them to protect your own feelings of insecurity.

To be a rebel, you need to act from your inner truth and take full responsibility for how you feel and what you say and do, regardless of how people receive it. To be a rebel you need to act out of consciousness, not out of your ego-mind.

*I feel like everything about me is a lie. I feel guilty about pretending to be somebody I am not. I hate myself for being phony and I can't forgive myself. I am scared to show my beauty and share my gifts with the world. Can you offer me some guidance?*

You are not the only one who feels this way. Society, organized religions, and those with vested interests have conditioned us to feel guilty for loving and appreciating ourselves and the beauty of our being. They have made us believe that it is egotistical to love oneself. This is how we are all controlled. We are all victims of the same collective mass hypnosis.

You need to break out of this unconscious belief that there is something wrong with you the way you are. You have been brainwashed to believe that if you love and respect yourself then there is something wrong with you. Your fear forces you to compromise and makes you phony. When you become conscious of your phoniness, you feel guilty. It is your responsibility to strengthen your awareness of yourself and remind yourself that no one can know you better than you know yourself. When you truly see your uniqueness and inner beauty, you will

also see the beauty and uniqueness within others and will not feel insecure or need to compete with them. Look inside, see your beauty, and
acknowledge to yourself and others that you are beautiful. Let go of the
belief that says otherwise.

Your courage in declaring your inner beauty will bring you closer
to your childlike innocence and will help to open your heart to yourself
and others. The moment you see and acknowledge your beauty and
other people's beauty without fear or competitiveness, your perception
of yourself and the world will change and you'll have more courage to
delve into the darkness of your unconscious. When you feel that you
don't need to suppress and hide either your beauty or your ugliness,
you conquer your ego-mind.

*Why can't I remember my past lives?*

Existence and your own higher self in their wisdom will not allow you
to remember your past lives until your witnessing awareness is strong
enough to remember them. If you start remembering your past lives
prematurely, you may become frightened and confused. Remembering
past lives before you have enough consciousness to understand and disidentify from them is like making a child who has not yet learned to
read, study a university text. First, the child needs to learn the alphabet,
then he needs to learn to read and develop his mind before he can comprehend a more complex document.

Before you can remember your past lives, you need to cultivate
your witnessing awareness and know what to do with the memories
when they surface. Witnessing awareness is necessary so you don't get
identified with the story that you see. If you become identified with
your past life memories and emotions on top of what you are struggling through in this life, you may become even more disturbed and
confused.

Remembering past lives is a necessary part of our spiritual development. However, we don't need to remember them to be entertained

by them. We need to remember them to understand the unconscious behavior patterns we are still repeating in this life.

You will be ready to remember your past lives when you can look into the darkness of your unconscious, observe what you see from a distance, understand the lessons it contains, and let go of any attachment to the memory and the experience.

*One interesting thing about the words you've spoken is their clarity, lightness, and simplicity. I don't feel I need to hang on to them. It's almost as if I can't remember anything you said.*

That's exactly what I mean when I say listen with your being. Even if you don't remember a single word I've said, something inside you gets the message.

# PART II

# 8 ONE SPIRIT'S JOURNEY

*"A man goes to sleep in the town where he has always lived, and he dreams he's living in another town. In the dream, he doesn't remember the town he is sleeping in his bed in. He believes the reality of the dream town ...*

*The world is that kind of sleep. The dust of many crumbled cities settles over us like a forgetful doze, but we are older than those cities. We began as a mineral. We emerged into plant life and into the animal state, and then into being human, and always we have forgotten our former states ...*

*Humankind is being led along an evolving course, through this migration of intelligences, and though we seem to be sleeping, there is an inner wakefulness that directs the dream, and that will eventually startle us back to the truth of who we are."*

—Rumi, translated by Coleman Barks

My purpose in writing this chapter is to give you a practical, down-to-earth example of how the concepts covered in this book manifested along my own journey. By sharing the story of my own path I hope to encourage you to delve deeper into yourself and examine your own life's path. There, you will find the thread that leads to your original face – the magnificent and miraculous eternal presence of your True Self.

## ONCE UPON A TIME

I was a black panther. There were many other animals living in the jungle with me, but I felt solitary and enjoyed my aloneness. I roamed in the jungle at night and rested high in the treetops during the day, watching the jungle life below me. There were no limits to my territory, and every tree was my home. I kept myself, and my strength, hidden.

@

I was a wolf. I remember catching my prey. Each time I sank my teeth into it and tore its flesh I felt love towards the animal that had given me its body so I could live.

@

I was a dolphin. I loved the ocean and its creatures. I felt free and one with the ocean. My moods mirrored the moods of the ocean. I jumped and played with the waves and my dolphin friends without a care in the world. The mighty whales were my guides and teachers. The ocean was my home.

@

I was an ape. One day I stood upright and suddenly saw the world all around me—a world I'd never seen before. It was magical. I felt in awe seeing the sun rays shining through the mighty trees surrounding the meadow. I was in wonder, and this planet was my home.

I was a Samurai general. I was loyal and passionate about the cause I was fighting for, and I was prepared to die for it. I demanded equal loyalty from others. Some people loved me and others feared me. I led my armies to victory after victory and felt invincible. Although many lives were lost in battles, I believed the deaths were justified by the cause they served.

Then, a woman came into my life. I fell deeply in love with her. I was prepared to do anything to win her heart, but no matter what I did she did not return my affection. I could not conquer her heart the way I won battles. With all the glory of worldly victory, for the first time I suffered the pain of rejection and loss and felt unfulfilled and empty.

She was a widow and had a son who was a rebellious and defiant young man. I intuitively knew that when he grew older he would one day overthrow me and have me killed. I knew that I should have him killed before he could kill me, but I spared him. I could not kill the son of the woman I loved, even if it meant losing my own life. I knew that killing him would make me nothing more than a murderer, and I would have dishonored myself. He grew older and stronger, and the day came when he did overthrow me. I was put on trial, humiliated, and sentenced to death.

I saw that no one cared if I died. Looking back at my life, I realized how unconscious I had been, and how many people had suffered because I had blindly followed an ideology instead of my heart. It was agonizing to see my ignorance. I felt deep sorrow for all the lives that had been cut short because of my unconsciousness. I saw the meaninglessness of my life's pursuit of power, and I vowed to never follow any ideology or be in a position of leadership again because I had realized that all ideologies were against life and true happiness. Before dying, I made a decision to come back and pay back my dues by helping the people I had hurt, though I had no idea how and what I could do for them.

As the day of my execution approached I welcomed my death, knowing that it would liberate me from the pain of my conscience. I asked for forgiveness but I knew it would not be enough to wash away all the blood that was spilled because of me. On the day of my execution, I was surprised to see that the woman I had loved was the only person who seemed to care about me. She cried at my execution. As I left my body I decided to search for the truth that transcends all ideologies and surpasses life and death.

I was a scholar living in an astronomical observatory high up in the mountains of China. A great wall was being built to protect us from the Mongols. I wanted to discover the meaning of life, and I thought I could do this by studying the stars. I was not interested in power, possessions, or worldly pleasures and enjoyed the quiet serenity of the mountains and the simplicity of my life. As I explored the mysteries of the universe, my life felt full of meaning. My days were abundant with wonder and excitement while studying the stars and the magical vastness of the cosmos. I enjoyed my solitary life. In fact, I felt relief at being undisturbed by social obligations and relationships.

Every now and then, I would go down to the village to fetch food or clothes, and I would think to myself that people were wasting their lives in futile worldly activities. In the village, there were many young girls interested in marrying me, for I was a tall, handsome, and charismatic young man. But I wasn't interested in any of them. I was convinced that an ordinary life of marriage, family, and earning a living was not for me and would in fact prevent my search for truth.

One girl was especially persistent in her pursuit of me. She came to the observatory one day with a basket of food and invited me to share it with her. We walked in the mountains and found a beautiful field of flowers where we sat for two hours, enjoying our lunch and the beauty of nature all around us. My mind stopped, and my search for truth completely disappeared for those two hours. I remember feeling present in a way that I had never felt before. I was empty of thoughts and felt very peaceful and at one with everything around me. I had nothing to observe or study. I had only to be there: alive, present, and enjoying myself, my female companion, and the serene nature surrounding us. The girl was very beautiful, and I genuinely appreciated her presence. The experience was intoxicating, but after she left I went back to my observatory and resumed my search, with no thought of pursuing a relationship with her.

I spent the rest of my life alone, studying the stars, but I never forgot those beautiful moments with that young woman. I was convinced I had made the right decision by pursuing my search for truth. It was only at the time of my death that I saw my ignorance. As my whole life flashed before my eyes, what I saw shook me to the core. I realized that I had wasted my whole life except for those two hours I had spent being fully present in the Now. I realized how wrong I had been in trying to find the meaning of life outside of what was in the present. I saw that those two hours were the only time I had truly known and lived the truth I'd been searching to find in the stars. In that instant, I understood that truth could never be known outside of myself, but only through living fully and spontaneously in the present.

I was a wife of an Indian chief. I spent most of my time working in the field, cooking, cleaning, and looking after my children. My husband liked to sit in the teepee, smoking his pipe, contemplating the spirit world and the meaning of life. He thought his search for truth was all that mattered, but I felt he was wasting his time trying to find it through contemplation. I tried to tell him that only ordinary living embodied the truth he was searching for but he would not listen. Sometimes I would say something to him about it, but he would stubbornly ignore me thinking I couldn't possibly understand his quest. In spite of this, I felt his love for me and respected his wisdom and understanding of life, and continued to serve him. The daily physical work exhausted me, but the love between us nourished me to carry on.

I was a wealthy man living in India. I had everything I could want or need, including many servants who took care of all my needs, but somehow my life felt empty and meaningless. One day I heard about a teacher they called the Buddha who was coming to visit my town. I went to see him and was instantly drawn to him. I felt his wisdom and compassion and intuitively recognized that he knew the truth and could help me find it for myself. I gave up my wealth and status and became one of his disciples. I loved the Buddha with my heart and being, and enjoyed being in his presence, but I struggled with having to beg for my food. When I chose to renounce my privileged life, I didn't realize that I would feel so humiliated begging for my daily meal. I hated begging so much that I finally left the life of a monk. I became a fisherman. I thought, "Buddha is in my heart. I can still follow his teachings, meditate, and live a simple life earning my living, but without having to beg."

Many years later, I heard that the Buddha had died. I took my little boat out into the lake and, sitting in the middle of the lake, cried with a deep sense of sorrow and loss. Here I was, surrounded by the incredible beauty and serenity of nature that I had loved and cherished above anything else, but the beauty of the lake, the trees, and the sky were nothing compared to the beauty of the Buddha. I grieved deeply that I had missed an exceptionally precious and once-in-many-lifetimes opportunity to be with such an extraordinary man like the Buddha, and all because of a small thing that my ego didn't want to surrender to. In that agonizing moment, I suddenly heard

Buddha's loving and compassionate voice next to my ear whispering: "charaiveti, charaiveti" (go on with your journey, go on with your journey). I realized that although I had physically left him, he had never left me and had been with me all these years. I knew then, that in his boundless wisdom, he had always known that I would not be able to stay with him and adapt to a monk's lifestyle. In spite of this he had still welcomed me, and even in his death helped to transform my pain into hope. Tears welled up in my eyes and my heart melted as I surrendered my being to his feet in eternal gratitude.

I was a Sufi dervish. I chose the path of love and surrender and sought a way to abandon my ego and find God, the Beloved. I tried to enjoy everything that life could offer me and live it fully. I reveled in my senses and the small pleasures of the ordinary world. I whirled, danced, and celebrated the richness of life and the heart. I was devoted to my master and never wanted to leave his sight. To me, he was the door to the divine. But my master, trying to break my attachment to him, decided to send me with a few other disciples on a journey across the desert.

I did not want to leave him and went reluctantly for I sensed it could be my last trip. I was afraid I would never see him again and that he would not be there to help me if I was to die. I knew the trip would be dangerous, and there was no guarantee that I would survive because the desert always hungrily devoured humans and animals. I intuitively knew that my master was testing my trust and trying to teach me acceptance and surrender. And even before he sent me away he already knew that this might be the last journey – of either my ego or my body.

Regardless of my inner knowing, I still struggled and resisted the journey instead of enjoying and surrendering into its mystery. I had difficulty trusting that my master would be there to help me. Several weeks later, I died as I felt I would. I remember the moment of my death vividly. It came as a sudden opening into the unknown. I hesitated, and

235

a moment later realized I could have been liberated from my ego had I trusted and surrendered to the unknown. I saw myself missing the precious moment of death and a possibility of awakening because of my mistrust and fear that I could not awaken on my own, without the help of my master. After leaving my body, I realized that he was there with me all along but the choice and responsibility to surrender was mine.

I was a monk in Tibet. I wanted to learn how to die consciously. The Tibetan masters understood the mystery of death and dying and were able to help people in their transition from one life to next. They called this transition the "bardo."

The snow-covered mountains isolated the monastery from the rest of the world. It was cold and physically challenging most of the year. Although in my heart I embraced the people, the wisdom, and the teachings, I struggled with the harsh weather. I felt deprived of the enjoyment of the senses: food, music, dancing, intimate relationships, daily bathing, the warmth of summer, and the green of the trees. I struggled with the rigorous demands of the practice and the long winters. I couldn't leave the monastery, yet at the same time I felt unable to surrender to its lifestyle.

It was customary for monks to often fast and meditate for twenty-one days in order to purify themselves. All we were given each day was water and a little piece of bread. During one such twenty-one-day fast, I felt extremely depressed. I thought my Rinpoche (teacher) was unaware of my difficulties and cared little about my suffering. I felt desperate and trapped. Death seemed the only way out of my misery. In my hopelessness and despair, on the seventh day of my fast, I jumped off a cliff and died.

It was only after I had left my body that I saw what my Rinpoche (Lama Karmapa) was trying to teach me. I watched an assembly of monks gather around him to hear what he had to say about my suicide.

It was like seeing him for the first time. Behind his detached appearance was a being of immense love and compassion. I saw my ignorance and how I had identified with my misery instead of simply observing my resistance with detachment and acceptance. He sat with the monks in silence for a while, then addressed one of them, saying: "Make sure you bring this monk back into the fold."

## ANOTHER OPPORTUNITY TO AWAKEN

It was now 1952. I delighted in the paradise of my mother's womb, a place where I could just be, without any fear or worry. I simply existed in bliss and a state of total surrender. Everything I needed was provided for and taken care of, without me needing to do anything. Suddenly, I felt a powerful and mysterious force pushing me out of the womb. At first I resisted it. I didn't want to leave the paradise I was in. But in spite of my best efforts, the force kept pushing me out. I finally realized I was powerless against it and gave up struggling. A memory of the Earth and its beauty suddenly came to my mind. I thought with excitement of once again seeing the vast blue sky, feeling the warmth of the Sun, and hearing the breeze in the trees. I surrendered, and I was born into this life.

I remember lying in a crib surrounded by many other cribs with babies lying in them. Some of them were quiet, others were crying. The only thing that seemed to distinguish us from each other were the names our parents had given us. Mine was Eliza.

The large hospital room we were all packed into never seemed to go to sleep. Bright fluorescent lights shone above us day and night. I cried and cried, desperately trying to tell the nurses that the lights were disturbing me, and that it was impossible to sleep. But no one understood my cries. In helplessness, I gave up and stopped crying. I concluded that people were unconscious, uncaring, and insensitive.

For twenty-four years, I lived in Yerevan, the capital city of former Soviet Armenia. It spread along a valley below the mysterious and majestic Mt. Ararat where, according to the Bible, the legendary Noah's ark rests. My parents, both of Armenian descent, had immigrated to Armenia in 1946 after the Second World War. My father was born in 1915 in what is now part of Turkey, and my mother was born in Athens, Greece, in 1930. It was an arranged marriage, and even though they were both kind people with an air of innocence about them, it was not a good match. My father was conservative and my mother liberal and free-spirited.

I was nine months old when I started to walk. I refused to have anyone hold my hand and learned walking by going back and forth holding on to the sofa.

When I was five, I saw my maternal grandfather die. He was struggling with cancer and was in pain. I saw him grab the bottle of morphine he used to use to help him ease his pain and start to drink from it while my mother and aunt tried to take it away from him. When he was done drinking he lay on his bed and became calm. Shortly after, he stopped breathing and died.

I lay awake that night feeling his presence in my room. I was afraid. Thinking of his motionless dead body, I realized that one day I too would die, and that the world would keep on going after my death just as it did after my grandfather's death. The sun would continue shining, trees would continue growing, and people all around the world would continue living their lives, regardless of whether I was here or not. I thought it was useless to fear death because just as it had happened to my grandfather, one day it was going to happen to me too. This realization made me wonder: *Who am I? Why am I here? Where have I come from? Where will I go when I die?*

Somehow, I knew I had died before and yet was still here. I understood that everything is temporary, including my own body. I thought that death could never separate me from myself, even though it would separate me from my body and the outside world. I relaxed and my fear of death subsided.

Although this experience profoundly changed my perspective on life, at the same time it estranged me from others who lived fearing death. I could no longer sympathize with those who mourned the dead because I knew that death was not the end, and it was better to live life fully instead of uselessly worrying about death.

I felt alone. There was no one who could understand me. Even though I felt things deeply, some people judged me as odd, saying I had no feelings. I gradually learned to remain detached and to simply watch what I was feeling.

※

The happiest times of my childhood were those I spent with my paternal grandmother. She always allowed me to explore whatever I was curious about and never scolded me for anything I did. In her presence I felt loved, accepted, nurtured, and free.

One night, when I was six, I was sleeping in her room and saw her sitting on her bed praying before she went to sleep. Although I couldn't hear what she was whispering, I thought that she was praying to some invisible person she called God. (Growing up in Soviet Armenia I had never seen my grandmother or my parents go to church. Religion was considered a poison to the people and those who had come from abroad after the war feared going to church and exposing their beliefs.) The next day I teased her and ran around our long dining room table shouting: "There is no God! Where is God? If there is a God, show him to me!" She playfully chased me around the table, got hold of me, tightly held my arms in her ancient wrinkled hands, and looking straight into my eyes said: "God is within you. God is within every human being. God is within every animal and tree and in everything you see all around you."

I became silent. Deep inside, I knew my grandmother had given me an answer that I could not dispute. I felt respect for her wisdom in considering me, a small child, mature and worthy enough to receive such an explanation. From that day on, I never teased her again and enjoyed spending as much time as I could with her.

When I was three my parents had their second daughter, whom I was excited about and loved to play with. When my sister was three and I was six, my parents who had been unhappy together for as long as I could remember, finally separated. My father asked me to choose whom I wanted to live with, but in spite of my wish to live with my mother, I was left in his care. My sister, however, went to live with my mother. My grandmother moved in with us to take care of me. She had already raised nine children of her own: three who had died in early childhood; three married daughters, two of whom lived in the U.S. and one in Lebanon; and three sons, with whom she had immigrated to Armenia. She had been living with her middle son one floor below us in the triplex my father had built for his two brothers and himself.

My father was very angry with my mother for leaving him for a younger man, so he would not allow her to see me. He also did not want to see my sister, thinking she was not his child.

A year later, I was of age to start school. My father, not able to decide for himself, asked me whether I wanted to go to Armenian or Russian school. This time he honored my wishes and allowed me to go to a Russian school. He seemed to always be concerned about what might happen to me if I was given too much freedom and often held me back from doing what I really wanted to do. He flatly refused to let me study ballet or to play on the school basketball team, and decided that I should take piano lessons instead. Even though as a youngster I felt my father's good wishes and his adoration of me, I could also feel his disappointment that I was not a boy. He thought that as a girl I could not be of much help to him, so he ignored my education and let me figure out what to do with it on my own.

My father remarried shortly after I started school, and my stepmother moved in. Like his marriage to my mother, this was an arranged marriage to a much younger woman. My grandmother lived with us for two years until my second brother was born. She not only took care of me and sheltered me from the dark side of my stepmother's personality but also cooked and washed for the whole family. When she was around seventy-seven or seventy-eight years old and could no longer help around the house, she went to live with one of my uncles who was married but had no children.

I was nine when my stepmother took full control of my life. She forced me to do all the housework that my grandmother had been doing while living with us. With the exception of cooking, I became the Cinderella who had to do all the household chores my grandmother once did: wash the dishes, clean the house, do the laundry, and look after my two younger brothers. When I turned twelve, I also had to do the grocery shopping for the family. It was exhausting. I was not allowed to rest until all my chores were done. In addition to these responsibilities, I was also expected to keep up with my schoolwork without any assistance from anyone.

My stepmother didn't teach me how she wanted things done. I had to figure it all out on my own. This was both a blessing and a curse. I had to learn to think for myself and rely on my own intelligence, but I also missed experiencing the playful, carefree childhood I saw my cousins and friends experiencing. At twelve, I had to think and behave like an adult.

I didn't mind doing the work, but no matter how many chores I completed, nothing I did seemed to please my stepmother. She was often angry with me, called me names, beat me frequently, and even threatened to kill me once. If I cried, it provoked her even more, so I learned to hide my tears. When I told my father that I was being beaten, he apologized and said: "What can I do, daughter? It is your fate, as it is mine." I felt hurt that he wouldn't protect me, but I also felt sorry for him and his weakness and never mentioned it again. I felt too embarrassed to tell anyone I was being abused and that my father was unwilling to protect me. I never talked about it, even with my close friends.

As a child I had the ability to intuitively know and hear the real thoughts and emotions behind people's words and actions. I felt my stepmother's jealousy, unhappiness, and frustration, and my father's difficulties with his wives and having me in the middle of them. I knew he cared about me but was unable to show it because of his need to please my stepmother and protect his marriage. Many times I felt like running away, but I knew I couldn't make it on my own. I kept silent in order to survive and developed an armor of cool aloofness that made people see me as cold and unreachable. Inside, however, I felt alone and helpless and would often retreat to my room and cry, thinking of my grandmother. The memory of her unconditional love saved me many times from suicide in my moments of despair. But no matter how bad it got, I never hated my stepmother, and many times even cared for her when she was ill.

When I was sixteen my struggles with my stepmother ended. The last straw came just before I finished high school, when she tried to arrange a marriage between me and a man twice my age. My stepmother could control me as a child, but I was now strong enough to not let her control my future. I wanted to continue my education and go to university, not become somebody's obedient wife. When I said "No," she tried to beat me again, but this time I stood up to her and threatened to hit her back if she hit me again. She knew I meant it and backed off. Soon after, I left my father's house and went to live with my mother and her family who lived in the same city. My father and stepmother tried to make me feel guilty for leaving, but they did not stand in my way.

My new life with my mother, stepfather, and two sisters (my mother had another daughter after she remarried) was completely opposite to my old one. For the first time since my parents' divorce, I had the freedom to do whatever I wanted. I could go to parties, participate in extracurricular activities, invite friends over, and even have a boyfriend. I was no longer responsible for any household chores or looking after my siblings. I had as much time as I needed for my studies. I reveled in my new freedom and felt as though the whole world suddenly opened its arms to embrace me, and I was eager to embrace it back.

The freedom my mother gave me to study fed my incessant hunger for knowledge. Even though I initially wanted to study cybernetics because of my love for math and physics, my mother encouraged me to study English instead and become a teacher like my cousin. To please my mother, I agreed. Three years later, my sister began her studies in architecture. I became fascinated by what she was doing, so I decided to continue with my studies and began to study architecture as well. Altogether I completed seven years of university studies: four years in education, and three years in architecture.

At the age of nineteen I began dating an architecture student in his second year. Soon after I discovered I was pregnant. Though we both had no idea what we were getting into, we decided to get married. Since we had only been together for two months, our relationship had yet to be tested.

I went to visit my grandmother to tell her I was getting married. She was very old by then and had difficulty recognizing people, but she quickly recognized me, asked about my mother and my sister, and lovingly gave her blessings. We sat together holding hands and singing.

It was the last time I saw her. Seven months later, she died. It was on the day and to the hour my daughter was born. For three days after my daughter's birth, she experienced digestion and elimination problems – the same physical condition my grandmother suffered from before dying.

Soon after my daughter's birth, I found myself once again burdened with responsibilities. I had to clean, wash, do dishes, shop for groceries, and study for exams. On top of that, I now had to look after my own daughter and be a wife. My husband helped with cooking and chores, but he was a student himself.

I would be so tired at the end of the day that at night I would collapse from exhaustion. Being sexually available to my husband whenever he wanted was the hardest part of being married. My priorities were my child and my education and I did not experience any sexual desire. He couldn't understand that I simply had no energy or interest, and this lead to many arguments. At times, I felt deeply depressed, even suicidal, but I would quickly come out of it because I literally had no time to stay depressed.

After my husband's graduation, when our daughter was four and I was twenty-four and in my fourth year of architectural studies, we decided to leave Armenia. We had a choice to immigrate either to the United States or to Canada. Not knowing much about the differences between these countries, I intuitively chose Canada because I felt that Canada would be the land of the future. In October 1976 we moved to Montreal, Quebec.

The culture shock of moving to a new country with no job and no money brought our marriage to a crisis point, and a year later we separated. Marriage had only moved me further away from myself, and it was clear to me that married life was not my calling. I was now alone with my daughter and felt a sense of renewed freedom to take back control of my life. Thanks to my architectural training, soon after my divorce I found a job in graphic design and was able to support my daughter and myself. I tried my best to give her the time and attention she needed and deserved, and I felt guilty for not being able to give more.

Even though I was only twenty-five, I began experiencing signs of chronic fatigue that lasted for many years. I often used the strength of my mind and spirit to push myself to accomplish simple tasks. Though this was difficult physically, it was also a blessing in disguise as it often helped me to experience the illusion of the world and reawaken the need to know myself.

# THE SEARCH

I used to take my daughter to Beaver Lake on top of Mount Royal dur-ing the winter months, so she could ice-skate. One day I decided to try it myself, and as I took my first step onto the rink I slid and fell right on my coccyx. An excruciating pain shot up my spine into my head like a bolt of lightening. The pain was so intense that I felt I would go mad if I stayed in my body for one more second. I fainted and lost consciousness. Then, I remember floating in a tunnel. The tunnel was dark but very peaceful. I was floating inside a grayish mass that both contained and supported me. I knew that, although I had no body, I still existed. The feeling was euphoric and blissful. All of a sudden, I felt I was being pulled back into my body. When I opened my eyes, I saw a woman slapping me hard on the cheeks. There were many people gathered all around looking down at me as I lay motionless on the ice. I closed my eyes, and feeling caught between two worlds, tried to hold on to the euphoric blissful state I was experiencing. Though I didn't want to come back, I suddenly remembered that my daughter was there alone, and it kept me from drifting back into the tunnel.

This experience made me pause and look more deeply at my life. The questions I had asked myself when I saw my grandfather die re-emerged: *Who am I? Why am I here? Where have I come from? Where will I go when I die? What is the purpose of my life?* Despite the challenges of being a single mother, I was prepared to do whatever it took to find the answers to these questions.

I knew I needed help, but I didn't know where to look. Soon after I met Lalito, a Russian woman in her late fifties. She was a Second World War survivor who had immigrated to Canada after the war. She became my angel. My daughter and I would spend our weekends at her country house in Rawdon, an hour away from Montreal, every summer for many years. We would go swimming in the nearby lake, walk through the woods, and she would cook us delicious vegetarian meals that I didn't know were possible. I soon became a vegetarian myself. From her extensive library of esoteric literature, I began to read books about reincarnation, life after death, near-death experiences, and the philosophies of different spiritual teachers such as Edgar Cayce, P. D. Ouspensky, Georges Gurdjieff, J. Krishnamurti, Lao Tzu, and the Indian mystic Osho. Reading these books intensified my thirst to find the truth they were pointing at for myself. Lalito also invited me to meditate with her, and I began to experience the bliss of my inner peace and a growing sense that I was back on track. This was the start of a new life.

Reading Osho's books in particular was like drinking from an inexhaustible wellspring of knowledge and wisdom, with every drop fresh and life-quenching. I felt a soothing sense of light radiating from his words. They awakened and confirmed what I had known deep inside but had been unable to express. Through his seven thousand hours of audio and video recordings published as 350 book titles and translated into more than fifty languages, he skillfully and with unparalleled insight brought the fragrance of all the past masters back to life. Hearing him speak on the Buddha's Dhammapada and the Diamond Sutra I felt as if I was sitting in the Buddha's presence once again. When he commented on the sayings of Lao Tzu, Chuang Tzu, Jesus, Pythagoras, Socrates, and other masters, I felt their unique essence and presence beside me, still fresh and very much alive. His talks on the Upanishads and the Indian mystics, the Sufis and Hasids, the Yoga sutras of Patanjali, the Tantric visionaries, and the 112 meditation techniques of Shiva shone a bright new light into my consciousness. And his discourses on the thunder and lightning of Bodhidharma and the Zen masters was like discovering a source of crystal pure waters that was out of this world.

Osho spoke about all the Eastern and Western flowers of human consciousness with such love and depth of understanding that it blew my mind and expanded my consciousness to heights I could not have been able to reach and experience on my own. The education I received from Osho did not exist anywhere else. His insights gave me a greater understanding of spirituality, religion, the world, and myself – that no single religious organization or university in the world could offer. There was no doubt in my mind that he was not only the intellectual giant of this century but also a great master of immense magnitude and compassion. With his curiosity, brilliance, and enlightened genius, he gathered the nectar of all the greatest spiritual teachers and minds this world has ever produced and lovingly offered it to the rising tide of the *novo homo* and the generations to come.

As Osho spoke on all spiritual paths and masters, he emphasized the bringing together of the paths of love (outer devotion) and meditation (inner discipline). He taught that taking one path would lead to the other and, ultimately, to self-realization, but living them together would enrich one's life even more. He taught that a life of devotion without the awareness and discipline of meditation is shallow, and a life of meditation without the heart of devotion is selfish. He also said that this new path would lead to the birth of the New Man whom he called "Zorba the Buddha." A "Zorba," the name of a character from the novel Zorba the Greek by Nikos Kazantzakis, is someone who embraces life and all it has to offer with a joyful heart and celebration, and a Buddha is someone who lives consciously with inner wisdom, awareness, and compassion. In essence, Osho encouraged us to live life fully and consciously without repression, preconceived ideologies, judgments, and conditionings. I found his message rational, radical, and refreshing. I understood that I could never experience unity and wholeness by denying any part of myself.

Not only did Osho teach this new path, he also devised new meditation techniques to help seekers experience the ultimate truth for themselves. The three meditations that I worked with the most and that affected me most deeply were Dynamic, Kundalini, and Nadabrahma active meditations. Practicing them, I quickly noticed an increase of energy in my body, and I felt my ability to witness my mind and emotions strengthen and grow.

The more I meditated and the deeper I went into myself, the more I realized I knew nothing. I felt that, unlike any contemporary teacher available on the planet, Osho was the only person who could help an extremely picky and demanding old seeker like me, find myself. I felt drawn to go to India to see him, but I couldn't afford it. I didn't despair, though, because somehow I intuitively knew he would one day come to North America, and I was not mistaken. Three years later, in 1981, he came to the United States.

In March of 1982, I sent a letter to Osho, asking him to initiate me with a new name to symbolize my commitment to my awakening journey. To describe my soul's potential in this life, he gave me a new name – Jivan Mada. In Sanskrit, Jivan means life and Mada means ecstasy. Soon after, I began my preparations to finally see him in person and fully plunge myself into meditation in his presence. Meditating on my own was good, but it was difficult to stay focused and continue my spiritual growth in a society that did not nourish and support a meditative lifestyle. In July of 1982, I arrived at the Big Muddy Ranch in Oregon, a sixty-five-thousand-acre desert-like ranch where Osho and five thousand of his resident disciples were building a small city for a community of meditators.

X

Upon arrival, everyone had to line up their luggage to be sniffed for drugs and weapons by specially trained dogs. Drugs were forbidden within the community and, because of death threats against Osho, security was stringent. In spite of these formalities everyone was warm and welcoming, and they made every possible effort to make all visitors comfortable. After passing through security, we were taken to our shared accommodations – large tents set up on wooden platforms. On each sleeping bag there was a handwritten note welcoming us.

Scattered throughout the ranch there were many one- or two-room A-frame cabins built into the mountainous landscape, several townhouses accommodating the residents, a small hotel, a mall with restaurants, a bookstore, and an ice-cream parlor, which seemed very popular during the hot summer months.

Not only did I feel welcomed by the people, but the desert landscape of the Oregon hills reminded me of my home in Armenia. During the day, the temperature would reach 113°F, but at night, it would drastically cool down to 50°F. The land was dry and barren, yet alive with an invisible undercurrent of life that fed the scattered all around juniper trees. The air was fresh and pungent with the fragrance of dried grass, and the sky seemed so close that at night I felt I could almost touch the stars. Deer and coyotes were also frequent visitors at night and during the early hours of sunrise: the deer looked for anything green to munch on and the coyotes searched for the abundant population of mice and water rats. There were also migrating Canada Geese that began to congregate around the small ponds created by the residents, which were beautifully landscaped and scattered along the streams passing through the ranch. In spite of the nearly twenty thousand festive people present all around, I also felt the profound stillness and silence surrounding the hills.

The next day, I saw Osho in person for the first time during one of his famous drive-by greetings. I was full of expectation that something miraculous was going to happen, and I had my eyes closed in anticipation. When I felt his car next to me, I opened my eyes, not realizing that he had already greeted me and was on to the next person. I was disappointed that I had missed looking into his eyes, and I lay down on the dry grass feeling deflated. When I closed my eyes, I suddenly saw a ball of bright light with his smiling face in the middle of it looking down at me and saying: "Don't be so serious. Enjoy, celebrate." Instantaneously I saw how serious I had been, and an uncontrollable laughter welled-up from deep inside my belly. I could not stop laughing and a profound sense of lightness and joy permeated my entire body.

I saw Osho again the following morning at a large assembly of seekers gathered in the biggest structure on the grounds called the "Buddha Hall," which accommodated close to twenty thousand visitors during the festivals organized four times a year. I woke up at 5:00 a.m. in anticipation of the morning meeting and saw that some people were already lining up in front of the Buddha Hall. Osho arrived at 8:00 a.m. While we sat in silent meditation with him and he looked at me (I was close enough to see his eyes), I began to cry for no apparent reason. I cried for the entire two hours he sat with us in silent meditation. I felt his unconditional love and acceptance washing away the centuries of old pain and suffering I'd accumulated living on this planet. Through the tears I also felt a deep knowing inside that I had known him before. It seemed that somehow he had called me back to my path.

There was a lot to explore at the ranch after the morning meditation. On several occasions I volunteered to help at a huge organic farm that grew a variety of vegetables and salads to feed the residents and visitors, or worked at a state-of-the-art greenhouse where everything was impeccably neat and clean. While recycling was not yet a common practice in North America, most everything at the ranch was being recycled, including leftover food, which went to feed the cows and chickens that produced milk and eggs as a source of protein to complement the community's vegetarian diet. I also took time to enjoy swimming in a man-made lake called Krishnamurti Lake, a popular spot in the summer months where we could swim or paddle a boat. My first visit to the ranch lasted a month. It was a magical time filled with friendship, dance, and celebration. I had never before seen a gathering of so many intelligent, loving, and happy people.

When I returned to Montreal and looked around my beautiful apartment on Forest Hill, my life seemed empty and meaningless in comparison to what I had experienced at the ranch. I missed the fullness of living in Osho's presence and the "Buddha-field" of seekers from around the world. I wanted nothing more than to return to the ranch and live there full time, but my daughter was still young and in school. I continued reading Osho's books, listening to his taped discourses, and kept on meditating.

One afternoon, during the Kundalini meditation, I observed in wonder as my body started to move on its own with no effort on my part. As the movements continued, I saw my body, thoughts, and emotions literally evaporate into nothingness. Instead of the body, there was only emptiness and consciousness of the emptiness. Although I was dancing and moving my body, arms, and legs, all movements were happening within the emptiness and without any effort on my part. I felt no physical sensation or movement. All I was feeling was a sense of "am-ness," within the emptiness. Suddenly, for the first time, I truly understood what Buddha meant when he said that our being is emptiness. While experiencing the emptiness, I also realized that this same emptiness exists within everyone and everything in this world and the entire universe.

Although the intensity of the experience gradually dissipated, the awareness I gained from it never left me. I did not think that this was the end of my search or that I had become enlightened. In fact, it felt like my real search had just begun.

I continued with my meditation and spiritual work while simultaneously working and raising my daughter. Two and half years later, existence gave me another opportunity to return to the ranch and continue my spiritual work in Osho's presence.

My daughter was now twelve and a half years old and decided to live with her father. I could feel her sadness about growing up without a father and her longing for the kind of attention I was unable to give her. Though it was difficult to let her go, I had to respect her wishes. I gave up my apartment, all my possessions, and returned to the ranch.

I arrived at the ranch in March 1985. Osho had come out of a three-year silence and had begun giving daily talks again at his residence. The talks were videotaped and shown every evening in the Buddha Hall. I was always eager to hear him speak because I never knew what new insights he would spontaneously share each day. Listening to him was a meditation. Most of the time I wouldn't even listen to his words but only relate to their meaning. Although Osho never worked with me directly, by simply living his own life's purpose he was helping me to find mine. I knew that the only way to find myself was to do my own work.

To further my understanding of myself, I enrolled in a three-month self-healing course called "De-hypnotherapy" facilitated by an American psychologist. In the course, which was from 10:00 a.m. to 4:00 p.m. daily, with a lunch break and Osho's drive-by at 2:00 p.m., we focused on looking at our early childhood conditionings and healing our childhood wounds. We also explored how our beliefs and past-life patterns were influencing our current lives and how we could break free from them. Alongside the course, I also continued practicing the Dynamic and Kundalini meditations every day. I would start my day with the Dynamic meditation at 6:00 a.m. and end it after Osho's discourse at 9:00 or 10:00 p.m.

After completing the course, I decided to enroll in a three-month volunteer work program. To be accepted and to participate in this program we had to pay a monthly fee for room and board and work eight hours a day, seven days a week. The atmosphere was very relaxed and festive, and it hardly felt like "work." There were half-hour tea breaks twice a day with delicious baked treats and fruit, which gave us an opportunity to socialize and make friends. After lunch, we would line up for Osho's afternoon drive-by. People would play musical instruments, sing and dance while waiting to see him. Everyone looked happy, and seemed to live spontaneously in the Now without any worry of the future.

I had three different jobs while participating in the work program. My first job was cleaning toilets in the toilet trailers. Hundreds of people used them daily, so they needed to be cleaned twice a day. It was not a glamorous job, but I loved it. I felt like a Zen monk in a monastery, cleaning for my fellow seekers with love and dedication. Alongside my work I also continued with my meditation routine I had created for myself during my De-hypnotherapy course. Between my meditations, work, and the evening discourses my day would start at five in the morning and end at almost eleven at night.

Once in a while, I would also go to the open-air disco at night and enjoy dancing under the stars. Most of the people at the ranch were young, and with so many vibrant and available individuals it was almost impossible to avoid "falling" into a relationship. I generally considered relationships to be a distraction from my path because I thought they required a commitment and compromises that I was not prepared to make. I also did not want anyone to hinder my freedom and interfere with my search. Deep down, I was a monk, focused on my search for enlightenment. I wasn't interested in how I looked or what I was wearing. I was just happy to have clean clothes, enough food to sustain me, and a place to sleep.

As with any group, everyone was functioning at different levels of consciousness, and naturally, not everyone gathered around Osho had the same agenda. There was a sense of competitiveness within the group for his attention and affection.

Although everyone was there because they had embraced Osho and his teachings, I felt there were three kinds of people around him: those who longed for power, those who were looking to be taken care of, and those who cherished their independence and singularly focused on their own transformation. Those who were hungry for power enjoyed controlling others and telling them what to do, while those who were looking to be taken care of would obediently follow their orders and avoid confrontation. Many seemed to be caught up in their spiritual egos and fell into the trap of feeling superior to the rest of the world, thinking that by repeating Osho's words they now knew the truth. To maintain the purity of my being and remain true to my own search, I lived for the most part avoiding the pitfalls of the social hierarchy.

Sometimes I bumped heads with the people in authority when I felt that what they were asking me to do or not do didn't make sense to me. When I would confront them, I was singled out as a troublemaker. The closer I came to myself, the more silent yet more rebellious I felt. Many times I felt like an outsider, as I had in my childhood, but feeling Osho's support for my individuality gave me the opportunity to experience my inner power and stand up for my truth. In spite of the occasional conflicts with those in charge, I never doubted the truth of Osho's teachings, and my love and trust for him only grew stronger.

Although he treated everyone with respect, it was easy to turn against him, as many people did when he didn't fulfill their expectations or exposed their egos. Regardless of whatever conflicts existed within the community, however, Osho's teachings and our love for him kept us united.

In spite of the controversy and accusations created around Osho as a "sex guru" and a "cult leader" who led his followers into "immoral" sexual behavior and encouraged drug use, the reality was far different. Although I and the community felt love and respect for Osho's wisdom and teachings, we didn't worship him as someone who was going to "save" us. Osho never asked to be worshiped, nor did he encourage subservience or following as most religions do. In fact, the very opposite was true; he warned against the dangers of getting attached to him and missing the truth that he was pointing to. Like the Buddha, he reminded us that if we saw him getting in the way of our own path, we should cut his head off immediately, meaning we should let go of our attachment to him and find our own truth.

He also never gave any system of beliefs. On the contrary, he often shocked everyone by shattering our old beliefs and stressing the importance of individuality and self-responsibility. He gave no commandments; rather he emphasized the importance of meditation and introspection above all else. No one was ever forced to be at the ranch. Everyone was always free to come and go as they pleased.

Sadly, Osho was also misunderstood when, in the early seventies, he spoke out against the sexual repressiveness of society and became known as the "sex guru," angering many people in India. He was accused of encouraging sexual perversions, but in fact, here too, the opposite was true. Through his fierce and fiery talks against sexual suppression he was in fact helping people free themselves of their suppressed sexual energy which otherwise might have led to sexual perversions. To help people practically break through their repressions, there were therapeutic Tantric workshops conducted by psychotherapists. The western media heard about these and latched onto the term "sex guru" used by the Indian media. They proceeded to sensationalize and feed the controversy by reporting that there were wild orgies happening in his community.

Although the media was preoccupied with sex, in truth, I actually saw the opposite. I remember once, during lunch, overhearing a visitor at my table say to another: "With all the publicity I'd been hearing, I finally came here to get laid, but no one seems to be interested. Now I have to leave this place in order to get laid." In fact, while the media was ignoring the burgeoning global AIDS epidemic, everyone at the ranch was being tested for HIV and were encouraged to practice safe sex. Osho began encouraging monogamy, or celibacy if one was ready and able.

As far as drugs were concerned, I personally never witnessed any drug use at the ranch. Osho taught that drugs could give only a temporary glimpse of no-mind and, in the long run, would lower the level of the user's consciousness. As I said earlier, drugs were forbidden at the ranch, and everyone had to be searched by drug-sniffing dogs before entering.

Another popular criticism directed against Osho was that he lived extravagantly and materialistically and that he financially exploited his followers. This belief was mainly due to the fact that he had a fleet of ninety-three Rolls-Royces, many expensive watches, and armed body-guards. Did he need all those watches and Rolls-Royces? Perhaps not, but personally I very much enjoyed seeing him drive by in a different Rolls-Royce every day, each painted in such loving and stunningly cre-ative ways that they would evoke a sense of awe and beauty within any viewer. One was decorated with peacocks, another looked as if it was on fire, and yet another was covered with flying swans or fluffy white clouds. If Osho enjoyed driving them, I enjoyed seeing them.

In my opinion all these cars humorously and tastefully exposed our own judgments, attachments, and unfulfilled desires. They did not seem to bother Osho, nor did they bother the rich or those who were enjoying their own lives. Looking beneath the surface, I could see that Osho lived exactly as he taught: to enjoy all the inner and outer riches that this world can offer: *"A new human being is needed on the Earth, a new human being who accepts both, who is scientific and mystic, who is all for matter and all for the spirit. Only then will we be able to create a humanity, which is rich on both sides. I teach you richness: richness of the body, richness of the soul, richness of this world and that world. To me, that is true religiousness."* (Osho, *The Wild Geese and the Water*)

Then, there was the criticism about his armed bodyguards. To me, anyone who has threats or attempts made on their life is in need of protection. For example, I was in Montreal during the Papal visit in 1984 when a ten-million-dollar, bulletproof "Popemobile" was built to protect the Pope from possible assassination. There were also many bodyguards around him, and heavy security everywhere. Thousands of Catholics had flocked to the streets, eager to get a glimpse of the Pope and demonstrate their faith. I'm sure that those present didn't mind seeing their spiritual leader ride in a protected car and wear luxurious clothes and jewelry. It is interesting that people who were so eager to criticize Osho's cars, watches, and bodyguards never noticed such similarities, nor did they criticize or condemn the people who crowded the streets as blind followers. If we truly wish to have peace in this world, we cannot achieve it by judging and criticizing each other's beliefs and differences but by embracing them and perhaps learning from them.

While at the ranch I was unaffected by the negative media coverage, but I did feel its effect on my personal life when I visited my father in California after leaving the ranch. My father, who had initially been open to Osho's views, changed his mind after seeing a tabloid TV program that described Osho as a "sex guru" and his followers as sex maniacs. He gave me an ultimatum to either drop my association with Osho or not come to his house again. I felt hurt that he could not trust me, and instead trusted the media. My choice was clear – I was not going to compromise myself again to appease him.

I attempted to connect with my father again five years later, but he still wouldn't see me. Eventually, I gave up trying. After another ten years, when he was eighty-three years old, I tried again. This time he was open to seeing me. With tears in his eyes, he expressed his deep regret that he had missed all these years that we could have shared together, and he apologized for my childhood suffering. A year later, he died.

## THE AWAKENING

Generally, while on my work program at the ranch, the controversy swirling around Osho and the community did not interest me. I carried on with my work and meditation, knowing there were more depths to explore. I felt as if I was standing on the edge of an abyss that was my unconscious, and I was excited to explore its depth. At times, It was agonising to feel the thin veil that was blocking me from living fully in the truth I had already glimpsed. I had many questions: *Is there anything more profound to experience beyond the emptiness that I had already experienced? What exactly is enlightenment? How is it supposed to feel? How does enlightenment apply to everyday living? Is there any guarantee that I will even experience it? How can I break through the veil? How does one get rid of the mind permanently?*

Even though many times I would hear Osho say that all the answers were inside us, I still felt I didn't really know them. I cried out for my mind to stop and leave me alone. In spite of my confusion, I persisted. I was exhausted and losing weight from my already-thin body, but as per my usual habit, I pushed myself, testing the limits of my physical endurance. I was feeling so light that I couldn't feel the weight of my body any longer. In a way this was freeing, but in another way it became more and more difficult to work physically. The strength of my spirit and my desire to be with Osho kept me going.

I continued meditating, and many times experienced my body becoming completely weightless and my energy expanding beyond its limits. The deeper I went into my center, the more joy and expansion I felt. Many times, I would feel my body dissolving into the empty space all around and I would feel such overwhelming joy that I would prevent myself from expanding any further.

Osho had now begun giving talks in Buddha Hall every morning, and one day during the discourse, he looked at me and said: "You are postponing enlightenment and waiting for the moment of your death to experience it. Why not enjoy it while you are still alive?" His words hit me like a powerful Zen stick. It was true that I had thought this many times. I had convinced myself that I would wait until the moment of my death to experience the enlightenment I was searching for. I realized that this was my excuse for avoiding taking on the responsibility that comes with enlightened consciousness while still alive. I decided to let go of this thought.

Ж

Three weeks later, on a full moon day at the end of July 1985, I got up to go to my regular morning Dynamic meditation. It was still dark outside. The morning chill filled the thin desert air and penetrated deep into my bones. I could see the full moon with thousands of flickering stars scattered all around the dark sky. There was a heightened sense of fullness and grandeur everywhere I looked. It felt magical and surreal standing on the Earth and being surrounded by all the moons, planets, and stars aimlessly floating within the universe.

I slowly made my way to Buddha Hall. Although I was feeling physically and mentally exhausted, I thought to myself, "If my body drops dead, I will not resist. I would welcome death with open arms." I was prepared to surrender everything, including my quest for enlightenment, and say goodbye to the world. There was nothing to hold me back. I had no material possessions to worry about, and no attachment to anyone. I knew that if I were to die, my ex-husband would take care of my daughter and the community would take care of my body.

I don't remember exactly how the first phase of the meditation, the chaotic breathing, started. I remember observing myself breathing. The breathing was happening on its own, without any effort on my part. As the music changed and the second phase began, my body started to shake and vibrate with the music. Waves of energy started moving up from my feet into my head and turning into a radiant white light as they reached my third eye. I was in a state of total let-go, just observing what was happening. Then came an enormous wave, which in a split second illuminated my entire body, transforming it into bright light. It felt as though thousands of suns suddenly arose from inside every cell of my body. The light was blinding but cool. It seemed as if the entire universe with all its suns and solar systems had suddenly jumped into my body. I was literally standing in light! I felt a sense of overwhelming Joy that I can only describe as *Absolute Ecstasy*. The entity that was known to me as the "I" disappeared. With the disappearance of the "I" there came

259

the awareness that the Universe was living and breathing in my body. I suddenly saw that everything within the Universe vibrates with Joy, and this Joy was a by-product of Creation. This Creation was God itself, living and breathing in my body and being, and in everything that exists. I saw that Joy is the source and essence of each and every one of us, and our worldly happiness seemed like a faint light compared to the *Absolute Joy of Creation* that permeates the entire Universe.

I surely would have died and would have not been able to endure the magnitude of experiencing this universal Joy and contain it within my body, if I hadn't practiced centering and grounding my energies for years. I quickly moved my awareness into my center, then into my feet and into the Earth. Just like the Bodhi tree that helped the Buddha anchor his awakening and stay in his body, the Earth helped me to stay in mine.

Uproarious laughter at the ridiculousness of my search for something that was already inside of me welled up as I stood witnessing the ignorance of my small ego-mind. I now clearly saw how my mind had been keeping itself alive by focusing on the goal of attaining enlightenment somewhere *there* and preventing me from knowing the truth of what is already *here* in this moment. I realized that my entire search had been an illusion. I was in the same place where I had always been from the beginning of time. I was looking for enlightenment somewhere outside myself so my mind could remain needed. I finally understood, first-hand, what the mystics throughout the ages had been saying about *the pilgrimage being the goal.* I had finally come home.

Having found what I had been searching for over many lifetimes, left me with nowhere to go and nothing more to look for. I realized that my being and the universe were inseparable. I now knew that the same ecstatic Joy, Light, and Love vibrates within everyone and everything in the universe.

The intensity of the experience faded with time, but the consciousness it evoked permanently remained ingrained deep within my cells. I felt something inside me had radically changed. My inner tension of looking to attain something outside had suddenly dropped. My self-imposed stress of having to get somewhere was no longer there because I had finally understood that existence is an eternal mystery that can never be solved, only lived moment to moment. I had realized that life was simply a series of moments without any goal, and that just living these moments was the goal.

Although this experience had altered my perception of reality, it took time to fully integrate it in my body and my life. Having had the experience did not mean that my life was now over and I had nothing else to learn, so I went on with my life, thinking of it as just another experience. There was one big difference, however. Now I had a sense of peace and wholeness within myself independent of what was happening in my life on the outside. I felt the Joy of my aloneness even stronger. I continued with my usual daily life of "chopping wood and carrying water from the well" as the Zen saying goes, but with a newly heightened awareness.

## THE WORLD

When my work program at the ranch ended at the end of August 1985, I left Oregon to visit friends in northern California. Two weeks later, I heard a news report that Osho's secretary, Sheela, had suddenly left the ranch with an entourage of a dozen or so people. I also heard for the first time that she had been orchestrating crimes against the residents of the nearby city of Antelope, Oregon, as well as against Osho and his community. She was accused of contaminating the salad bars of several nearby restaurants to prevent people from voting in the local election. It was also said that she had attempted to poison Osho's caretaker and personal physician, bugged Osho's room to monitor all of his conversations, and embezzled money from the community. She was arrested and sentenced to five years in prison. Through her unconscious actions, Sheela not only betrayed Osho but also the entire community, helping to further fuel the fire of controversy that surrounded him.

Although Osho himself invited the FBI to come to the ranch and investigate the matter, they eventually accused him and his followers of bio-terrorism so they could then have a reason to destroy him and his community.

On October 28, Osho was arrested without a warrant, handcuffed, and chained. While in jail he felt that he was being poisoned through his food and with radiation. Soon after, his health began to quickly deteriorate and he showed symptoms of Thallium poisoning. He was eventually forced out of the country in mid-November. As the American author Tom Robbins put it: "If crucifixion were still in vogue, of course Osho would've been nailed up. But, since we're civilized, they had to force him into exile instead. I'm sure they would have much preferred to crucify him on the White House lawn."

Some of Osho's followers blamed him for everything that had happened at the ranch. They criticized him for being a failed guru and were disillusioned, disappointed, or just plain angry. They did not realize how dependent they had been, and how much they had expected from Osho and the community without taking responsibility for their own lives.

After his deportation from the U.S., Osho toured the world looking for a new home. Under the influence of the Reagan administration, twenty-one countries rejected him, and eventually he had to return to his native India. Although the Indian government initially received him with hostility, four years after his death they recognized him as one of India's "great sons" and "one of the ten people alongside Gandhi, Nehru and Buddha who have changed the destiny of India." His books are now displayed in the Indian Parliament – an honor shared by very few. Indian newspapers referred to him as someone who helped to "liberate the minds of future generations from the shackles of religiosity and conformism." The *Sunday Times* of India described Osho as one of the 1,000 Makers of the Twentieth Century. Of his teachings it wrote:

"Drawn from a variety of ideologies and religious traditions, but bearing their own stamp, Osho's teachings are uncompromisingly radical, anti-rational, and capricious. They invite the individual to free him or herself from all social conditioning: the only commitment is to be open and honest, to enjoy life, and to love oneself."

X

In September 1986, I visited Osho in Bombay, India, and spent three months there. Six months later, in July of 1987, after he moved from Bombay back to his ashram in Pune, I returned to India and over the next three years, until his death in 1990, I spent most of my time in India with occasional short trips back to Montreal. While at the ashram, I volunteered to work in a number of departments: the Osho Times International newspaper, the kitchen, The Rebel Publishing House (GmbH), and the press office.

Osho had resumed his daily talks, which in the beginning were twice a day: at eight in the morning and seven in the evening. Due to the side effects of the poisoning in the U.S. jail, his health was compromised, forcing him to stop his morning discourses. There were many days when he didn't come out at all. Once, a simple ear infection that would normally take seven days to heal, kept him from speaking for forty-five days.

His final discourses were called *The Zen Manifesto: Freedom from Oneself*. This was his last spoken book. He stopped speaking altogether after this and due to his fading health would only come out in the evening to sit with us for ten minutes in meditation in Buddha Hall. Looking at his frail body, I knew he was living his last days. As he entered and left the hall, he would, as usual, have his hands folded in namaste to greet us and to say goodbye. Every time he looked at me, I would feel a rush of Joy inside my body and would begin to laugh loudly for no reason at all. It often felt as if he was encouraging me to live the Joy I had experienced at the ranch in Oregon.

Two days before he died, he took an extra long time to leave after the evening's meditation. He slowly moved his eyes from person to person, and when our eyes met he silently said goodbye to me. I whispered: "Goodbye, Osho," and in that moment I knew I would not see him alive again.

The next day, to my surprise I heard that he was still alive and would be attending another assembly. He sent out a message that he would be coming only to greet us but would not sit in meditation with us. He also requested that we keep our eyes open. On the night before, many had missed their chance to see him for the last time because, normally, when he would leave the hall, many people would still be sitting in meditation with their eyes closed.

When he came out he could barely stand. He looked as if he was in deep pain. Seeing the depth of his compassion brought tears to my eyes. He had forced himself to stay in his body so everyone could see him for the last time. The following day, we meditated in Buddha Hall without him, and the day after he left his body.

Most people, especially those in the West, never realized how much unnecessary pain he had to endure to help others come out of their unconscious sleep and suffering. Helping others to awaken from their ignorance required a tremendous output of his own life force. It also made him vulnerable to persecution by those who were threatened by the light of his consciousness. Just like the Buddha and Christ, he gave of himself and his own energy, motivated only by his compassion for the suffering of those who were still searching. Not only did he have to contend with the weight of the collective unconscious, but he also felt the continual pain of enduring the confinement in his own body.

Osho asked that his body be displayed in Buddha Hall for ten minutes and then taken to the burning ghats, not too far from the ashram. He also asked that we celebrate his death with music and dance. I walked alongside his body as it was carried on a bamboo stretcher in a procession from the Buddha Hall to the burning ghats.

At the ghats, I saw the last log placed on his funeral pyre covering his face before it would be consumed by fire. While people sang and played music in the background, I sat by the burning pyre feeling grateful that I could be there during his last moments. I felt that the time I had spent in his presence had been the most precious time of my life, for he had brought such light and joy into it. Without his guidance and his new active meditation methods, I would have been still groping in the dark to find myself. Now, without the possibility of sitting with him again, I couldn't even imagine what life could offer me that would be greater than what I had already experienced. I sat by his burning body until the early hours of the morning, and finally went back to my room at around 4 a.m.

Before his death, Osho had distilled his whole life's teaching into the one phrase on his epitaph: *"Never Born, Never Died, only Visited this Planet Earth Between December 11, 1931 and January 19, 1990."* After Osho's death, I and many others in the community continued to feel his presence around the ashram for many days. I felt his Joy and bliss at finally being freed from the limitations of his body and the restrictions of this world. I was deeply happy for him. On the ninth day, I felt his energy begin to lift off from the gravity of the Earth and felt that I had to be more sensitive to stay in tune with it.

For twenty-one days after his death, I felt a constant flow of Joy and bliss inside me. I would simply sit on the low marble wall that curved around the marble pathways of the ashram and would only move when the energy moved me. Everything I needed to do would get done, even though I just sat and did nothing. Those who needed to see me about something would find me wherever I was sitting. When I would move somewhere else, other people who needed to talk to me would be there, and things would get done absolutely effortlessly.

These twenty-one days allowed for all my previous experiences of Joy to settle and integrate more deeply into my psyche and daily life. I saw how my consciousness deepened, grew, and expanded. Each new experience would create a new depth of understanding and wisdom, helping to ground consciousness more deeply within my body.

With Osho gone, I now had to stand entirely on my own and find a new direction for my life. His words, "If you see me on your path, cut off my head immediately" kept resonating in my mind. I knew I had to let go of my attachment to him so I could live my own destiny.

# NEW BEGINNING

Six months after Osho's death I felt it was time to return to Montreal. At first it was not easy being back in the world. The city was busy and noisy, with almost no space for inner silence. My daughter was now seventeen and about to finish high school. She was eager to live with me once again.

After some difficulty in trying to re-adapt to the Western lifestyle, I made a spontaneous decision to seclude myself from the world to fast and meditate. I was going to turn forty in twenty-one days and felt that I needed to gain more clarity for the next phase of my life. For twenty-one days, almost twenty-four hours a day, I meditated. I started at six in the morning with Dynamic meditation, followed by Vipassana meditation (sitting and watching my breath), then Vipassana walking (focusing on the ground two feet in front of me while walking). I did some more Vipassana sitting throughout the day, then Kundalini meditation, followed by more Vipassana. I would end my day with an evening bath and more sitting.

My watchful awareness would carry over through the night and I would remain alert and aware while I was asleep. I would spontaneously wake up again at three in the morning, sit in Vipassana for an hour, and then go back to sleep until six. Physically, I felt a noticeable change in my body.

Although I had been living a healthy vegetarian lifestyle for sixteen years, during the fast I felt my body getting healthier and younger. I started to feel like a twenty-year-old again: strong and full of life. This not only due to the physical cleansing of the fast, but it was also the result of remembering and releasing many past life memories, including my animal lives, from my body's cells.

By the seventh day of my what I called "urban retreat," I felt unusually light and full of energy. Coming out of a hot bath that evening, I felt a sudden rush of energy suddenly move up my body. I once again felt the familiar feeling of Joy but this time I couldn't remain standing. I fainted and fell on the bathroom floor. When I regained consciousness after about fifteen minutes, I was surprised to see myself lying on the cold tiles. There was blood on the floor, and I had broken my tooth. I called out for my daughter who helped me to my bed and brought ice for my bruised face. She asked if I was going to continue with my meditation and I said, "Yes." She sat silently by my bedside for a while then left. We didn't see or speak with each other again until I completed my full twenty-one days.

The following morning, as I walked on the freshly fallen snow and heard the rhythmic crunching sound under my feet, I was suddenly transported into a different time and space. A memory of a snow-covered mountain range came to my consciousness. I knew it was from my life in Tibet. My life as a Tibetan monk flashed before my eyes in vivid detail. At that moment I understood why I fell unconscious on the seventh day of my fast, and why it was now necessary to complete what I'd left unfinished in Tibet. I also recognized Osho as the monk in Tibet that my Rinpoche had addressed, asking him to bring me back into the fold. Osho had kept his promise, and the circle was now complete.

I was on my own once again, with a deep sense of gratitude and responsibility to share what I'd learned from Osho and all my past teachers. But what and how was a mystery yet to unfold. One day during the retreat I heard a voice. The voice was clear and strong, though outwardly inaudible. Hearing it so unexpectedly and with such authority, I couldn't reject or distrust it. I realized that I was hearing the voice of my own inner master.

Had I heard this voice earlier, I would have been unable to recognize it, or may have simply dismissed it. Recognizing the voice now helped me to also recognize the mysterious doorway to the universe, swiftly propelling me to the next phase of my journey. It was now time to say goodbye to my life as an eternal seeker and begin helping others to also awaken.

)( 

When I came out of my twenty-one day seclusion and walked out onto a busy street, I was astounded to see that everyone around me was sleep-walking. I could see people's bodies moving, but they were lost in the clouds of their many thoughts. No one was present where their body was standing. In their thoughts, they were all going somewhere else. I felt like an alien. I didn't know how to reach them or relate to them. I wanted to shake them out of their sleep, but I knew that no one can be forced out of their sleep unless they are ready and willing to wake up. I could only share the wisdom I'd gained on my own journey, but only with those who were searching for awakening themselves.

Shortly after this retreat, I began looking for a job. Two months later I was hired as a social worker in Northern Ontario. My job was counseling and conflict resolution for parents and their teenage children. Sixty percent of my job, however, was spent dealing with bureaucracy and paperwork. I was responsible for documenting all the cases and meetings, preparing court documents and going to court in cases of child apprehension, and doing foster-home evaluations and placements. On top of my regular nine-to-five duties, for six days a month I was also required to be on-call after-hours, often working through the night, and then starting another regular workday in the morning. Twice a week I also voluntarily offered evening workshops for parents and teens.

It was the most heartbreaking, challenging, exhausting, and thankless job I had ever done in my life. I dealt with familial dysfunctions, child abuse and neglect, teen pregnancies, substance abuse, and criminal and anti-social behavior. I witnessed continual power struggles between teens and their parents, and their inability to understand each other. As a counselor, I would pour my energies into trying to get people to understand that they were responsible for improving their own lives, but no one seemed to hear me. Everyone saw the other as the source of their problems, often also throwing the blame onto the counselors. I felt myself as a vacuum cleaner continually trying to clean up after people's problems. People would feel relieved and lighter after leaving my counseling sessions, but I would be completely drained and depleted.

I began suffocating under the weight of the job and the responsibility I was taking for people who didn't want to help themselves. Physically I was getting weaker and weaker. I began losing my eyesight and experiencing aches and pains in my body. No matter how hard I tried to help, not much was changing for my clients. Most of them were unwilling to commit to doing the needed work to change their lives, and some actively resisted it. And even if a few people wanted change, they seemed unable to let go of their old behavior patterns. I felt caught between the dysfunctions of my clients and the limitations of the social service system, which wasn't designed to truly help people transform, nor was it interested in doing so. At its best, it provided no more than band-aid solutions.

Through this job, I learned that most humans are not interested in or able to make an effort to improve their lives. They cannot see the need for self-improvement, not to mention self-realization. The light finally came on: "I am doing it all wrong! I can't help people by taking on their problems and pain." I understood that each person needed to learn through their own pain and suffering. I realized I could only guide people to becoming more aware, but ultimately everyone had to take responsibility for the work needed to improve their own lives.

I finally understood that I needed to begin working with people who were functioning at a higher level of consciousness and were open to the self-transformation that only meditation can bring. I approached the local college about teaching an eight-week course that I called *The Art of Meditation.*

269

To my surprise eighteen people registered, most of them educated professionals. It was refreshing and rewarding to meet people who were interested in their growth and transformation. When the course ended, some even asked to continue meeting and meditating with me. We formed a small group that met regularly in the recreation room of my apartment building. Between my meditation group and my social work, I was amazed at how human beings were capable of living and functioning in such varied ways and at so many different levels of consciousness.

※

In 1995, after two years of child protection work, I was in desperate need of a long vacation. I decided to return to the ashram in Pune, India, for a month to rejuvenate my body and soul by bathing in the ashram's supportive and nurturing energy field. To make my stay even more meaningful, I enrolled in an energy-healing course called Star Sapphire.

During the course I was surprised to rediscover my childhood ability to hear the thought-forms hidden in people's body and energy. As a child I had always felt confused when hearing people say one thing outwardly but thinking something else inwardly. Not knowing what to do with what I was experiencing, I learned to suppress my ability and at times even learned to play dumb when I knew that people were being insincere. At the same time, however, this ability also helped me to recognize and appreciate the people who were honest and sincere, and I always enjoyed their company.

When I first connected to the energy of my practice partner during the course, a Japanese man in his mid-thirties, to my surprise I immediately and effortlessly heard a stream of thought-forms emanating from his body and energy. It seemed as though he was subconsciously trying to communicate what he had been shy to expose for many years. There were so many thought-forms in his body that I couldn't remember them all. I decided to stop looking and relay back to him what I was hearing. I was doubly surprised when he confirmed in amazement that everything I said was true.

As I went on practicing with other partners, I continued to hear the overwhelming stream of thought-forms in each person's energy, and everyone confirmed that what I was hearing was true. Through working with many other partners, I realized that unlike me, others were unable to hear any thought-forms in my body, but had a visual image or intuitive sense of what was in my energy. For example, my Japanese partner, after connecting to my energy, suddenly bowed down to me in a gesture of reverence and said he saw me as an oracle and teacher surrounded by many people who were learning from me.

At the time I didn't think that my ability was anything special or could be something useful in helping others. After the training I went back to my job and resumed my regular duties as a social worker. After a year, when I eventually felt completely burnt out, I applied for a three-month unpaid leave of absence. My request was denied, and after many bureaucratic hassles I finally left my job.

X

I once again returned to the ashram in India and started giving Star Sapphire sessions based on the course I had taken a year earlier. My sessions were received extremely well, both by other practitioners and clients. I was excited to work with my newly re-discovered ability, and I was happy that I could help make a difference in the lives of those people who were eager to help themselves. After three months in India, I returned to Ontario, gave up all my possessions again, and in July of 1996 moved to Vancouver, British Columbia. There, I began to see clients and gradually established a healing practice.

A few months into my practice, I realized that the method I'd been practicing with in India was limited and did not produce the kind of results I wanted. I was not happy with just partial success and wanted to find a way to quickly help people achieve a complete and permanent energetic shift in consciousness in just one session, instead of working on the same issue session after session.

I began experimenting with different ways of accessing the core thought-forms and emotions hidden in the person's body that were causing their emotional and mental problems on the surface. As I went on experimenting with different ways of working with the suppressed thought-forms and emotions in the body, I realized that the new system I was developing was not only helping to transform people's emotional and psychological problems into more consciousness, but it was also helping eliminate the cause of their physical pain and ailments.

By 1997, I had developed a completely new and powerful healing method that worked with the person's entire energy system: body (head to feet), mind, emotions, spirit, and their past unconscious history all at the same time. At first, I called it Psychi-energetic Healing, but in 2000, I changed the name to the Dalian Healing Method® (DHM) on the recommendation of several clients and friends.

Over time, I saw more and more clients with various physical and psychological ailments. They came to me because they had been unable to resolve these problems, despite the many conventional and alternative treatments they had tried before.

I worked with chronic pain, cystitis, MS, asthma, chronic fatigue, Crohn's disease, diabetes, cancer, anxiety, depression, childhood trauma, physical and sexual abuse, pregnancy, chronic fear, digestion, thyroid, lumps and tumors, panic attacks, past life patterns, relationship issues, rosacea, sexuality, self-esteem issues, weight loss, prostate problems, and many others.

Sometimes, it took only one session to clear what months and years of other forms of therapy had not been able to accomplish – and the results in energetic shift and transformation in consciousness were permanent. Several people were able to avoid surgery as a result of working with me and others who came after a surgery, which had strangely intensified their pain, experienced complete recovery.

Not only did I witness startling physical changes, but more

importantly, I saw profound spiritual changes. Seeing people quickly transform in front of my eyes was the most rewarding part of my work. When they would first come to see me, they would be depressed, fearful, hopeless, and have clouded eyes. After the session, they would walk out with shiny eyes, feeling a new sense of direction, clarity, and strength. Most people would say that they felt as though they were learning to walk for the first time. And those who had never meditated before began experiencing deep meditative states and glimpsing the emptiness of their being – something that usually only comes after years of arduous discipline in self-awareness and meditation. People reported experiencing a simultaneous sense of elevation, expansion and groundedness that they had never experienced before. Many had their view of reality radically altered and as a result changed their lifestyle and their relationship with themselves and the world.

Although the results of the sessions were outstanding, in my mind this was only a small step towards a complete transformation into enlightened consciousness. I encouraged my clients to continue with their spiritual work by incorporating meditation into their daily lifestyle. Some people took this seriously and went on with their inner exploration. For those who continued working with me personally, I gradually found myself becoming a teacher as much as a healer.

Feeling a sense of obligation and responsibility to assist people further on their journey to awakening, I also began offering twenty-one-day intensive meditation workshops twice a year alongside my healing practice. At first I called them Breath Awareness Intensives and later changed this to Self-Awareness and Enlightenment Intensives. During these workshops, I used the Osho Dynamic and other active meditations as well as my ability to see and guide people through the multitude of the suppressed thought-forms and emotions in their body and energy. This was an ideal combination for anyone seriously working on their transformation to quickly and easily see and move through their unconscious darkness, which they otherwise were afraid or unable to go into on their own.

With time, many of my clients who were healers, yoga teachers, counselors, therapists, and psychologists began asking me to train them with my healing method. Some called the method evolutionary, and others thought it was a new paradigm in healing that needed to be shared with the world. I felt an urgency in sharing it with as many people as possible.

At first I began to simply demonstrate the method in seminars by asking for volunteers from the audience. I would educate people about how their suppressed thought-forms and emotions create most of their physical ailments and psychological problems. I demonstrated how once the unconscious thought-forms and emotions were released from the body, the energy in the body would immediately begin to flow, creating a possibility for physical and psychological healing to happen instantaneously and without any effort. I tried to help people understand that only their own awareness and consciousness were the ultimate healing force that can help them find healing and happiness.

I simultaneously also felt the need to train other therapists to practice with this method. The challenge, however, was to find the right people capable of working with it. Though simple in its structure, the method required therapists who were conscious enough to recognize their own ego-mind and disidentify from their own thoughts, emotions, and judgments before they could work with other people's thought-forms and emotions. The therapist had to be capable of accepting everything that was within the client's energy without any judgment or condemnation, in order for the needed healing to take place. Also, the method required the therapist to stay absolutely present, centered, and grounded within herself or himself throughout the session so they could know how to work with the many contradictory thought-forms and emotions that would unexpectedly surface in different parts of the client's body.

Before beginning the training, I felt the need to give potential therapists something they could use as a manual so they would first understand how their own ego-mind and consciousness work and how these relate to their own healing.

274

My practice was growing rapidly, so it was not always easy to find time to write. To allocate more time, I began to discourage people from coming for sessions by raising my fees. This didn't seem to work at first, but eventually, as I went on raising the fee, it became manageable and I was able to find more time to focus on writing.

At first I started writing about the process I had experienced while developing the complete method, hoping to take the reader on the same journey I had traveled. At times, I felt overwhelmed with the enormity of the task. I felt it was impossible to put everything I had come to experience and understand into words. In the process of writing, I also realized that I was not a writer but a mystic – a very old soul with unbound earthly experience to share.

I tried my best to make this book as comprehensive and complete as possible, but everything I wrote seemed incomplete. I often felt I was conveying only parts of the truth while most of it remained unsaid. What I originally planned to cover in one book gradually expanded into three, and what I thought would take only a couple of years to complete took seven.

As the years went by, I realized the need to make my new healing method available to more people who are looking for ways to take charge of their own healing and transformation. As a result, a self-healing version of my method was born. I began using it with extreme success in my workshops, and eventually created self-healing seminars and retreats using this light-speed method.

There is no doubt in my mind that if used by thousands of people simultaneously, this method has the explosive power to instantaneously transform the collective pain and suffering of humanity, and allow people to quickly step into their individual power and creativity. And the beauty of it is that anyone can practice it in the comfort and privacy of their own home.

I'll follow up on the concepts covered in this book with two other books in the near future. In the meantime, whatever you can practice and integrate from the teachings of this book will lay a wonderful and solid foundation for the material that will soon follow. You can also participate in the *Healing into Consciousness On-line Courses* and *Monthly Tele-classes,* which are designed to support you with hands-on practical guidance so you can deepen your self-awareness, strengthen your inner witness, and heal into joy and consciousness.

I hope that reading the story of my personal journey of awakening will encourage you to explore the unique treasures of your own being and help you realize that regardless of any hardships or pain you may have experienced, you can, at any moment, transform your suffering into the Joy of awakened consciousness.

May your healing journey into consciousness be light and playful!

# EPILOGUE

## EMBRACING THE LIGHT

In January 1990, a few days after Osho's death, I had a vision. I was within a boundless cosmic darkness, waiting for something to happen. Suddenly, there appeared a small ball of light shining brightly in the darkness. The Light was like the Sun, illuminating the surrounding darkness and giving life to everything in its sphere. The energy of Light was the collective consciousness of all the enlightened beings that had, at one time, lived on the planet Earth. They were now united as one source of energy, light, and consciousness.

The energy of Darkness was the energy of all the unconsciousness within the universe, including the unconsciousness of all humans living on the planet Earth. Light was aware of Darkness and conscious of itself, and Darkness was aware of Light but it was unconscious of itself. Darkness was threatened by Light and thought that Light was its enemy. Light knew it was once part of Darkness and wanted Darkness to know that they were not separate. Darkness, however, was afraid of Light's power to expose things hidden in the darkness.

Feeling threatened by Light, Darkness tried to suppress it in order to maintain control and rule the Earth. The Light, attempting to grow in size and brightness, was patiently waiting for other beings to awaken and join in its endless celebration of Joy. Suddenly, within seconds, many small light streams emerged out of Darkness and at the speed of light began entering into the ball of Light from all directions. As the light of each awakened being merged with the collective Light of the Awakened Ones, it lost its separate identity as an "I" and became one with the collective consciousness of Light. Light quickly grew in size and strength.

Then, all movement stopped just as suddenly as it had begun, and everything came to a standstill. Light, though visibly smaller compared to the Darkness that prevailed on the planet Earth, was now as powerful as Darkness. A question stood hanging in the air: Who would win the battle and tip the scale, to determine how humanity would live for the next 2,500 years? Who would rule life on Earth? Would it be the creative and compassionate consciousness of Light or the destructive unconsciousness of Darkness? Darkness struggled to maintain its power, while Light, with its now greater size and strength, almost forcibly pulled one more light stream out of Darkness. As this last light stream entered the Light, it tipped the scale of power and Light became victorious.

This vision filled my heart with joy. Deep in my soul I knew that in spite of the much-talked about coming doomsday that the unconscious powers are preparing for, the Light will overcome Darkness and humanity will enter the Enlightened Era of greater consciousness – a consciousness that cares for all fellow humans, the Planet and all its creatures. Although it may seem like life on Earth is becoming grimmer, I believe, as do many others, that the foundation of our collective consciousness is strong, and the new dawn of a more aware and loving humanity is just around the corner.

Every one of us can make a difference in our common future by courageously transforming the unconscious darkness of our own ego-mind into consciousness. Conscious people don't create wars – they strive for unity. Only consciousness can help us live in peace, freedom, love, and brotherhood, and make this planet a better place for ourselves and the generations to come. I hope this book is an invitation and a supportive guide in your journey from Darkness into Light.

For more information about
*Self-healing Seminars, Self-awareness* and *Meditation Intensives,*
*Retreats,* and *Active Meditation Teacher Training* courses
with Eliza Mada Dalian, or to enroll in the
*Healing Into Consciousness Home Study Course* and *Monthly Teleclasses*
to gain a practical experience of the material covered in this book,
visit *www.madadalian.com.*

For educational videos, pod casts, interviews,
and to sign up for a newsletter, visit
*www.madadalian.com.*

To schedule Eliza Mada Dalian for a talk, seminar, or
healing demonstration with
DHM – the Dalian Healing Method® –
email *seminars@madadalian.com.*

For the e-book *Healing Into Consciousness Through Active Meditation*
*& Visualization,* visit *www.madadalian.com.*

For information about forthcoming books, e-books,
CDs and DVDs, or to sign up for newsletter updates, visit
*www.ExpandingUniversePublishing.com.*

**FSC**

**Mixed Sources**
Cert no. SW-COC-00127
© 1996 FSC